STUDIES IN SOVIET HISTORY AND SOCIETY
General Editor: R. W. Davies, Professor of Soviet Economic Studies, University of Birmingham

The series consists of works by members or associates of the interdisciplinary Centre for Russian and East European Studies of the University of Birmingham, England. Special interests of the Centre include Soviet economic and social history, contemporary Soviet economics and planning, science and technology, sociology and education.

Gregory D. Andrusz
HOUSING AND URBAN DEVELOPMENT IN THE USSR

John Barber
SOVIET HISTORIANS IN CRISIS, 1928–1932

Stephen Fortescue
THE COMMUNIST PARTY AND SOVIET SCIENCE

Philip Hanson
TRADE AND TECHNOLOGY IN SOVIET–WESTERN RELATIONS

Jonathan Haslam
SOVIET FOREIGN POLICY, 1930–33
THE SOVIET UNION AND THE STRUGGLE FOR COLLECTIVE SECURITY IN EUROPE, 1933–39

Malcolm R. Hill and Richard McKay
SOVIET PRODUCT QUALITY

Peter Kneen
SOVIET SCIENTISTS AND THE STATE

Nicholas Lampert
THE TECHNICAL INTELLIGENTSIA AND THE SOVIET STATE
WHISTLEBLOWING IN THE SOVIET UNION

Robert Lewis
SCIENCE AND INDUSTRIALISATION IN THE USSR

Neil Malcolm
SOVIET POLITICAL SCIENTISTS AND AMERICAN POLITICS

David Mandel
THE PETROGARD WORKERS AND THE FALL OF THE
OLD REGIME

THE PETROGRAD WORKERS AND THE SOVIET SEIZURE
OF POWER

E. A. Rees
STATE CONTROL IN SOVIET RUSSIA

Christopher Rice
RUSSIAN WORKERS AND THE
SOCIALIST-REVOLUTIONARY PARTY THROUGH
THE REVOLUTION OF 1905–07

Richard Sakwa
SOVIET COMMUNISTS IN POWER

Roger Skurski
SOVIET MARKETING AND ECONOMIC DEVELOPMENT

Daniel Thorniley
THE RISE AND FALL OF THE SOVIET RURAL
COMMUNIST PARTY, 1927–39

J. N. Westwood
SOVIET LOCOMOTIVE TECHNOLOGY DURING
INDUSTRIALISATION, 1928–52

Series Standing Order

If you would like to receive future titles in this series as they are published, you can make use of our standing order facility. To place a standing order please contact your bookseller or, in case of difficulty, write to us at the address below with your name and address and the name of the series. Please state with which title you wish to begin your standing order. (If you live outside the UK we may not have the rights for your area, in which case we will forward your order to the publisher concerned.)

Standing Order Service, Macmillan Distribution Ltd,
Houndmills, Basingstoke, Hampshire, RG21 2XS, England.

Soviet Product Quality

Malcolm R. Hill
and
Richard McKay

in association with the
CENTRE FOR RUSSIAN AND
EAST EUROPEAN STUDIES
UNIVERSITY OF BIRMINGHAM

©Malcolm R. Hill and Richard McKay 1988

All rights reserved. No reproduction, copy or transmission of this publication may be made without written permission.

No paragraph of this publication may be reproduced, copied or transmitted save with written permission or in accordance with the provisions of the Copyright Act 1956 (as amended), or under the terms of any licence permitting limited copying issued by the Copyright Licensing Agency, 7 Ridgmount Street, London WC1E 7AE.

Any person who does any unauthorised act in relation to this publication may be liable to criminal prosecution and civil claims for damages.

First published 1988

Published by
THE MACMILLAN PRESS LTD
Houndmills, Basingstoke, Hampshire RG21 2XS
and London
Companies and representatives
throughout the world

Printed in Hong Kong

British Library Cataloguing in Publication Data
Hill, Malcolm R.
Soviet product quality.—(Studies in
Soviet history and society)
1. Quality Control—Soviet Union
I. Title II. McKay, Richard
III. Series
658.5'62'0947   TS156
ISBN 0-333-43591-5

To E. Flavell

Contents

List of Tables ix

List of Figures xi

Preface xii

Acknowledgements xv

1 Introduction 1
   Concepts of Product Quality 1
   Previous Studies of Soviet Product Quality 3
   The Case for Further Research on Soviet
      Product Quality 7
   Standardisation in the Soviet Economy 8
   Conclusions 15

2 General Purpose Machine Tool Type Standards 17
   Introduction 17
   Previous Studies on Machine Tool State
      Standards 17
   The Current Study 18
   Results 22
   Conclusions 28
   Trends in Accuracy Improvement in Soviet
      Machine Tool State Standards 31

3 Machine Tool 'Mark of Quality' Standards 35
   'Mark of Quality' Standards 35
   An Analysis of the Requirements of Machine Tool
      'Mark of Quality' Standards 38

4 'Squirrel Cage' Electrical Motors 50
   Introduction 50
   Squirrel Cage Motors 50
   The Quality Characteristics of Soviet Squirrel
      Cage Motors: A Comparative Study 52
   Comments and Conclusions 65

Contents

5 Automotive Products and Components — **68**
Introduction — 68
Passenger Cars — 69
Trucks — 77
Engine Components — 86
Conclusions — 90

6 Domestic Refrigerators — **92**
Introduction — 92
The Domestic Refrigerator — 92
The Soviet Domestic Refrigerator Industry — 93
Quality Levels of Soviet Refrigerators — 94
Comparative Assessment of the Quality
 Indicators of Soviet Refrigerators — 96
Comments and Conclusions — 108

7 Cameras — **111**
Introduction — 111
Technical Appraisal of Soviet Cameras — 112
Conclusions — 123

8 Comments, Conclusions and Further Research — **126**
General Comments and Conclusions — 126
Further Research on Soviet Advanced
 Manufacturing Technology — 135

Appendix — 142

Notes and References — 182

Bibliography — 198

Index — 203

List of Tables

2.1	Soviet state standards and British national standards for selected machine types	20
2.2	Soviet output of specific machine tool types	21
2.3	Selected lathe parameters for accuracy comparison	24
2.4	Comparison of accuracy requirements specified by British and Soviet standards for machine tool alignment tests	29
2.5	Comparative accuracies of normal precision lathes specified by GOST 42–56 and GOST 18097–72	32
2.6	Comparative accuracies of normal precision knee and column milling machines specified by GOST 13–54 and GOST 17734–72	32
2.7	Comparisons of accuracy requirements in current and previous Soviet state standards	33
2.8	Current and previous state standards for machine tools	34
3.1	'Mark of quality' standards for machine tools	39
3.2	'Mark of quality' specifications for machine tools	41
4.1	Operational characteristics for squirrel cage motors (0.5–9 kW rated output)	53
4.2	Operational characteristics for squirrel cage motors (10–45 kW rated output)	55
4.3	Operational characteristics for squirrel cage motors (45–160 kW rated output)	58
4.4	Operational characteristics for squirrel cage motors (200–1100 kW rated output)	60
5.1	Soviet passenger car collision resistance	70
5.2	Comparative technical data for passenger cars	71
5.3	Moskvich 412 – test results	73
5.4	Soviet 'type standards' for goods vehicles	77
5.5	Comparative output of trucks by weight (USSR and selected Western countries, 1970)	80
5.6	'Mark of quality' standards for Soviet trucks (1982)	83
5.7	Technical specifications of the ZIL 130 truck range (to GOST 5.979–71)	84
5.8	Steel crankshafts	87

List of Tables

5.9	Gudgeon pins	89
5.10	Gudgeon pin tolerances to BS 3537:1979	90
6.1	Comparison study results: small to medium capacity refrigerators	98
6.2	Comparison study results: medium capacity refrigerators	100
6.3	Comparison study results: medium to large capacity refrigerators	102
6.4	Comparison study results: large capacity refrigerators	104
6.5	General technical conditions for Soviet and British domestic refrigerators	106
6.6	Comparative weights of Soviet and Western refrigerators	108
7.1	Comparison of Soviet and British standards requirements for photographic equipment	115
A.1	Comparative lathe accuracies	142
A.2	Comparative milling machine accuracies	149
A.3	Comparative accuracies for vertical drilling machines	152
A.4	Comparative accuracies for radial drilling machines	153
A.5	Comparative accuracies for surface grinding machines	155
A.6	Comparative accuracies for cylindrical grinding machines	158
A.7	Comparative accuracies for internal grinding machines	163
A.8	Comparative accuracies for semi-automatic vertical broaching machines	167
A.9	Comparative accuracies for vertical gearhobbing machines	168
A.10	Comparative accuracies for horizontal gearhobbing machines	170
A.11	'Mark of quality' standards – selected turning machines	172
A.12	GOST 5.4–67	175
A.13	Comparative assessment of electrical rotating machinery	178

List of Figures

1.1	The Soviet mark of quality	13
4.1	Comparative motor parameters	63

Preface

This book is an account of research carried out by the authors on the theme of product quality in the Soviet planned economy. Although this topic has been previously discussed by a number of scholars and industrialists who are either studying, or trading with, the USSR, this present research has followed a distinctive approach to the understanding of Soviet product quality.

The methodology used in this research has consisted of the comparative assessment of technical data contained in Soviet documentation, for a selected sample of industrial and consumer products. In most cases, these documents have been Soviet state standards in view of their legal status in the Soviet economy, and their availability for study as openly published documents. The information contained in these documents has been compared with their British counterparts as typical examples of standards used by an advanced industrialised Western country. In several cases, the use of these documents has been supplemented by data in other Soviet and British published materials, and the use of expert opinion. Previous publications by the present authors have given an introduction to this methodology, and provided an insight into its potential application.[1] This book, however, provides a broader account of the application of the methodology through the selection of a wider product sample.

The relatively smooth progress of the research has been greatly facilitated by three main factors. The first of these has been the existence of an agreement for the exchange of standards and relevant information between the State Committee of Standards of the USSR (*Gosstandart SSSR*), and the British Standards Institution (BSI). This has led to a comprehensive collection of Soviet state standards being held in the UK by the latter organisation, and the authors have been allowed complete access to this collection by the BSI. The third factor which has significantly helped this research has been the cooperative working climate created by the Anglo-Soviet Working Group on Metrology and Standardisation. As the authors' research fell within the terms of reference of this group, it was possible to hold discussions with Soviet specialists in this field in their research institutes, factories and product testing establishments in Moscow.

The book is divided into eight chapters. The first of these is an

Preface xiii

introductory chapter with a brief summary of Soviet concepts of product quality, followed by a survey of previous research on this theme. These sections are then followed by an account of the role played by state standards in the Soviet economy, and the growing importance of the quality attestation system.

The following six chapters then present the results of research into the assessment of Soviet quality for five product groups, namely machine tools, electrical motors, automotive products, domestic refrigerators and photographic equipment. The first two of this set of chapters, namely those dealing with machine tools, consider 'type standards' and 'mark of quality' standards separately.

The book closes with the major conclusions emerging from this research. These can be summarised as an apparent similarity between the technical requirements for quality as specified by standards, in both the Soviet and British documents for the sample of products which have been surveyed. This conclusion contradicts many of the previously published views on Soviet product quality, and suggestions are consequently advanced for further research to widen the sample of products selected; and to consider other quality-related factors which it is difficult to regulate by means of standards documentation.

The results of the research should be of interest to three main groups of readers. The first of these are students of the Soviet economy, who are concerned with an accurate assessment of the technical capability of that economy. The second are students of quality management systems who are interested in the approach to this topic in different economic, political and social systems. In recent years, Western publications in the production and quality management fields have tended to concentrate on the results of Western, and particularly Japanese, experiences in these areas. It is unfortunate that the Soviet experience is sometimes dismissed as being irrelevant to the market economies, when it is remembered that the manufacture and distribution of many products and services in the West are carried out in market conditions very far removed from those of perfect competition. This book shows, therefore, that the USSR's expertise in this field has an important perspective to offer to international discussions on the role of standards in quality management systems. The third group of readers for whom this book is addressed are industrial executives and government officials with interests in trade with the Soviet

Union. A better understanding of Soviet product quality capabilities can significantly help the establishment of market opportunities for both imported and exported products.

MALCOLM R. HILL
RICHARD MCKAY

Acknowledgements

The authors wish to acknowledge the assistance of a number of organisations and individuals throughout the project described in this book. The project was financially supported during 1984–5 by the Joint Committee of the Science and Engineering Research Council (SERC) and the Economics and Social Research Council (ESRC) through the provision of funding for a full-time research worker, and for travel costs. Without this financial support, the scope of the project would have been severely limited.

The progress of the project depended to a very great extent on the provision of Soviet state standards from the collection maintained in the library of the British Standards Institution. The library staff were always quick to respond to the researchers' requests, and the Head of Information Services at the BSI, Mr B. D. Roden, gave his full support to the project. Materials were also used from the Centre for Russian and East European Studies, University of Birmingham, and the authors acknowledge the assistance provided by Professor R. W. Davies, Professor R. Amann, Dr P. Hanson, Dr J. M. Cooper, Mr P. Snell, Mr M. J. Berry and Dr J. Brine.

Dr Hill wishes to particulary thank Mr R. Foxwell, Joint Chairman of the Anglo-Soviet Working Group on Metrology and Standardisation, for the support of an application to visit the USSR during February 1985. The State Committee of Standards of the USSR arranged a comprehensive and relevant programme of visits to the All-Union Scientific-Research Institute of Metrological Services (VNIIMS), the All-Union Scientific-Research Institute of Standardisation (VNIIS), the All-Union Scientific-Research Institute of Engineering Standardisation (VNIINMash), the Moscow Centre of Standardisation and Metrology, and the 'Manometr' factory. Useful discussions were held with specialists at each establishment.

Finally, the authors wish to acknowledge the provision of facilities by Loughborough University of Technology, to carry out the research project described in this book; and the support of Professors J. Sizer and G. Gregory, Heads of Department of Management Studies at Loughborough during 1984 and 1985–6, respectively. The manuscript was prepared for publication by Miss F. Nash, Mrs C. Darbyshire and Mrs S. Garner, to whom the authors are obliged for their patience and efficiency.

1 Introduction

CONCEPTS OF PRODUCT QUALITY

During the late 1960s a leading Soviet economist, D. S. L'vov,[1] observed that 'the word "quality" figures frequently in economic literature. Dozens of different definitions of this concept exist, each of which have their own particular feature different from the others'; and he then went on to discuss the term from the philosophical, engineering, legal, economic and social points of view. Looking at the engineering aspect of quality in more detail, L'vov considered that '[this] aspect of quality is related to research into technical, quantifiable laws covering the formation and manifestation of physical, mechanical, chemical and other properties, of items of identical functional purpose. From this point of view, quality is commonly considered as the totality of properties of a product, which determine the possibility of its utilisation in service.'[2]

L'vov's definition of quality is also similar to that frequently quoted by Western writers on this topic at about the same time, namely 'fitness for purpose'. Lockyer[3] in his widely read general textbook on production management, published in 1969, described the quality of a product by that term as did another leading writer in this field, namely J. M. Juran.[4] Furthermore, the latter sentence of L'vov's definition is almost identical to that quoted for 'quality' in a British Standard published in 1972, namely 'the totality of features and characteristics of a product or service that bear on its ability to satisfy a given need'.[5] It is evident, therefore, that by the early 1970s, similar concepts of product quality were held in both the USSR and the UK.

The similar concepts of product quality held by the two countries have also been maintained throughout the 1970s and into the 1980s. For example, a Soviet state standard (GOST 15467–79) published some ten years after L'vov's book also provides a similar definition of quality, namely 'the totality of properties of a product, determining its suitability to satisfy defined requirements in accordance with its purpose.' There is a close resemblance between this definition, and what is referred to in BS 4778:1979 as the 'quantitative sense' of quality or 'quality level', where product requirements can be expressed according to technical concepts and quantitative parameters. The definition of 'quality level' given in this standard is 'a general indication of the extent of departure from the ideal: usually a numerical value indicating either the degree of conformity or the degree of nonconformity'.[6] The present authors also consider that a quantitative assessment of quality level can be obtained from the 'tolerance zone' for products, (i.e.: 'the zone of values in which a measurable characteristic is in conformity with its specification')[7], and the 'specification tolerance' (i.e.: 'the permitted variation in a process or a characteristic of an item'). This latter approach is used for comparative quality assessment purposes throughout this book.

The economic aspects of product quality, however, are normally considered more difficult to define, since they require detailed information on manufacturing costs, which can vary with volume of production and capital investment; and customers' utilisation costs, which the seller is not always in a position to know. Furthermore, it is even more difficult accurately to define the effect of quality on profits and profitability of the manufacturer and user; although these two indicators are considered to influence the survival of a Western company, and the success of a Soviet enterprise. In the research programme which this book describes, therefore, particular attention has been paid to the technical, rather than the economic, aspects of product quality. It may be argued that such an approach may provide an incomplete picture of product quality, but the present authors considered it better to reflect usual industrial practice in this present research by focusing on technical indicators. In practice, these indicators are established at values considered to provide economic utilisation of a product in the most commonly expected range of applications, although products may also be ranked into 'grades' where this is feasible.[8] This latter practice then permits the selection of a higher (and probably more expensive) grade of product to meet a more demanding application.

L'vov also discussed the legal aspect of product quality, which he considered to 'be related to the manner in which legally, or contractually, specified technical requirements are adhered to by the relevant manufacturing organisations'.[9] This, in its turn, can be related to his concepts of 'engineering quality' when 'the properties of functional purpose' are included in 'appropriate legal and contractual technical documentation.' These Soviet concepts of the legal aspects of product quality are probably not very different in day-to-day practical application from those encountered by Western industrial managers in their own experience in their own countries. What does differ in this field between the Soviet and Western economies, how-

Introduction 3

ever, is the legal status of various technical documents and the associated parameters specified within them, in view of the different roles played by government bodies in the USSR and the West in the planning and control of industrial activities. This theme of the legal status of various technical documents is referred to again in more detail in a subsequent section of this chapter.

PREVIOUS STUDIES OF SOVIET PRODUCT QUALITY

Many of the first economic studies of Soviet industrial development[10] were concerned with the measurement of industrial growth in appropriate physical output and aggregated economic indicators based to a very great extent on published Soviet statistics. Later studies,[11] either separately from or as corollaries to economic investigations of the type mentioned above, attempted to value Soviet output and capital accumulation in financial terms appropriate for purposes of comparison with other countries. In more recent years, the Soviet economy has also been studied from the viewpoint of its scientific, technological and industrial design capabilities. The first major study[12] in this field was concerned with an understanding of the administrative framework and procedures by which research and development has been executed in the USSR, whilst subsequent research has investigated the technological[13] and design[14] capabilities of a range of Soviet industries. The most recent studies have concentrated on extending this work to explain the effects of the USSR's research and development system on its industries' technological performance,[15] and the options open to Soviet policy-makers to improve that performance.[16] In parallel with investigations into Soviet technological capability, attention has also been paid to the role played by international technology transfer to and from the Soviet economy;[17] this topic also being of major concern in the West in view of changing government policies towards East–West trade.

In addition to the above-cited studies which have attempted to quantify the economic and technological capabilities of the Soviet economy, and the effects of the planning systems for manufacturing and product development on these capabilities, research has also been carried out on the political and managerial contributions to Soviet industrial performance. Publications on these latter topics have focused on the role of the Communist Party and its officials at local levels,[18] and the economic, social and political constraints within which a Soviet industrial manager is expected to perform successfully.[19]

All of these approaches to the study of the Soviet economy have provided valuable insights into the planning and operation of Soviet industry, and most of them also refer to one important factor relating to Soviet industrial performance, namely Soviet product quality. In addition, several other researchers have addressed themselves to the specific problem of the assessment of Soviet product quality and its effect on Soviet economic performance.

The general view of these latter Western researchers is that the quality levels of Soviet industrial products are generally lower than their Western counterparts as a result of the influence of several factors. According to Berliner,[20] the major factors can be summarised as the low levels of labour skills during the early years of Soviet industrialisation, problems encountered in the allocation of supplies in a centrally planned economy, and the continued existence of a seller's market in the Soviet Union. Since the publication of Berliner's book in 1976, there have been two further studies by Grant,[21] and Treml,[22] which also appear to further substantiate the view of a generally low level of Soviet product quality in particular sectors of industry. A study by Gorlin[23] on consumer goods also reaches similar conclusions, although that publication is more concerned with product style than technical specification.

Grant's conclusions will be considered first, since his is the earliest of the studies. Grant pays particular attention to the Soviet machine tool industry, classifying machine tools into two broad groups, namely 'conventional' and 'advanced' machine tools. Conventional machine tools are defined by Grant as those types that have traditionally been produced, namely lathes, drilling, boring, grinding, and milling machines, and also transfer lines; whilst 'advanced' machine tools are defined as conventional types that have been enhanced in one or more key aspects (flexibility, productivity, precision) through the application of electronics and computers. Considering conventional machine tools first, Grant concludes that 'most of the machine tools that reach Soviet standards can be assumed to be less precise than their Western counterparts. That is because Soviet accuracy requirements for precision machine tools tend to be less stringent than corresponding Western requirements'.[24] In the same paper, Grant also cites several Soviet and Western sources including those compiled by Berry[25] which claim that certain Soviet machine tools lose their initial accuracy in a shorter time than their Western counterparts, lack certain design features, and are also less reliable and durable. Grant summarises his view of these sources by stating that 'Soviet conventional machine tools do not differ technologically from those of the developed West – in design and principle of operation they follow world-wide practice – but mainly in quality; that is in performance, durability and reliability'.[26] Finally, Grant also claims that there are major technological lags in Soviet 'advanced' machine tools compared with their Western counterparts, caused mainly by technical deficiencies in control equipment.

Grant's conclusions on the accuracy of Soviet conventional machine tools were not supported by any associated technical data, however, but partly by the citation of a previous study carried out by one of the present authors[27] on a sample of Soviet state standards which had been approved before 1970; although that same study went on to show that improvements in state standards were apparent after 1970. It is our view, therefore, that some of Grant's conclusions on Soviet standards for ex-supplier machine tool precision, and his associated conclusions on machine tool quality, should be reconsidered.

On the other hand, a study carried out by one of the present authors[28] on a small sample of Soviet milling machines, drilling machines and grinding machines purchased by a British factory in the late 1960s would certainly support Grant's second cited conclusion relating to performance, durability and reliability. That study revealed certain shortcomings in the design and manufacture of those machines which subsequently affected their working speeds, continued accuracy, reliability, and down-times; even though the initial tolerances as specified in the state standards, and achieved in the alignment tests, were reasonably satisfactory. If several of these 'design-based' shortcomings (e.g. thermal distortion of grinding-head spindle bearings) were not rectified on machinery specially tooled for use in the intensive production conditions of the high volume industries,[29] problems of manufacturing efficiency would almost certainly occur. In addition a sample of British machine tool engineers with experience of selling into the Soviet market from the late 1960s to the mid 1970s, when interviewed by one of the authors in 1978, were of the opinion that Western machine tools designed for use in the high volume industries were more productive than their Soviet counterparts. This was due to greater Western experience in the design and use of specialised tooling; and the use of more reliable and durable assemblies, components and materials.[30] The importance of numerical control interface component performance and reliability was also raised by one engineer with experience in this field. Few of the engineers, however, raised serious doubts over the initial accuracy of Soviet machine tools.

Treml's paper[31] is an informative account of the price supplements received by Soviet enterprises to cover the costs associated with modification of their products for sale in export markets. These supplements average out at 24 per cent for 'general destination' exports and 58 per cent for 'tropical destination' exports; and a Soviet source[32] cited by Treml indicates similar levels of price supplements for machine tools. Treml relates these price differences to quality differences, stating that 'export price supplements appear to be used, that is quality improvements and modifications are required for practically all machine exports, which suggests that the quality gap between domestic and world standards pertains to most machinery produced in the USSR, except possibly military products'.[33] This view also appears to be supported by the comparatively low market shares achieved by Soviet engineering exports in the Western economies[34] even after supplementary work for export has been carried out by their manufacturer.

It is our opinion, however, that additional costs are incurred by many exporters in Western countries also, as a consequence of such factors as differences in electrical equipment specification, special safety and testing procedures required in certain markets, and other technical regulations which sometimes appear to be specifically designed to protect domestic producers and to discourage the penetration of the market by imported products.[35] Consequently, similar additional costs might also be faced by Soviet enterprises producing machinery for the export market. It is Treml's view, however, that for American computers, aircraft, electronic components and machine tools, the need for modification for other markets is minimal; whilst Swedish products usually only cost about 4 per cent[36] more to adapt for export markets. The magnitude of the additional costs in the Soviet case, therefore, does lend strong support to Treml's view that the major factor influencing price differences between machine models for domestic and export markets, is the quality difference; but this still requires testing by information from more actual cases. Furthermore, it is important to note that the comparatively low market shares achieved by Soviet products may not be entirely attributable to quality levels, since there may be many marketing factors worthy of further study such as range, accessories,[37] service, and customers' perceptions.[38]

THE CASE FOR FURTHER RESEARCH ON SOVIET PRODUCT QUALITY

The studies referred to in the previous section have provided some useful insights into the quality of articles manufactured in the Soviet economy, but few of them have carried out investigations into the quality of specific products. It is considered, therefore, that further research is necessary for a number of reasons, as outlined in the following paragraphs.

It is difficult, for example, accurately to assess the performance of the Soviet economy and to compare it with its Western counterparts, if the quality of industrial production is omitted from economic and financial calculations. If poorer quality items are manufactured in the USSR there may be an overall decrease in industrial efficiency, whilst if items of too high a quality are manufactured a waste of valuable resources may result. The study of aspects of quality of Soviet manufactured articles is therefore of possible use in more realistically assessing Soviet growth rates, capital accumulation, and industrial efficiency for comparative purposes.

Secondly, it is of general interest to study the methods of product quality regulation in a centrally planned economy where, compared with Western economies, there is limited opportunity for purchasers to transfer their buying power between different suppliers. This latter aspect may be particularly relevant in the purchase of capital goods, the quality of which can subsequently affect the quality of items produced by them.

A third reason for further research in this field is that it is likely that particular Soviet import objectives have been related to the country's need for certain high quality capital goods which it has not yet sufficiently developed for manufacture on a wide scale, but which are required for the expansion of a priority industry. Thus, it is useful for prospective and current exporters to the USSR to be acquainted with the current quality levels of similar Soviet-produced articles, and the ways and means that such parameters are maintained and modified, in order that market requirements may be more clearly defined.

Fourthly, the success of industrial products in Western markets is influenced to a very great extent by non-price factors, such as quality and service. It is useful, therefore, to assess the degree to which Soviet shares in Western markets[39] for industrial products may be influenced by the mix of their quality, price and service indicators; and the extent to which Soviet manufacturers may need to modify products for export to the market economies. Finally, it is useful to explore more thoroughly the relationships between Soviet product quality and Soviet industrial innovations, to determine comparative performance characteristics for novel products, and those products at a mature stage of their life cycle.

This chapter, however, is more concerned with comparative aspects of product quality management, and specific ways in which product quality can be comparatively assessed as a means of providing information to answer some of the questions raised in the previous paragraphs. The next section of this chapter, therefore, considers product standards as convenient sources for comparative quality assessment.

STANDARDISATION IN THE SOVIET ECONOMY

Soviet Standards

Engineering standard specifications are documents approved by a recognised authority at the relevant level, which specify rationalised dimensional parameters and defined quality characteristics of industrial articles. Standardisation is used in all industrial countries as a means of promoting production specialisation through variety reduction, and ensuring that the quality of manufactured articles is of an acceptable level.

It will be appreciated that standards can be published by many different bodies in market and mixed economies.[40] Individual Western companies may, for example, publish standards for components and materials drawn up by the company's standards department for their own internal use, in order to obtain a more intensive use of a restricted variety of these items and hence reduce production costs. Furthermore, such standards may form the basis of purchasing orders to ensure the quality of incoming raw materials and components. The majority of Western companies also produce what they refer to as 'standard items', which are frequently those made in batches for serving customers from stock, or those items which have been manufactured previously for which relevant technical documentation exists. In such cases, it is usually the company's sales department which is the 'recognised authority', on which products can be considered as 'standard'. A further set of standards in use in Western companies are those approved by a national standardising body (e.g. British Standards Institution) in a Western country. It is unusual for these documents to have legal status in their own right and they are usually applied voluntarily by those companies to which their requirements apply. They may, however, form the basis of a purchasing contract and thereby assume legal status, or they may be incorporated into a country's legislation covering such items as safety.

In the USSR, individual industrial enterprises, like their Western counterparts use standards for the purpose of attempting to reduce manufacturing costs and particularly to help to guarantee the quality of sources of supply. These documents are referred to as 'enterprise standards' (*standarty predpriyatiya*), and may form the basis of a purchasing contract. Similarly, industrial ministries may also publish standards for use by those factories responsible to them, and these are frequently referred to as 'industrial standards' or 'branch standards' (*otraslevye standarty*). The national standards used in the USSR, (referred to as 'state standards' or *GOSTy*, the abbreviation for *gosudartstvennye standarty*), however, have legal status in their own right[41], since they are considered to be a means of ensuring that the national economy is provided with a supply of products of adequate quality. They automatically form a legal framework for purchasing contracts between Soviet enterprises, as well as carrying penalties for non-observance. Hence, it is important for 'industrial' and 'enterprise' standards to conform with state standards for those products specified by the latter. Most state standards specify major parameters for defined types of articles, and relevant tests and acceptable tolerances to be observed during the product's manufacture and final test. These standards can be conveniently referred to as 'type standards' since they refer to article types, and they can be viewed as useful instruments for establishing the major features of product types as manufactured. Another group of state standards has been introduced since 1967 known as 'mark of quality' standards which refer to specific models of a product, manufactured in a particular factory, rather than the generic product group referred to in 'type standards'. These 'mark of quality' standards are discussed later in this section of the chapter.

For both 'type standards' and 'mark of quality' standards, it is normal Soviet convention for the last two digits of the standard designation to denote the year in which the standard was published. For example 'type standard' GOST 18097–72 was published in 1972, and 'mark of quality' standard 5.806–71 was published in 1971. Implementation of the standard into industrial practice normally occurs during the following year, or possibly two years.

Organising Framework

The current framework for publishing state standards in the USSR has emerged since 1965, following the re-establishment of the ministerial system of industrial management,[42] and the passing of two resolutions by the Council of Ministers of the USSR to strengthen the role played by standardisation in Soviet economic development.[43] Many of the features of this current framework are not new, however, since standards have been published for national use by Soviet industry for some sixty years, the first central organisation responsible for standardisation being set up by government decree in 1925. This organisation, named the All-Union Committee of Standardisation, was responsible for the approval of industrial standards which had legal status throughout the national economy. The Committee underwent several organisational changes, until in 1954 it was made responsible to the Council of Ministers of the USSR, (the highest government body in the Soviet Union) and its title changed to the Committee of Standards, Measures and Measuring Instruments under the Council of Ministers of the USSR.[44] Since the beginning of 1971, its title has been modified to the State Committee of Standards of the Council of Ministers of the USSR, (*Gosstandart SSSR*) and its Chairman elevated to membership of the Council of Ministers of the USSR. In spite of the Committee's apparent improvement in status, however, there appeared to be little change in many of its administrative frameworks formalised between 1966 and 1970, although its powers to arbitrarily inspect the quality of produce of industrial enterprises were increased.[45]

The organisational structure of the State Committee of Standards is divided into administrations or departments, which carry out overall co-ordination of the drafting of standards for particular sectors of industry. The State Committee has also established a number of scientific-research institutes (probably about twenty in total) to assist its relevant administrations and departments by executing research work into problems of standardisation and metrology, and checking the technical content of draft standards prior to approval. The practical work of drafting standards is delegated by the State Committee to research and development organisations already established within the appropriate industrial ministries and responsible to these for product and process development. These establishments are frequently referred to by the State Committee of Standards as 'base organisations for standardisation', or 'head organisations for standardisation' in those cases where a particular industry may be large enough to require close co-ordination of its several base organisations. Over 400 research and technological organisations throughout the USSR have been designated in this manner.[46]

State standards are introduced into industrial practice by means of factory standards, published by the standards department of a particular enterprise and approved by its chief engineer. The technical requirements of these documents should coincide with the relevant state standards, but specify in more detail those quality parameters required for particular manufacturing and testing operations.[47] They are introduced into factory practice by the standards department which in a large enterprise may also supervise the work of small groups of standards engineers employed in different departments. In an attempt to ensure that all enterprises carry out this work, and hence produce articles to the quality level of the relevant state standard, a system of local inspection organisations ('laboratories of state supervision') responsible to the State Committee of Standards' Department of State Supervision has been established in all industrial areas throughout the USSR.[42] The main duty of these organisations is that of supervising the observance of relevant standards for finished products and measuring equipment by factories within their industrial location, by means of inspection as and when they choose; but they also have the right to confiscate sub-standard production through the authority of the office of the Chief State Inspector who is a Deputy Chairman of the State Committee of Standards.[49]

'Quality Attestation'

As mentioned in a previous section of this chapter, most state standards specify major parameters of types of articles and relevant tests and acceptable tolerances to be observed during the product's manufacture and final test. These 'type standards', therefore, can be considered as useful instruments for establishing the major quality features of a product as manufactured. In practice, however, the quality in service, or the performance, of a product will also be dependent upon many other factors which it is difficult to standardise. In a Western-type economy, it is assumed that market pressures force manufacturers to take account of these factors during the design and manufacture of their product range in order to remain competitive; but in a tightly planned Soviet-type economy, with its associated seller's market, these market pressures are almost absent since purchasers have restricted choice in their buying activities. The USSR has consequently attempted to reduce this problem by means of a 'mark of quality' or 'quality attestation' system. The main feature of the 'mark of quality' system is that it is a serious attempt to improve the quality of Soviet industrial production by granting an award to those products which are considered to meet the same requirements as similar advanced products sold by other non-Soviet manufacturers in the world market.

The Soviet 'quality attestation' and related 'mark of quality' systems were introduced after a 1965 decree of the Council of Ministers of the USSR which related specifically to product quality. ('On the improvement of planning and the strengthening of incentives for industrial production'.)[50] This system of quality attestation divided products into three main quality categories, namely 'highest', 'first', and 'second'; and overall responsibility for the allocation of products to the appropriate category was to rest with the Committee of Standards.[51] This allocation was determined according to the following criteria:

(a) all products allocated to the 'highest' category were to exceed the demands of appropriate state 'type standards' and correspond to the highest indicators of reliability and durability, convenience of manufacture, style, and the use of standard and common parts. In addition, such products were to provide economic advantages to the purchaser.[52] Products that were considered to meet these requirements were to be submitted by their manufacturing ministry or enterprise. An 'attestation commission' was then set up by the manufacturing ministry and approved by the Committee of Standards to investigate the product, and if the outcome of this investigation was satisfactory, the product was to be stamped with a state 'Mark of Quality' (see Figure 1.1). A premium was to be awarded to the manufacturer to cover the additional costs required for quality improvements, and also to provide increased profitability; but the size of this premium was also to be influenced by the economic advantages to buyers.[53]

(b) all products designated as 'first category' were to correspond to

the requirements of contemporary 'type standards' and to meet the demands of the national economy and the population,[54] but were not considered to meet the demands of the 'highest category' products outlined in (a) above.
(c) all products designated to the 'second category' were considered not to correspond to contemporary demands, were obsolete, and considered to require modernisation or removal from production. The time for the completion of modernisation, or removal from production was agreed between the manufacturing ministry, the chief customer ministry, and the State Committee of Planning (*Gosplan SSSR*).[55]

Figure 1.1 The Soviet 'Mark of Quality'

From 1967–71, the objectives of quality attestation were quite narrowly defined, namely the awarding of the 'Mark of Quality' to products made in high volumes in factories recently transferred to the post-1965 method of planning and economic incentives.[56] From 1971 onwards, however, the intention has been to extend the range of products receiving 'Mark of Quality' approval.[57] In general, those products receiving such approval were considered to be equivalent in specification to other similar products made for the world market by foreign producers.

Since 1981, following the December 1979 decree of the Council of Ministers (No.1093), the State Committee of Science and Technology, and the State Committee of Planning have also become engaged in the product categorisation process along with the State Committee of Standards.[58] Furthermore since 1984, the role of the Ministry of Foreign Trade has been strengthened in the product approval process, to increase the likelihood that highest category products match the specifications of the most advanced similar products sold on the world market.[59]

In future the system of approval is to be more tightly controlled by closer state supervision, as distinct from branch supervision, of the approval process, mainly through the designation of 'approval centres' for certain product types. Although these centres are to be research and technical establishments nominally responsible to industrial ministries, the approval procedure is to be more tightly controlled by *Gosstandart SSSR* to ensure that products do not receive the award without being rigorously tested.[60]

Since 1984, the 'second category' of quality has also been gradually abolished to put increased pressure on industrial enterprises and ministries to remove obsolete products from their product lines.[61] This new procedure is currently being introduced following the 1983 decree of the Central Committee of the CPSU, and it is intended that a comprehensive list will be compiled of agricultural and industrial products which must be submitted for categorisation into either the 'highest' or the 'first' level of quality. The only exemptions to this list are defence equipment, and a range of foodstuffs, cosmetics and medical goods, which are presumably assessed by other procedures.[62]

Those products which fail to be categorised as 'highest' or 'first' quality under the new procedure, and are consequently defined as 'second' category, are to be removed from production within two months unless special permission to continue production is granted by the State Committee of Planning for a two-year interval.[63] Products which have been attested to meet 'first' or 'highest' category are thereby listed for three years or two years in the case of consumer products; although in some cases 'highest' category products may receive the 'Mark of Quality' for five years.[64]

The quality attestation procedure is to be given increased importance from 1986 onwards as a result of the joint decree of the Central Committee of the CPSU and the Council of Ministers of the USSR. This decree provides for a price increase for 'highest category' products and a discount for 'first category' products.[65]

The 'attestation' system consequently differs from 'type standardisation' which has attempted to stabilise the technical level of all factories producing a specific type of item. The 'mark of quality' system on the other hand, attempts to create incentives for factories in a leading position in Soviet technology to manufacture products to the highest international levels. These levels may be higher than those previously specified by the product type standards, and include a detailed assessment of various product parameters, methods of manufacture and quality control which it may be too time-consuming to include in a 'type standard'. In addition, some assessment is made of product style, and the degree of use of standard and common parts. The 'quality attestation' process, therefore, assists in attempting to guarantee a mix of high quality products being delivered to the national economy. In addition, under possible new procedures currently being considered in the USSR, quality attestation may be carried out at the design, pre-production and final manufacturing stages of most industrial products for purposes of classification into the 'highest' or 'first' categories of product quality. Approval at the design and pre-production stages will be considered as 'hurdles' which the product must clear before commencement of manufacture, but the final decision on quality attestation will still be deferred until the product is manufactured under batch-production conditions.[66]

CONCLUSIONS

It can be seen from the previous sections of this chapter that the Soviet authorities have made serious efforts to develop and implement a comprehensive system of standardisation, and to use this system to stabilise and improve product quality in the economic conditions prevailing in the USSR. The following chapters of this book consist of a discussion of particular case studies of the use of state standards to evaluate Soviet product quality, to demonstrate the use of these openly-published documents to evaluate product parameters, and to contribute to the Western debate on Soviet product quality as outlined in the first section of this chapter. The particular cases considered are those of general purpose machine tools, asynchronous electric motors, automotive products, refrigerators and photographic equipment. In each case reference has been made to 'type standards' and 'mark of quality' standards since a complete range of these documents were available from the library of the British Standards Institute (BSI).

Where possible, the requirements of these Soviet documents have been compared wiht their British counterparts, as typical examples of standards published by an advanced industrialised Western country. This extensive data base of Soviet state standards has been facilitated by an agreement to exchange standards information between the BSI and *Gosstandart SSSR* through the Anglo-Soviet Working Group on

Metrology and Standardisation. In some cases, particularly for consumer products, the use of standards as data sources has been supplemented by the use of 'expert assessment' by technical journalists and consumers' associations.

2 General Purpose Machine Tool Type Standards

INTRODUCTION

General purpose machine tools are widely used in almost every industrial sector in the USSR, as in the Western industrialised economies, to produce engineering components in unit, small batch and medium batch production conditions. The basic requirement of any general purpose machine tool, assuming that it has adequate overall capacity, is its capability to produce components of the required accuracy. This capability depends, in its turn, on the precision with which major elements can be moved and positioned in relation to one another. Standards relating to machine tool quality, therefore, specify relevant tests and acceptable tolerances of error for the alignment of those major elements from which the machine tool is constructed.[1]

PREVIOUS STUDIES ON MACHINE TOOL STATE STANDARDS

A study was initially carried out by one of the present authors in 1969[2] to determine the range of products manufactured by the Soviet machine tool industry, for which state standards had been published. Since it appeared from this survey that approximately 90–95 per cent of the Soviet output of general purpose machine tools was specified by appropriate state standards, it was considered to be important to evaluate the technical requirements specified in these documents. Time did not permit a complete study of standards relating to every product type, and hence attention was concentrated on knee and column milling machines and centre lathes, as examples of widely used types of general purpose metal cutting machinery.[3]

The Soviet machine tool standards were technically assessed by comparing the technical requirements embodied in these documents, with those adhered to by British manufacturers of similar machine models to which the Soviet standards related, since there were no relevant British national standards for milling machines and centre lathes at that time.[4] Consequently, the accuracy requirements specified in the Soviet documents (GOST 13–54 for milling machines and GOST 42–56 for centre lathes) relating to 1250mm table size milling machines and 400mm swing centre lathes, were compared to those adhered to by British manufactures of similar models. From this comparative assessment it was concluded that although there were many tests for which similar tolerances were specified by both the appropriate Soviet state standard and the British manufacturers' testing documents, there were also some important tests for which closer tolerances were required by the British-built machines.

A subsequent study[5] was made of new Soviet standards published in 1972 for the accuracy of milling machines and centre lathes, for introduction into industrial practice at the beginning of 1974. These standards included tests and tolerances similar to those specified in the previous standards, although some important tolerances were also more demanding. The general trend was towards improving accuracy requirements, with many tests approaching the requirements of the British models selected for comparison. In addition to these accuracy requirements for 'machines of normal precision' (*stanki normal'noi tochnosti* ('N' Class)) the new standards also contained provision for the requirements of machines conforming to 'improved precision' (*stanki povyshennoi tochnosti* ('P' Class)) in which the alignment tolerances were usually 0.6 of those allowed for in 'normal precision' machines; whereas the requirements of 'improved precision' machines had previously been published in separate standards. Consequently, many of the test tolerances for these latter machines were more demanding than those of the Western models selected for comparison. Furthermore, in the case of centre lathes, tolerances were also included for 'high precision machines' (*stanki vysokoi tochnosti* ('V' Class)) which were even more demanding than those for 'improved precision' machines.

THE CURRENT STUDY

The method used in the previous studies consisted of a comparison of alignment tolerances specified in a Soviet state standard for a particular type and size of machine tool, with those adhered to by the manufacturer of a 'typical' British model of machine of the same type and size. In other words, the alignment tests for the British machine models were used as criteria against which to compare requirements of Soviet standards, in both the late 1960s and the mid-1970s.

In recent years, however, the British Standards Institution has published a series of standards relating to the accuracy requirements of many types of general purpose machine tool. A comparison of the accuracy requirements specified in these standards with their selected Soviet counterparts should consequently form a better basis for assessment than the previously used 'selected typical model' approach, since:

(a) national standards for similar machines can be compared;
(b) both sets of standards use similar tests and metric tolerances;
(c) both sets of standards are up-to-date, and should consequently represent contemporary machine tool standardisation in both countries;
and
(d) a sufficient time has elapsed to enable the requirements of the standards to be absorbed in both countries.

Consequently, it was initially decided to compare the alignment accuracies of knee and column milling machines and centre lathes, as specified in the relevant Soviet and British standards, in order to extend the previous studies described in the previous section of this chapter (see Tables A.1 and A.2 in the Appendix). As these pilot studies showed that comparative analysis was possible using the Soviet and British documents, the methodology was extended for the following types of machines which had not been compared previously:

radial drilling machines,
vertical drilling machines,
surface grinding machines,
external cylindrical grinding machines,
internal cylindrical grinding machines,
vertical broaching machines,
vertical gearhobbing machines,
horizontal gearhobbing machines.

The documentary sources used for comparative analysis are listed in Table 2.1.

These machine types were selected since they process the bulk of general purpose machining work carried out by the majority of

Table 2.1 Soviet State Standards and British national standards for selected machine types

Machine type	Soviet standard	British standard
Centre Lathes	GOST 18097–72	BS4656 Part 1 1970 (±ISO 1708)
Knee and Column Milling Machines	GOST 17734–72	BS4656 Part 3 1971 (±ISO 1701)
Radial Drilling Machines	GOST 38–71	BS4656 Part 10 1974 (±ISO 2423) (#ISO 2772 I&II, ISO 2773)
Surface Grinding Machines	GOST 273–77	BS4656 Part 7 1971 (±ISO 1986)
External Cylindrical Grinding Machines	GOST 11654–72	BS4656 Part 9 1974 (#ISO 2433)
Internal Cylindrical Grinding Machines	GOST 25–72	BS4656 Part 8 1974 (#ISO 2407)
Vertical Broaching Machines	GOST 16025–79	BS4656 Part 17 1973
Vertical Gearhobbing Machines	GOST 659–78	BS4656 Part 19 1976
Horizontal Gearhobbing Machines	GOST 18065–72	BS4656 Part 19 1976

Notes: ± denotes that the British national standard covers similar subject matter to that covered by the appropriate international standards, although there is not full technical equivalence between the two documents; # denotes that the national standard corresponds in all technical respects to the appropriate international standards, although wording and presentation may differ.

industrial users. This machining work includes the generation of plain cylindrical and flat surfaces, which act as envelopes for most engineering components, the generation of external helical gear teeth, and the generation of complex-shaped surfaces. In the light of available estimates (see Table 2.2), it is considered that the selected types of machines account for 65 per cent of the total annual quantity of metalcutting machine tools produced in the Soviet Union, or more than 75 per cent of the total Soviet annual output of 'standard' (i.e. 'non-specialised') machine tools, for which it is feasible to publish standardised alignment accuracies.

It is necessary to point out, however, that some further selection has been carried out when comparing the alignment accuracies specified in each of these documents, in view of the wide range of major product parameters used by the engineers responsible for drafting the

General Purpose Machine Tool Type Standards

Table 2.2 Soviet output of specific machine tool types

Machine type	1965 output in thousand units (1)	1970 output in thousand units (2)	1975 output in thousand units (3)
General purpose & Capstan Lathes	55.5	65.4	78.6
Automatic and semi-automatic Lathes	4.7	5.1	5.9
Boring Machines	3.2	5.0	5.7
Drilling Machines	28.3	24.0	27.6
Planing & Slotting Machines	4.3	4.8	5.6
Broaching Machines	1.5	n.a.	n.a.
Milling Machines	22.3	21.0	22.5
Gear Cutting Machines	3.5	4.0	4.6
Grinding Machines	12.3	13.7	13.8
Tool and Cutter Grinding Machines	11.0	n.a.	n.a.
Special purpose Machines	26.1	31.2	35.9
Sharpening Machines, Sawing Machines, Thread-cutting Machines, Others	13.6	28.0	30.4
Total	186.1	202.2	230.5

Notes: (1) Source for 1965 output data: Oznobin, N. M. *et al.* (eds), *Sovershenstvovanie struktury proizvodstva* (Moscow, 1968) p. 136, cited by Berry, M. J., Cooper, J. M., 'Machine Tools', in Amann, R., Cooper, J. M., Davies, R. W. (eds), *The Technological Level of Soviet Industry*, (New Haven and London: Yale University Press, 1977) p. 155. From this data, it can be seen that the output of the selected machine types in Table 2.1, (i.e.: general purpose lathes, drilling machines, milling machines, grinding machines, broaching machines and gear-cutting machines) accounted for 123 400 within a total output of 186 100 machine tools, or within a total of 160 000 machine tools excluding special-purpose types, (i.e.: 66 per cent of the former, and 77 per cent of the latter); (2) Source for 1970 output data: Institut fur Ost-Marktforschung GMBH; *Der Bedarf der Sowjetischen Volkswirtschaft an Werkzeugmaschinen und die Vorgesehene Bedarfsdeckung 1976–1980* (Hamburg, 1976) p. 25. From this data it can be seen that the selected machine types accounted for an output of 128 000 within a total output of 202 200 machine tools, or within a total of 171 000 machine tools excluding special purpose types (i.e.: 63 per cent of the former, and 75 per cent of the latter); (3) Source for 1975 output data. See (2) above. The selected machine types accounted for an output of 147 100 within a total output of 230 500, or within a total of 194 600 machine tools excluding special purpose types (i.e.: 64 per cent of the former, and 76 per cent of the latter); (4) Although the source cited in (2) above does not quote any published Soviet figures, the stated output figures for milling machines, grinding machines and total machine tool output for 1970 and 1975, coincide almost exactly with those quoted in the COMECON annual statistical handbooks published in 1974 and 1976 (*Statisticheskii ezhegodnik stran-chlenov Soveta Ekonomicheskoi Vzaipomoshchi*, (Moscow), pp. 88–9 (1974) and pp. 82–3 (1976)). The present authors were provided with this data by M. J. Berry of the Centre for Russian and East European Studies, University of Birmingham.

appropriate standards. In spite of the necessity of this selection, it is still considered by the authors that a valid comparison has been achieved over a wide range of diverse machine types.

These comparisons are shown in Tables A.1 to A.10 in the Appendix, with a discussion on these Tables given in the following section of this chapter. It will be noted that the tables in these appendices refer to a permitted tolerance for each test; these tolerances are usually measured by the difference between the maximum and minimum readings of a dial indicator or similar measuring instrument. The indicator is clamped at some fixed point on the machine with its measuring probe in contact with the relevant machine element which is traversed or rotated for the specified testing distance (e.g.: a machine table traversed along a slideway for a specified distance, or a mandrel mounted in a spindle which is rotated through a complete revolution). It is important to remind the reader that, when studying these tables, a smaller specified value of tolerance denotes an increased level of accuracy! Each of the tolerances are quoted to the nearest micron (i.e.: millionth part of a metre).

RESULTS

Centre Lathes

Centre lathes are one of the most widely used types of machine tool encountered in the engineering industry. Their universal design makes them capable of generating external and internal cylindrical surfaces, and screw threads, usually on workpieces which are themselves cylindrical or symmetrical about an axis of rotation. The major parameter usually selected by engineers responsible for drafting standards for these machines is the maximum diameter of workpiece that can be accommodated, which is frequently referred to as the 'swing'. Secondarily, the maximum length of workpiece that can be accommodated is also of importance, and this parameter can usually be defined by the 'distance between centres'.

It is usually the case that tolerances for some accuracy tests of centre lathes increase as the major parameters of the machine also increase, since it is generally more difficult to maintain a particular geometric tolerance over a longer distance. It is consequently important to select tolerances for machine alignment accuracy for machines of similar size, in order to obtain valid comparisons. Unfortunately, there are some differences between the major parameters used in the Soviet standards, and those used by their British counterparts, namely:

for the Soviet standard:
   up to 400 mm swing
   400–800 mm swing
   800–1600 mm swing
   1600–3200 mm swing
   3200–6400 mm swing
and for the British standard:
   up to 500 mm swing for 'precision lathes'
   up to 800 mm swing for 'other lathes'
   and 800–1600 mm swing for 'other lathes'

Taking these differences in parameters into account, and the Soviet practice of classifying machines by precision, the basis selected for comparison was as shown in Table 2.3.

The results for comparative lathe accuracies are shown in Table A.1 in the Appendix below, using alignment accuracies specified in GOST 18097–72 and BS 4656 Part 1 (1970) respectively. In general we can conclude from Table A.1 that Soviet state standards for centre lathes in the 'normal precision' class are at least as demanding as their British Standard counterparts, and in some cases even more demanding, particularly for centre lathes of less than 400 mm swing. Similarly, Soviet state standards in the 'improved precision' class are at least as demanding as their British Standard counterparts ('precision lathes') and in a few cases even more demanding, particularly for machines having a maximum workpiece diameter of less than 400mm. Soviet standards also provide for even more demanding tests in their 'high precision' machines category, for which there are no comparable tests available in British Standards.

Table 2.3 Selected lathe parameters (for accuracy comparison)

'Precision Lathes' (BS 4656 Part 1) and 'Machines of Improved Precision' ('P' Class GOST 18097–72)		'Other Lathes' BS 4656 Part 1 and 'Machines of Normal Precision' ('N' Class GOST 18097–72)	
GOST 18097–72	BS 4656 Part 1	GOST 18097–72	BS 4656 Part 1
up to 400mm swing) 400–500mm swing)	up to 500mm swing	up to 400mm swing) 400–800mm swing)	up to 800mm swing
		800–1600mm swing	800–1600mm swing

Knee and Column Milling Machines

Knee and column milling machines are used for the generation of external planar surfaces, chiefly on cubic or irregularly shaped components of small and medium size. To a lesser extent, they can also be used for the generation of internal cylindrical surfaces. In view of the large number of these types of component encountered in engineering practice, and their universal design, knee and column milling machines are widely used. Their production capacity depends, in the first place, upon the size of the table used for securing the workpiece to be processed and the distances over which this assembly can be traversed in relation to the tool-holding spindle. Consequently, table size and table traverse are frequently considered as major parameters for these types of machine tool.

The results for the comparative alignment accuracies of knee and column milling machines are shown in Table A.2 in the Appendix, using specified tolerances from GOST 17734–72 and BS 4656 Part 3 (1971) repectively. As in the case of centre lathes referred to in the previous subsection, it was found that the Soviet state standard for the accuracy of knee and column milling machines of the 'normal precision' class was at least as demanding as its British Standard counterpart, and in some cases, even more demanding. There is not, however, any 'precision milling machine' class in BS 4656 Part 3, and hence no comparison can be made for the 'improved precision' class of Soviet machine, although it is important to note that these more exacting requirements do exist in the Soviet document.

Drilling Machines

Drilling machines, as their name clearly suggests, are used for the generation of internal cylindrical surfaces, using the drilling process. In engineering production practice, general purpose drilling machines are usually divided into vertical drilling machines used for the smaller type of engineering component, and radial drilling machines provided with the means of radially traversing the drilling head along its supporting arm, thereby providing the means of producing holes in larger components. In general the production capacity of the machine is influenced by the maximum size of drill that can be fitted into the machine, and consequently this is frequently taken as a major parameter for the machine.

The results of the comparative studies are shown in Tables A.3 and A.4 in the Appendix with specified accuracies quoted from GOST 370–76 and BS 4656 Part 11 (1974) for vertical drilling machines; and GOST 98–71 and BS 4656 Part 10 (1974) for radial drilling machines. For 'normal precision' machines, it is apparent that the accuracy requirements of the Soviet standards are at least as high as their British Standard equivalents, and even higher in a few cases, particularly for vertical drilling machines. Furthermore, Soviet state standards for vertical machines include an even more demanding set of requirements in the tolerances for machines of improved precision.

Grinding Machines

General purpose grinding machines used universally in engineering production can be divided into three main groups, namely:

(a) surface grinding machines with a horizontal spindle, used for the generation of flat surfaces using an abrasive grinding wheel;
(b) external cylindrical grinding machines, used for the generation of external cylindrical surfaces by means of an abrasive grinding wheel;
(c) internal grinding machines, used for the generation of internal cylindrical surfaces by means of an abrasive grinding wheel.

It can be seen, therefore, that the general aims in the use of these types of machine are not dissimilar from the lathes, drilling machines and milling machines that have been described previously in this chapter. For example, both surface grinding machines and knee and column milling machines are used to generate flat surfaces; external cylindrical grinding machines and centre lathes are used to generate plain external cylindrical surfaces; and internal grinding machines, centre lathes, drilling machines and milling machines can be used to generate plain internal cylindrical surfaces.

In general, however, the use of an abrasive grinding process facilitates the production of surfaces of more precise dimension, accurate form and smoother finish than the lathes, drilling machines and milling machines referred to above, provided that the appropriate machine tool is designed and built to the requisite precision; although the rate of generation of the requisite surface dimensions is usually slower. Consequently, in engineering practice, precision grinding machines are usually kept specially for the accurate finishing of precision components, previously semi-finished to almost the requisite precision by a lathe, milling machine or other type of metal-cutting machine tool, but with a sufficient amount of metal remaining for economic removal during the abrasive finishing process.

The results for the comparative accuracies of grinding machines are shown in Tables A.5, A.6 and A.7 in the Appendix, as follows:

GOST 273–77 and BS 4656 Part 7 (1971) for surface grinding machines with a horizontal spindle and reciprocating table;
GOST 11654–72 and BS 4656 Part 9 (1974) for external cylindrical grinding machines;
GOST 25–72 and BS 4656 Part 8 (1974) for internal grinding machines.

As in the case of the metalcutting machines previously surveyed, it has been necessary to quote appropriate tolerances for machines having a particular major parameter. For surface grinding machines, this parameter was usually table width, and maximum workpiece diameter for cylindrical and internal grinding machines. From this data it is possible to draw the following conclusions with respect to the accuracy requirements of grinding machines specified by Soviet state standards:

(a) the Soviet state standard for the accuracy requirements of surface grinding machines specifies tolerances for 'high precision' ('V' Class) and 'ultra-high precision' ('A' Class) machines only. These tolerances are usually far more demanding than those specified by the British Standard, which are approximately equal to what would be expected from Soviet 'improved precision' ('P'

Class) machines if such requirements had been drafted, although the British Standard tests for finished workpiece accuracy appear to be almost as demanding as the Soviet 'V' class counterparts;
(b) the Soviet state standard for the accuracy requirements of external cylindrical grinding machines specifies tolerances for 'improved precision' ('P' Class) machines which are similar in requirement to the British standard, although the tests are sometimes less demanding for the 400–800 mm maximum workpiece diameter machines, and usually more demanding for those machines having a maximum workpiece diameter of less than 400 mm. In addition to these tolerances, however, the Soviet document also specifies even more demanding tests for 'high precision' ('V' Class) and 'ultra-high' ('A' Class) precision class machines;
(c) a similar situation was also apparent with regard to internal grinding machines, namely the similarity in tolerances between 'the improved precision' ('P' Class) machines and tolerances specified in BS 4656 Part 8 (1974), with the Soviet document also specifying even more demanding tests for 'high precision' ('V' Class) and 'ultra-high precision' ('A' Class) machines.

Broaching Machines

Broaching machines are used under conditions of repetitive production for the generation of flat or internal circular shapes, or the generation of complex external or internal shapes. The major factors influencing the accuracy of the broaching tool are the correct positioning and clamping of the workpiece in relation to the tool path, and the accuracy of movement of the tool slide (for external surfaces) or the tool puller (for internal surfaces) relative to the workpiece.

Broaching machines are classified according to three parameters, namely whether they are capable of carrying out external work, or internal work, or both; whether they have a horizontal or vertical configuration; and the magnitude of broaching force. For the purposes of this comparative analysis, vertical universal broaching machines have been selected, which are capable of carrying out both external and internal operations, with a broaching load range of 50–800 kN.

The results of the comparative studies are shown in Table A.8 in the Appendix, with specified tolerances quoted from GOST 16025–79 and BS 4656 Part 17 (1973). For 'normal precision' machines, it is apparent that the accuracy requirements of Soviet standards are higher than their British Standard equivalents for 50 per cent of the tests, and lower for the remaining 50 per cent. In conclusion, therefore, it would appear that neither the Soviet nor the British standard appears to be consistently higher than the other.

Gearhobbing Machines

Gearhobbing machines are used to generate external helical teeth on gear wheels using the hobbing process, in which the tooth is generated using a hardened high speed steel hob ground to the requisite profile. The hob and gear wheel are then rotated in a precise motion relative to each other such that the hob feeds through the component and generates the required tooth shape. The hobbing process is the fastest method of gear tooth generation, but its application is limited in practice due to the necessity of requiring an adequate clearance each side of the gear rim to feed the hob through the component.

Gearhobbing machines are classified into two groups in terms of their general configuration, namely vertical and horizontal gearhobbers. In this comparative analysis, both types of machines have been investigated with tolerances specified by GOST 659–78, GOST 18065–72, and BS 4656 Part 19 (1976). The Soviet standards specify tolerances for four classes of precision, namely 'normal precision' ('N' Class), 'improved precision' ('P' Class), 'high precision' ('V' Class), and 'ultra-high precision' ('A' Class), whilst the British Standard specifies requirements for 'normal' and 'high' accuracy machines for which many of the tolerances are identical.

From the results given in Tables A.9 and A.10 in the Appendix, it can be seen that the requirements of the British Standards are usually more demanding for the normal accuracy machines than their Soviet counterparts for both vertical and horizontal machines; whilst for 'high accuracy' (UK) and 'improved precision' (Soviet) machines, neither standard appears to be consistently higher than the other, although the British Standards for horizontal machines do appear to be slightly more demanding than those of their Soviet counterparts.

CONCLUSIONS

Table 2.4 is a summary of the results discussed in the previous section, and presented in detail in Tables A.1 to A.10 in the Appen-

Table 2.4 Comparison of accuracy requirements specified by British and Soviet standards for machine tool alignment tests

Machine type	Soviet standard more demanding (number of occurrences)	Equal tolerances (number of occurrences)	British standard more demanding (number of occurrences)
Normal Precision Centre Lathes	3	11	0
Improved Precision Centre Lathes	4	10	0
Normal Precision Milling Machines	0	16	0
Normal Precision Vertical Drilling Machines	3	1	0
Radial Drilling Machines	2	3	0
High Precision Surface Grinding Machines	8	0	0
Improved Precision Cylindrical Grinding Machines	3	7	3
Improved Precision Internal Grinding Machines	2	7	2
Vertical Broaching Machines	5	0	5
Normal Precision Vertical Gearhobbing Machines	1	6	7
Improved Precision Vertical Gearhobbing Machines	5	2	6
Normal Precision Horizontal Gearhobbing Machines	0	2	6
Improved Precision Horizontal Gearhobbing Machines	0	5	3
Totals (not counting surface grinding machines)	28	70	32
Totals (counting surface grinding machines)	36	70	32

dix. This table shows that for the total of more than 130 alignment tests relating to the ten machine tool types and sizes selected for comparison (not counting surface grinding machines, since there were no directly comparable classes of machine accuracy), similar tolerances were specified for over 50 per cent of the tests in both the Soviet and British Standards, with the Soviet tests being more accurate in 22 per cent of the cases, and the British tests being more accurate in 25 per cent of the cases. If surface grinding machines are included, the proportion of tests for which the Soviet tests were more demanding is marginally higher (26 per cent), compared with their British counterparts (23 per cent of the tests more demanding).

It can be concluded, therefore, that the alignment accuracies specified in Soviet state standards for centre lathes, drilling machines, milling machines, grinding machines, broaching machines and gear-cutting machines are generally as high as those specified in British national standards. If it is assumed that these alignment accuracies are an indicator of quality for general purpose machine tools, and that they are also an indicator of minimum quality requirements for the machine tool industries in the respective two countries, then there is strong evidence to suggest that the quality of Soviet-produced general purpose machines is similar to those of their British-manufactured counterparts. Furthermore, since many of the requirements of the British Standards are based on the recommendations of the International Standards Organisation, and the UK machine tool industry is a long-standing supplier to international markets, it would appear that the USSR can now be viewed as a potential international supplier of general-purpose machine tools of adequate quality.

It is necessary, however, to sound a note of caution over the use of these documents to obtain a total picture of product quality, since there may be several characteristics of a product which affect its quality in use, but which are difficult to specify quantitatively in a state standard. For example, if quality is viewed as total 'fitness for purpose',[6] it is apparent that in addition to alignment accuracy, the 'fitness for purpose' of a general purpose machine tool is also influenced by such factors as rigidity, ease and speed of setting, operation and control, and reliability and durability in service.

Moreover, some British machine tool factories may also claim that market forces require their products to be far more accurate than the minimum requirements laid down by national standards, whereas such forces are considered to be absent from the centrally planned Soviet economy. The validity of such a claim could only be verified by comparative analysis of individual machine models, which would require a very extensive study. In view of the comparatively recent publication of the British national standards, however, and the participation of the British machine tool industry in the drafting of these documents, the present authors are inclined to the view that their requirements should be typical for the industry.

TRENDS IN ACCURACY IMPROVEMENT IN SOVIET MACHINE TOOL STATE STANDARDS

The previous section of this chapter has demonstrated the apparent capability of the Soviet machine tool industry to meet contemporary international requirements for quality as defined by machine alignment accuracy. In addition, a previous study by one of the present authors,[7] described in the second section of this chapter, found that several tolerances for 'normal precision' class centre lathes and milling machines had been reduced in contemporary standards compared with those specified in their predecessors published some fifteen years earlier. A summary of these changes is presented in Tables 2.5 and 2.6 for centre lathes and milling machines of defined sizes (400 mm workpiece diameter and 320 mm table width milling machines, respectively) selected to reduce the time required to carry out the comparative survey. In addition, it is also apparent that the overall effect of this reduction in acceptable error has been to change the alignment accuracies for these machines from a position of 'equal to or worse than' to a position of 'equal to or better than' the corresponding requirements specified in the British Standard.

This survey has been extended to other types of machine tool for which information has been found to be available, namely cylindrical grinding machines and vertical gearhobbing machines. In the case of this set of machines, however, a different methodology has been followed to that used for centre lathes and milling machines to counter any bias which may have been created by selecting machines of a defined size. Each tolerance was taken for each defined machine size and accuracy class of cylindrical grinding machines and vertical gearhobber, and the contemporary standard compared with its predecessor where possible. The results of this survey are summarised in Table 2.7, together with those for the defined centre lathes and milling machines using the same methodology.

From this table it can be concluded that for three of the four

Table 2.5 Comparative accuracies of normal precision lathes specified by GOST 42–56 and GOST 18097–72

Test	Tolerance to GOST 42–56	Tolerance to GOST 18097–72	Tolerance to BS4656 Part 1
Spindle nose run-out	15	10	10
Spindle axial slip	15	10	10
Camming of spindle face plate	25	20	20
Run-out of spindle axis			
(a) at face	15	12	10
(b) 300mm from face	25	20	20
Parallelism of spindle axis to carriage over 300mm longitudinal movement			
(a) vertically	30	20	20
(b) horizontally	15	12	15
Parallelism of tailstock sleeve axis to carriage over 100mm movement			
(a) vertically	30	20	20
(b) horizontally	12	12	15
Accuracy of pitch generated by leadscrew over a 300mm length	50	40	40
Thrust bearing axial displacement	15	10	15
Roundness of machined test piece	15	10	10

Notes: (i) all tolerances in microns; (ii) tolerances selected for lathes having a maximum workpiece diameter within the range 400–800mm.

Table 2.6 Comparative accuracies of normal precision knee and column milling machines specified by GOST 13–54 and GOST 17734–72

Test	Tolerance to GOST 13–54	Tolerance to GOST 17734–72	Tolerance to BS4656 Part 3
Spindle axial slip	20	10	10
Camming of spindle nose face	25	20	20
Radial run-out of spindle nose external face	15	10	10
Parallelism of spindle axis to table surface	30	25	25
Parallelism of arbor support to spindle axis	25	20	20

Workpiece flatness	40	25	20
Workpiece parallelism	40	25	30
Workpiece squareness	20	20	20

Notes: All tolerances in microns.

Table 2.7 Comparisons of accuracy requirements in current and previous Soviet State Standards

	Number of tests		
Machine type	Previous standard more accurate	No difference between current and previous standard	Current standard more accurate
Cylindrical Grinding Machines:*			
'P Class'	0	51	19
'V Class'	0	39	11
'A Class'	0	29	7
Sub-total	0	119	37
Vertical Gear-hobbing Machines:**			
'N Class'	4	106	2
'P Class'	3	118	1
'A Class'	7	110	5
Sub-total	14	334	8
Centre Lathes 'N Class' (400mm Maximum Workpiece Diameter)***	2	5	8
Knee and Column Milling Machines, 'N Class', (1250mm Table Size)****	2	6	6
Total	18	464	59

Notes: * Previous Standard: GOST 11654–65; Current Standard: GOST 11654–72; ** Previous Standard: GOST 659–67, Current Standard: GOST 659–78; *** Previous Standard: GOST 42–56; Current Standard: GOST 18097–72; **** Previous Standard: GOST 13–54, Current Standard: GOST 17734–72.

Table 2.8 Current and previous State Standards for machine tools

Machine type	Current Soviet State Standard	Previous Soviet State Standard
Vertical drillers	GOST 370–76	GOST 370–67
Radial drillers	GOST 98–71	GOST 98–59
Surface grinders	GOST 273–77	GOST 273–67
Internal grinders	GOST 25–72	GOST 25–65

machine types studied (centre lathes, milling machines and grinding machines) there was a clear improvement in the contemporary standards for many of the tolerances specified. This improvement was not so apparent in the case of gearhobbing machines, where the tolerances appear to have been maintained or marginally modified to introduce a new precision class, namely 'high precision' or 'V' class machines. In addition, a very small number of tolerances appear to have been slightly eased, possibly as a result of difficulties encountered in meeting these requirements in practice.

It would clearly be useful to extend this study for other machine types using the documents listed in Table 2.8. A practical constraint to such a study, however, is the difficulty in locating copies of the older documents, since they are defined as obsolete and removed from circulation as soon as a new standard becomes operational.

3 Machine Tool 'Mark of Quality' Standards

'MARK OF QUALITY' STANDARDS

As outlined in Chapter 1, the main feature of the 'mark of quality' system is that it is a serious attempt to improve the quality of Soviet industrial production by granting an award to those products which are considered to meet the same requirements as similar advanced products sold by other manufacturers in the world market. The system consequently differs from 'type standardisation' which attempts to stabilise the technical level of all factories producing a specific type of item. The 'mark of quality' system on the other hand, attempts to create incentives for factories in a leading position in Soviet technology to manufacture products to the highest international levels. These levels may be higher than those specified by the product type standards, and include a detailed assessment of various product parameters, product style, the degree of use of standard and common parts, and methods of manufacture and quality control which it may be too time-consuming to include in a 'type standard'.

Soviet publications frequently cite evidence of the successful diffusion of the state attestation system throughout the Soviet national economy. In 1972, for example, the proportion of total sales turnover in the national economy accounted for by 'highest category' products was only some 2 per cent[1] but this had increased to 6.5 per cent by 1976,[2] 13.7 per cent by 1979,[3] and 15.7 per cent in 1981.[4]

In specific industrial ministries, the proportion of 'highest category' items in the product mix has been considerably higher than the national average. For example, the share of output to highest category levels in 1978 were 42.9 per cent for the Ministry of the Electrical Engineering Industry, 37.5 per cent for the Ministry of the Automobile Industry, 30 per cent for the Ministry of Consumer Products Engineering (*Minzhivmash*), 28.5 per cent for the Ministry of Heavy Engineering, and 25.3 per cent for the Ministry of the Instrument Building Industry.[5] Certain industries have also attempted to reduce their proportion of 'second category' output in the product mix as their proportion of 'highest category' output has increased. In 1968, for example, the Ministry of the Electrical Engineering

Industry produced 8.3 per cent of its sales turnover to the 'highest category' of quality, and 27.8 per cent to the second category. By 1980, the targetted proportion of highest quality output was 45 per cent, whilst second category output was less than 5 per cent.[6]

These claims have to be treated with a certain amount of caution, however, since 'Mark of Quality' products are probably some of the most expensive in the product range manufactured by the appropriate ministry. In the case of the Ministry of the Motor Industry, for example, none of the cars in the industry's product range have so far been awarded the 'Mark of Quality', although several trucks have (BelAZ–540 and 540A, GAZ–66, ZIL–130 and TSV–6). (See Chapter 5 below.) Consequently, although total truck output by the ministry's factories is probably about half that of cars in physical units (600 000 per year compared with 1 200 000 per year, approximately) the unit sales value of a truck is far higher. Furthermore, it is likely that high total growth rates in highest category products would be achieved in the late 1970s, compared with the early part of the decade, as the first 'highest category' product was not approved until 1967. Finally, some claims do not appear to be totally accurate. One such claim is that the 'Krasnyi Proletarii' factory intended to produce 90 per cent of its output to the 'highest category' by 1980,[7] even though the only three of the factory's products which have received the Mark of Quality award (1K282 and 1K283 eight spindle vertical autos and 1622 screwcutting lathe)[8] are probably smaller demand items compared with the more conventional centre lathe. If the 90 per cent target is true, the prices of the approved products would appear to be extremely high, or the Soviet economy is to be poorly served for conventional centre lathes unless they are now to be sourced from many other factories. Alternatively, the report may be misleading and refer to 'factory attestation', which would appear to be an internally administered and less rigorous system than 'state attestation' with its associated external controls.

Claims for success of the system also have to be balanced against frequent notes of criticism, mainly related to shortcomings in the manner by which the system is operated. For example, Ushakov[9] complains that a trailer was approved at the 'highest' level of quality without any comparative analysis being supplied on foreign equivalents; and the 'Bukovinka' hand-knitting machine was also approved without any data on reliability and service life. Furthermore, Treml quotes two Soviet authors who 'frankly admit that the quality-seal programme has not succeeded in bringing Soviet products up to world standards. They attribute this failure to the fact that representatives of foreign-trade agencies do not take an active part in quality certification, that certification commissions do not have adequate information on the technical specifications of advanced models on the world market, and that the State seal of quality is often awarded to products that already lag behind world technology'.[10] In addition, Lapusta and Nikitin also report that during 1975 and 1976, the right to use the Mark of Quality was removed from 168 enterprises making 333 products.[11]

There is also some evidence to suggest that enterprises have aimed to achieve high quality and state attestation without due regard to the associated costs; and the product's economic benefits to the user. For example, it is claimed that more than one half of products made to the highest category of quality received wholesale price supplements unrelated to their national-economic benefits,[12] and that the price of the KamAZ truck was raised by 40 per cent without due account being taken of the full economic effect.[13] This is referred to by Shteingauz as 'quality at any price',[14] but this criticism needs to be tempered with an appreciation of the problems of attempting to gauge utilisation costs with associated difficulties of gauging performance in practice and gathering data.

Finally, it would also appear that an insufficient proportion of new products are being manufactured to sufficiently high levels. For example, none of the sixty new products assimilated by enterprises in the tractor and agricultural engineering industry in 1980, were awarded the 'Mark of Quality';[15] whilst on the national average, only one in five of new products are approved to the highest quality level,[16] and conformance of new products to such requirements is not obligatory.[17]

In view of these differing viewpoints on the success of the mark of quality system, it was considered to be important to attempt to obtain an assessment of the quality levels of products awarded a 'mark of quality' by the state commission. Consequently, 'mark of quality' standards were initially selected for machine tools to extend the research described in the previous chapter. The results of this research are given in the next section.

AN ANALYSIS OF THE REQUIREMENTS OF MACHINE TOOL 'MARK OF QUALITY' STANDARDS

This section of the chapter is a study of the quality requirements of those models of machine tool which have been awarded a 'mark of quality' by the State Committee of Standards, following approval by a competent state certification mission. 1982 has been selected as a sample year for study, since this was the year for which the most complete listing was available at the commencement of this stage of the research.

The range of machine models which had received the 'mark of quality' by 1982 is listed in Table 3.1. A total of thirty-seven models had been approved by the certification commission, and the models receiving approval were spread over a broad machine range. It is important to note that almost one third of the total number of models of machine tool receiving 'mark of quality' approval were grinding machines for producing both flat and cylindrical surfaces. This has probably had a significant affect on the quality level of Soviet engineering production, since grinding machines usually carry out those processes at the final stages of component manufacture to achieve the requisite surface accuracy and smoothness. In addition, this suggests a high-precision technological capability of certain Soviet machine tool factories, since grinding machine design and production usually requires expertise in precision manufacture. This high precision capability is further suggested by the seven models of gearcutting machine which have received a 'mark of quality', since gearcutting machinery usually requires complex mechanisms and precision manufacture. It is also important to note that all of the attested machine models are general purpose machine tools using conventional metal-removal processes and methods of setting and control. Consequently, although the individual attested machine models are apparently of high quality as discussed below, they are all at a comparatively mature stage of the product life cycle compared with the more technologically advanced numerically controlled types of machine tool. It can be tentatively concluded, therefore, that attestation is intended more for the quality improvement of products at the mature and established stage of the technology life cycle, than the innovation of new products at the vanguard of advanced technology.

Table 3.2 contains comparative data on the technical requirements of 'mark of quality' standards, both in terms of quality requirements compared with appropriate type standards, and also between various

Table 3.1 Mark of Quality Standards for machine tools (1982)

Turning Machines	
GOST 5.81–68	Ultra-high precision centre- and screwcutting lathe, Model 1V616
GOST 5.1012–71	Screwcutting lathe, Model 1622
GOST 5.1347–72	Horizontal six-spindle bar auto, Model 1A225–6
GOST 5.1696–72	Vertical eight-spindle chucking auto, Model 1K282 and 1283
GOST 5.2130–73	Semi-automatic copy auto, Model 1B732
Drilling and Boring Machines	
GOST 5.1348–72	Bench-mounted drilling machines, Model 2N106P
GOST 5.1366–72	Horizontal-boring machine, Model 2B660 F1
GOST 5.1804–73	Single-column jig-boring machines, Model 2421
GOST 5.1915–73	Single-column jig-boring machines, Model 2411
Grinding Machines	
GOST 5.15–71	Ultra-high precision surface grinding machine, Model 3711
GOST 5.110–72	Cylindrical grinding machine, Model 3B151P
GOST 5.148–69	Universal cylindrical grinding machine, Model 3A10P
GOST 5.358–70	High precision profile surface grinding machine, Model 3B70P
GOST 5.359–73	Centreless grinding machine, Model 3D180
GOST 5.481–70	Cylindrical grinding machine, Model 3A164
GOST 5.482–70	Ultra-high precision cylindrical grinding machine, Model 3E153
GOST 5.727–71	Ultra-high precision surface grinding machine, Model 3701
GOST 5.806–71	Cylindrical grinding machine, Model 3A164A
GOST 5.1367–72	Cylindrical grinding machine, Model 3A172
GOST 5.1573–72	Special grinding machine, Model SSLP–1
Gearcutting Machines	
GOST 5.802–71	Ultra-high precision spur gearcutting machine, Model 5851
GOST 5.803–71	Gear-hobbing machine for worm-driven indexing wheels
GOST 5.804–71	Spur gear-grinding machine (abrasive hob), Model 5B832
GOST 5.1152–71	Semi-automatic gearshaving machine, Model 5701
GOST 5.1349–72	Spur gear grinding machine (abrasive hob), Model 5V830
GOST 5.1881–73	Semi-automatic horizontal gear hobbing machine, Model 5V370
GOST 5.1882–73	Vertical gear-hobbing machine, Model 5A342

continued on p. 40

Table 3.1 continued

Milling Machines	
GOST 5.919–71	Vertical knee and column milling machine, Model 6S12
GOST 5.1086–71	Disc milling machine, Model KZh–20M–Kh
GOST 5.1151–71	Plano-milling machine, Model 6605
GOST 5.1364–72	High precision toolroom milling machine, Model 6T75
GOST 5.1608–72	Key milling machine, Model 6D92
Planing and Shaping Machines	
GOST 5.1155–71	Hydraulically driven shaping machine, Model 7D36
GOST 5.1171–71	Twin-column planing machine, Model 7216
GOST 5.1171–71	Twin-column planing machine, Model 7212
Cut-off Machines	
GOST 5.702–70	Circular-saw cutt-off machine, Model 8A641
Other Machines	
GOST 5.1346–72	Screwcutting machine, Model RT 474

Source: *Ukazatel' Gosudarstvennykh standartov, 1982.*

'mark of quality' standards in terms of the specified requirements for a maintenance of accuracy, service life, guarantee and completeness (see Table A.11 in the Appendix, for two translated standards). The sample of fourteen machine models selected included four lathes, six grinding machines, two milling machines, and two gearcutting machines. These models were considered to be a representative sample of the range of machines covered by 'mark of quality' requirements, and the mix of machine tool types produced by Soviet industry.

When comparing quality requirements of the 'mark of quality' document with the 'type standard', test workpiece accuracy has been chosen as a basis for comparison, together with surface finish in the case of grinding machines, since these parameters are specified in every case, whereas a complete set of alignment tolerances for major machine elements is cited in only a few cases.

From the data shown in Table 3.2, therefore, it is evident that:

(a) in every case where comparison is possible, the workpiece accuracy and surface finish requirements are more demanding for the machine model specified by an appropriate 'mark of quality' standard than for the appropriate 'type standard' to which that machine model belonged at the time that the product was tested. Taking test workpiece accuracy as an indicator of initial

Table 3.2 'Mark of Quality' specifications for machine tools

Machine model	'Mark of Quality' State Standard number	'Type' Standard number	Accuracy requirements of 'Mark of Quality' Standards	Accuracy requirements of Type Standard	Maintenance of accuracy	Service life (to first overhaul)	Guarantee	Requirements for complete delivery
Screwcutting & centre lathe, model no. 1V616. 'A' class (Srednevolzhsk Factory)	GOST 5.8-68	GOST 18097-72	Ovality 2 Parallelism 3	2 (estimated from 'V' class tolerance) 5 (estimated from 'V' class tolerance)		11.5 years (double shift working)	1.5 years service or 2 years from delivery	—
Screwcutting lathe, model no. 1622. 'V' class (Krasnyi Proletarii Factory, Moscow)	GOST 5.1012-71	GOST 10897-72	Accuracy of threaded workpiece 5 9	12 25	5 years (to TU-024-25 08-70)	10 years	1.5 years service or 2 years from delivery	—
Eight-spindle vertical semi-automatic indexing lathe, model no. 1K282 & 1283. 'N' class (Krasnyi Proletarii Factory, Moscow)	GOST 5.1696-72	GOST 6820-75 (replaces GOST 6820-54)	Diameter consistency 80 (1K282) 100 (1283) Cross-sectional diameter consistency 15 (1K282) 20 (1283) Longitudinal diameter consistency 20 (1K282) 24 (1283) Face flatness 15 (1K282) 15 (1283)	80 (1K282) 100 (1283) 25 (1K282) 100 (1283) 25 (1K282) 30 (1283) 20 (1K282) 25 (1283)	4.5 years (to GOST 6820 -54)	8 years (for machining iron) 9.5 years (for machining steel)	1.5 years service	Corresponding to GOST 2.601-68
Six-spindle bar automatic model	GOST 5.1347-72	GOST 43-73 (replaces	Cross-sectional diameter consistency		(i) 1.5 years (to GOST	9 years	1.5 years service	Fast drill drive, screw

continued on p. 42

Table 3.2 continued

Machine model	'Mark of Quality' State Standard number	'Type' Standard number	Accuracy requirements of 'Mark of Quality' Standards	Accuracy Requirements of Type Standard	Maintenance of accuracy	Service Life (to first overhaul)	Guarantee	Requirements for complete delivery
no. 1A225-6. 'N' class (Ordzhonikidze Factory, Moscow)		GOST 43-65	8 Longitudinal diameter consistency 12 Batch diameter consistency 60 Batch stop-feed consistency 60	12 20 65 65	5.1347-72 (ii) 4.5 years (to GOST 43-65)			cutting drive, spindle tool, clamping collet, feed collet, set of change gears, set of hand tools, set of quick-wearing components
Surface grinding machine, model no. 3711. 'A' class (Orsha Machine Tool Factory)	GOST 5.15-71 (replaces GOST 5.15-67)	GOST 273-67	Flatness and parallelism of test piece per 400mm 2 Surface finish (to GOST 2789-73) by wheel periphery Ra = 0.063 Ra = 0.08 by wheel side face Ra = 0.25	2.5 Ra = 0.32	3.5 years to requirements of GOST 273-67	7.5 years (two-shift working)	1.5 years service	
Profile grinding machine, model no. 3B70V. 'V' class (Orsha Machine Tool Factory)	GOST 5.358-70	GOST 273-67	Surface flatness and parallelism of test piece over a length of 300mm 2.5 Surface finish by wheel periphery Ra = 0.16 Ra = 0.16 Side face by wheel periphery Ra = 0.64	3 Ra = 0.64	3.5 years to requirements of GOST 273-67	7.5 years (two-shift working)	1.5 years service, or 2 years from delivery	–
Cylindrical grinding	GOST 5.110-72	GOST 11654-72	Cross-sectional diameter consistency		(i) 1.5 years to	11.5 years (for grinding	1.5 years service	steady, wheel dressing-

Machine	Standard	Specifications	Life	Accessories
machine, model no. 3B151P. 'V' class (Kosior Machine Tool Factory, Khar'kov)	(replaces GOST 5.110–69)	3 Longitudinal diameter consistency 1.2 Surface finish Ra = 0.12	3 2 Ra = 0.16	requirements of GOST 5.110–72 (ii) 5.5 years to requirements of GOST 11654–72	steel) 9.5 years (for grinding iron)	tool, hand tools and accessories, table indexing indicator, clamping accessory, wheel balancing mechanism centres, wheel flange remover, wheel balance mandrel, magnetic coolant separator
Vertical knee and column milling machine, model no. 6S12. 'N' class	GOST 5.919–71	GOST 13–54 (replaced by GOST 17734–72)	Workpiece flatness per 300 mm 15 25 Parallelism of upper surfaces per 300 mm 20 25 Perpendicularity of side faces and upper surface 15 (per 150mm) 20 (per 150mm) 25 (per 300mm) 25 (per 300mm)	4.5 years to requirements of GOST 13–54	9 years	1.5 years or 2 years from delivery	—
Toolroom universal knee and column milling machine, model no. 6175. 'V' class (Enterprise P.ya 8889)	GOST 5.1365–72	—	Workpiece flatness 5 Surface finish Ra = 2.5	No equivalent standard	2 years to requirements of GOST 5.1364–72	9 years	2 years from time of introduction into service	vertical boring and milling head, vertical drilling and milling head, parallel bars, accessory cabinet, boring chuck, chuck for mandrel drilling, collet chuck, set of setting tools and fixtures, set of hand tools

Table 3.2 continued

Machine model	'Mark of Quality' State Standard number	'Type' Standard number	Accuracy requirements of 'Mark of Quality' Standards	Accuracy requirements of Type Standard	Maintenance of accuracy	Service life (to first overhaul)	Guarantee	Requirements for complete delivery
Surface grinding machine, model no. 3701. 'A' class	GOST 5.727-71	GOST 273-67	Flatness and parallelism of test piece per 250 mm 1.5 Surface finish by wheel periphery Ra = 0.063 Ra = 0.08 by wheel face Ra = 0.25 Ra = 0.32	2	4 years to requirements of GOST 273-67	7.5 years	1.5 years service	—
Cylindrical grinding machine, model no. 3A172. 'P' class. (Kosior Machine Tool Factory, Khar'kov)	GOST 5.1367-72	GOST 11654-65	Diameter consistency in any section 8 Diameter consistency in any cross section 3 Ra = 0.24	Diameter consistency in any section 16 7 Surface finish Ra = 1.25	(i) 1.5 years to the requirements of GOST 5.1367-72 (ii) 5.5 years to equirements of GOST 11654-65	11.5 years (for grinding steel) 9.5 years (for grinding iron)	1.5 years service	centre grinding attachment steady, wheel dressing attachment, wheel flange, set of grinding wheels, coolant tank, magnetic separator, wheel balancing mechanism, indicator, set of measuring tools. set of hand tools

Machine	Standard	Specifications	Requirements	Period 1	Period 2	
Cylindrical grinding machine, model no. 3A164A. 'P' class (Kosior Machine Tool Factory, Khar'kov)	GOST 5.806.71	Diameter consistency in any section 9 11 Diameter consistency in any cross section 3.5 4.4	GOST 11654–65	5.5 years to requirements of GOST 11654-65	11.5 years	1.5 years, or 2 years from delivery	—
Cylindrical grinding machine, model no. 3A164. 'P' class (Kosior Machine Tool Factory, Khar'kov)	GOST 5.481–70	Diameter consistency in any section 9 11 Diameter consistency in any cross section 3.5 4.4	GOST 11654–65	5 years to requirements of GOST 11654-65	11.5 years	1.5 years service, or 2 years from delivery	—
Cylindrical grinding machine, model no. 3E153 'A' class (Vil'nyus Grinding Machine Factory)	GOST 5.482–70	Diameter consistency in any section 2 3 Diameter consistency of any cross section 0.8 1.2 Surface finish Ra = 0.08 Ra = 0.16	GOST 11654–65	5.5 years to requirements of GOST 11654-65	11 years	1.5 years service, or 2 years from delivery	—
Universal cylindrical grinding machine, model no. 3A10P	GOST 5.148–69	Diameter consistency in Longitudinal section 3 3 Diameter consistency in cross section 2 2	GOST 11654–72	5.5 years to GOST 11654-72	11 years	1.5 years service	—

Table 3.2 continued

Machine model	'Mark of Quality' State Standard number	'Type' Standard number	Accuracy requirements of 'Mark of Quality' Standards	Accuracy requirements of Type Standard	Maintenance of accuracy	Service life (to first overhaul)	Guarantee	Requirements for complete delivery
			Flatness of end face					
			5	5				
			External surface finish					
			Ra = 0.16	Ra = 0.32				
			Internal surface finish					
			Ra = 0.32	Ra = 0.64				
			Face surface finish					
			Ra = 1.25	Ra = 1.25				
Horizontal gear-hobbing machine, model no. 5V370, 'N' class (Kolomensk Heavy Machine Tool Factory)	GOST 5.1181–73	GOST 18065–72	Profile accuracy of adjacent teeth		7 years to GOST 18065–72	14 years	1.5 years service	to documentation standard. GOST 2.601–68
			20 seconds	25 seconds				
			Profile accuracy of teeth over complete rim					
			66 seconds	80 seconds				
Vertical gear-hobbing machine, model no. 5A342, 'N' class (Kolomensk Heavy Machine Tool Factory)	GOST 5.1882–73	GOST 659–67	Positional limits of adjacent teeth		7 years to GOST 659–67	14 years	1.5 years service	to GOST 2.601–68
			6.8 seconds	12 seconds				
			Positional limits of teeth around rim					
			27 seconds	40 seconds				

Notes: (1) All tolerances are given in microns (mkm); (2) The definitions of machine tool accuracy defined in Table 3.2 above follow the usual Soviet definition, namely:

Normal Precision	'N' Class	(*Stanki normal'noi tochnosti*)
Improved Precision	'P' Class	(*Stanki povyshennoi tochosti*)
High Precision	'V' Class	(*Stanki vysokoi tochnosti*)
Ultra-high Precision	'A' Class	(*Stanki osobo-vysokoitochnosti*)

(3) All 'Mark of Quality' standards specify the overall capacity of the machine (e.g. maximum workpiece size, table size, spindle speeds, range of feeds, etc.); (4) Additional requirements are also specified for the motor drives and magnetic starter frequencies for grinding machines, namely:

(a) for surface grinding machines (model 3711) built to GOST 5.15–71 electric wheelhead drive and electric hydraulic drive motors frequency must not exceed the 2.8 class to GOST 16921–71; magnetic starters must not have a noise level greater than 65 dB.

(b) for surface profile grinding machines built to GOST 5.358–70 electric wheelhead drive motor must not exceed a frequency level of 3 mkm;
electric drive motors for hydraulic drive, grinding head fast return, and cross feed must have a level of vibration lower than the first class in the established procedure;
magnetic starters must not have a noise level greater than 65 dB.

(5) For machines built to GOST 5.1012–71 (Model no.1622 screwcutting lathe) the high precision set of alignment tests to GOST 18097–72 appear to have been selected, although the critical accuracy is the screwcutting accuracy test, since this machine is intended for the cutting of precision lead screws; (6) Surface finish requirements are defined by means of 'centre line average'(Ra) (see Mamet, O.P.: *Kratkii spravochnik konstruktorastankostroitelya* (Mashinostroenie, Moscow, 1964) p. 306); (7) Newer type standards are signified by later years in the last two digits (e.g. 659–78, published in 1978 replaced 659–67, published in 1967); (8) In these cases where a type standard has been replaced by a newer version, the tolerances of the newer type standard are generally equivalent to those of the 'Mark of Quality' standard; (9) – Denotes that the parameter is not quoted by the source.

quality, it can be concluded, therefore, that the initial quality requirements of attested or 'highest grade' machine tools are more demanding than their 'first grade' counterparts, as specified by the Soviet system of quality categorisation at the time that a product's quality attestation is carried out.

(b) In those cases where new 'type standards' have been drafted after a product's date of attestation, the requirements in the 'mark of quality' standard generally remain equal to or better than those specified in the new 'type standard.'

(c) Since a previous investigation reported in Chapter 2 has shown Soviet 'type standards' for machine tools to be generally similar in accuracy demands to British national standards, which in turn are based upon ISO documents, it is strongly suggested that Soviet claims that attested products meet contemporary international quality standards appear to be true for general purpose machine tools.

(d) In almost every case, a minimum time limit is specified for which machines should hold a defined level of accuracy, assuming that they are used in accordance with manufacturers' instructions. In some cases, this maintenance of accuracy is based on tolerances to the initial requirements of the 'mark of quality' standard, and also of the appropriate 'type standard' category to which the machine model belongs. The minimum time limit for the latter is of the order of five years on average, and would appear to be satisfactory according to normal international practice.

(e) In almost every case, a minimum service life of some nine years to first major overhaul is specified. Again, this requirement would not appear to fall short of international practice.

(f) In every case, a minimum guarantee period of one and a half years service is specified. This would also appear to conform with international practice.

(g) In certain cases, requirements for the complete sales package are specified, including accessories and tooling. This would appear to be a serious attempt to rectify the problem of incomplete deliveries from Soviet industry,[18] which is an aspect of the general supply problem in the USSR caused by taut planning and a seller's market.[19] Although aggrieved Soviet customers have the right to pursue compensation for faulty delivery through the arbitration courts, this legal activity is as apparently complex, time-consuming, and uncertain in outcome as similar procedures in any other country.[20]

Machine Tool 'Mark of Quality' Standards

(h) The majority of machines obtaining 'highest category' approval received their awards in the early 1970s and in several cases, the relevant 'type standard' has been superseded. The momentum of this quality attestation in the early 1970s does not therefore appear to have been maintained in the machine tool industry.

(i) In conclusion, therefore, adequate evidence exists to strongly suggest that the requirements of Soviet 'mark of quality' standards are contemporary with the demands of the international market for those machine models of the appropriate vintage to which they relate. Many of these machine models are of a complex and precision type (e.g. grinding machines and gearcutting machines) although at a comparatively mature stage at the machine tool technology life cycle. Machines embodying the most advanced machine tool technology (e.g. unit heads and numerical control) however, have not yet received 'mark of quality' approval.

4 'Squirrel Cage' Electrical Motors

INTRODUCTION

This chapter is an account of research carried out on the quality levels of 3-phase Asynchronous AC Induction Motors, having rotors of a 'squirrel cage' construction. These products were selected for study because the present authors considered it to be important to assess the quality of Soviet design and manufacture in the field of electrical technology. Electrical motors are typical examples of products using widely-diffused and standardised electro-mechanical technologies, and squirrel cage motors in their turn are the most widely used type of electrical motor in industry.[1]

A second factor influencing the selection of squirrel cage motors for further study was the approval of a range of these products as the first items to receive a 'Mark of Quality' in 1967 under the Soviet quality attestation system. These products have retained their 'Mark of Quality' since that time, and were consequently considered by the present authors to be a suitable sample of Soviet electrical engineering products. A full translation of the 'mark of quality' standard is given in Table A.12 in the Appendix.

The remaining sections of this chapter consist of a short introduction to the technical features of squirrel cage motors, and a comparison of these features with those of selected Western counterparts. This is then followed by comments and conclusions from the comparative study.

SQUIRREL CAGE MOTORS

The widespread popularity of squirrel cage motors arises mainly from their simple design and robust physical construction. They are suitable for high-speed operation and for use in environments where severe operating conditions are encountered. The absence of sliprings, brush gear and electrical connections to the rotor creates a motor of low cost, requiring the minimum amount of maintenance; and also ensures that during normal operation, little or no sparking occurs, thus greatly reducing the risks of fire and explosion. Other inherent advantages include power factor ratings close to unity enabling the circuit cables to supply comparatively large loads without overheating;[2] and high values of operational efficiency, both of which depend on the rated power output and synchronous speed of the motor.[3] Finally, the relationship between torque and speed for squirrel cage motors creates an approximation to a constant speed machine over the designed operating range of the motor.

There are many standard electrical designs of squirrel cage induction motors depending on the special load requirements, with each design characterised by a specific shape of torque-speed curve. The electro-magnetic relationship causing an induction motor to develop rotational force or torque, and deliver horsepower to a load involve physical reactions of magnet to magnet or, as in the case of squirrel cage motors, the reactions of a rotating magnetic field to rotor conductors. Squirrel cage motor design consequently depends primarily on the selection of rotor resistance and inductive reactance, which are influenced by the amount of bar material and total cross-section of the conductors. There are, however, certain limitations on the application of these machines, associated with the starting process and resulting from the standard 'low-resistance' cage of the rotor. These disadvantages take the form of large starting currents and low starting torques, but continual developments in squirrel cage design have been aimed at minimising these shortcomings. The changes in the values of rotor resistance and reactance which result from these developments have a direct bearing on the relationship between torque and speed for these motors. This, relationship, in turn, alters the values of other indices (or operational parameters) that normally influence the correct selection of a squirrel-cage motor for a particular task. The most important of these indices are:

> the percentage slip at full (or rated) load;
> the ratio of initial starting current to rated current;
> the ratio of initial starting torque to rated torque;
> the ratio of maximum torque to rated torque.

These indices, together with power factor and operational efficiency referred to in the previous paragraph, were selected for comparative study in the next section of this chapter.

Another prominent indicator of the motor's operational performance is the 'power to weight' ratio. Firstly, it gives a good indication of whether or not a machine is rated at its full potential and, secondly, its value provides a measure as to the level of technology incorporated in the design and construction of the motor (i.e.: the design techniques employed and the raw materials involved.) The practical reality of meeting the requirements of a particular load (i.e.: the type of starting and character of duty cycle) invariably requires that a compromise must be found to achieve the best optimum balance in the operational performance of the motor. For example, machines capable of attaining high starting torque and low starting current, whilst still retaining acceptable values of efficiency and power factor, may require an increase in the active material of the rotor or frame size of the motor. This invariably leads to increased cost and motor weight which, in turn, effectively reduces the motor's 'power-to-weight' ratio. Technically advanced design and construction, therefore, attempts to maximise power to weight, whilst still retaining high performance levels for the other technical parameters. 'Power to weight' has consequently been selected as a further parameter for comparative study in the next section of this chapter.

THE QUALITY CHARACTERISTICS OF SOVIET SQUIRREL CAGE MOTORS: A COMPARATIVE STUDY

This section describes a comparative assessment of the technical characteristics of over forty different models of squirrel cage motor: thirteen Soviet, three Polish and the remainder from Western motor manufacturers. Their rated output in kilowatts ranged from less than 1kW up to over 1000kW, and this range was covered in twelve separate steps of power output groupings. At each step it was ensured that motors selected for comparison were also of the same synchronous speed rating, (with the exception of the 11kW grouping where speeds vary from 348rpm to 1000rpm), this having a direct bearing on the weights of individual machines (i.e.: the machines with higher synchronous speeds having fewer pairs of poles and vice versa). Although information on all the fifteen selected operational parameters appears at least once in the Tables 4.1 to 4.4 details on only seven to ten indices were normally obtainable from either Soviet state standards or individual motor manufacturers. The seven most-quoted indices, the importance of which have been discussed in the previous section of this chapter, are listed below:

motor efficiency;
power factor;

Table 4.1 Operational characteristics for squirrel cage motors (0.5 – 9 kW rated output)

Index or operational parameter	GOST 5. 2051-73 Motor type KD6-4 single phase capacitor	Parvalux SD21 Capacitor Motor 10	GOST 19713-81 Series 4A	Elektrim Motor Type Se71-2B	B.C.P.M. Motor Type D71b	NEMA.1.5 Hf Design B 50 Hz	GOST 22185-76 Motor Type VRM10052	GEC Alpak Motor Type D112M	NEMA 5HP Design B 50 Hz	Leroy Somer Motor Type LS 112M
Rated Output (kW)	.006	0.009	0.55	0.55	0.55	1.1	4.0	4.0	3.73	4.0
Synch. Speed (RPM)	1400	1400	3000	3000	3000	3000	3000	3000	3000	3000
Efficiency (%)	29	24.5	77	75	68	–	85	81	–	83
Power Factor	0.86	0.84	0.84	0.87	0.74	–	0.87	0.89	–	0.88
Ratio Start Torque/Rated Torque	0.65	1.1	2.5	2.4	2.5	1.75	2.0	2.4	1.5	3.2
Ratio Max. Torque/Rated Torque	1.9	–	3.5	2.3	–	2.75	2.8	2.6	2.25	3.0
Ratio Start Current/Rated Current	–	–	8.5	4.7	4.5	7.0	6.5	6.0	6.2	9.03
Slip (%)	5.3	6	4.0	6.0	4.0	less than 5	4.4	6.0	less than 5	3.6
Weight (kg)	1.1	1.7	12.0	7.3	6.6	–	84	31.8	–	27.5
Factor of Fault Free Operation	–	–	–	–	–	–	–	–	–	–

continued on p. 54

Table 4.1 continued

Index or operational parameter	GOST 5.2051-73 Motor type KD6-4 single phase capacitor	Parvalux SD21 Capacitor Motor 10	GOST 19713-81 Series 4A	Elektrim Motor Type Se71-2B	B.C.P.M. Motor Type D71b	NEMA.1.5 Hf Design B 50 Hz	GOST 22185-76 Motor Type VRM10052	GEC Alpak Motor Type D112M	NEMA 5HP Design B 50 Hz	Leroy Somer Motor Type LS 112M
Period of Service	5 years	–	18 years	–	–	–	30 000 hrs	–	–	–
Mean Time Between Failures (MTBF)	–	–	–	–	–	–	–	–	–	–
Bearing Life (hours)	–	5000	10 000	–	20 000	–	–	12 000	–	15 000
Manufacturer's Guarantee Period	2.5 years	–	2 years	–	1 year	–	2 years	1 year	–	1 year
'Power to Weight' Ratio (kW/kg)	0.0055	0.005	0.046	0.075	0.083	–	0.047	0.125	–	0.145

Notes: (a) The GOST 5.2051–73 and the Parvalux motors are induction type with the capacitor permanently connected. The Soviet motor is specially designed for sound-recording equipment and merited a 'Mark of Quality' Award. (b) The Soviet 'Series 4A' motor is specially designed for driving commercial sewing machines. (c) 'Elektrim' is a Polish exporter of electrical and other industrial products. (d) Leroy-Somer is a French manufacturer of electrical motors. (e) The Soviet type 'VRM' motor is designed for operation with ventilation fans. (f) A hyphen denotes that the parameter is not quoted by the source.

Table 4.2 Operational characteristics for squirrel cage motors (10–45 kW rated output)

Index or operational parameter	GOST 185-70 Crane Motor	GOST 5.1686-72 Type VSO 10-19-16	NEMA 15HP design B50HZ	FENNER Gear Motor Type 160LB	GEC Motor Style CM180M	RENOLD Gear Motor GM5D	GOST 20818-75 Motor Type 4A 160 M4Y3	NEMA 25HP Design B 50 A7	BCPM Type Motor D180 M (Alum.)	BCPM Type 7-D180M (Cast Iron)
Rated Output (kW)	11	11	11.1	11	10	11	18.5	18.6	18.5	18.5
Synch. Speed (RPM)	1000	375	720	372	750	348	1500	1500	1500	1500
Efficiency (%)	–	88	–	–	84	–	88.5	–	89	89
Power Factor	–	0.61	–	–	0.70	–	0.87	–	.89	.86
Ratio Start Torque/Rated Torque	2.8	1.0	1.05	1.8	1.5	–	2.0	1.5	2.5	2.25
Ratio Max. Torque/Rated Torque	2.8	2.0	2.0	–	2.0	–	2.2	2.0	–	–
Ratio Start Current/Rated Current	–	4.0	4.4	5.2	4.5	–	7.5	5.0	7.0	7.0
Slip (%)	–	–	less than 5	3.0	4.0	–	2.3	less than 5	2.6	3.3
Weight (kg)	163	620	–	330	168	143	160	–	158	160
Factor of Fault Free operation	–	0.8	–	–	–	–	0.9	–	–	–
Period of Service	15 years	10 years	–	–	–	–	15 years	–	–	–
Mean Time Between Failures (MTBF) (hrs)	60 000	–	–	–	–	–	–	–	–	–
Bearing Life (hrs)	10 000	–	–	–	40 000	–	14 000	–	20 000	20 000
Manufacturer's Guarantee Period	2.5 years	2.5 years	–	–	1 year	–	2 years	–	1 year	1 year
'Power to Weight' Ratio (kW/kg)	.067	.018	–	.03	.06	.077	.115	–	.117	.115

continued on p. 56

Table 4.2 continued

Index or operational parameter	Manufacturer or GOST no. (USSR) and type of motor							
	NEMA 50HP Design B 50HZ	ELEKTRIM Motor Type Se180M-4	GOST 23111-78 Motor Type V&VR 250M8	GEC 'Flowpak' Range Motor Style D280S	ELEKTRIM Motor Type Se280M-8	BCPM Motor Type D280S (Cast-Iron)	BCPM Motor Type 7-D280S (Hollow Steel)	LEROY-SOMER Motor Type N280M	NEMA 60HP Design B 50HZ
Rated Output (kW)	37.3	18.5	45.0	45.0	45.0	45.0	45.0	45.0	44.7
Synch. Speed (RPM)	1500	1500	750	750	750	750	750	750	750
Efficiency (%)	90	91	90.7	92	93	91.0	92	94.0	–
Power Factor	.875	0.88	0.78	0.79	0.82	0.77	0.75	0.72	–
Ratio Start Torque/Rated Torque	1.85	2.0	1.8	2.0	1.8	1.3	1.8	2.1	1.25
Ratio Max. Torque/Rated Torque	2.0	2.3	2.0	2.4	2.1	–	–	2.4	2.0
Ratio Start Torque/Rated Current	5.85	6.0	5.0	6.0	5.7	6.0	5.25	5.1	5.0

Slip (%)	3.3	3.0	2.0	2.0	1.3	2.0	2.0	2.0	3
Weight (kg)	–	182	815	727	650	856	580	630	–
Factor of Fault Free Operation	–	–	0.95	–	–	–	–	–	–
Period of Service	–	–	15 yrs (V) 10 yrs (VR) 30 000 (V) 20 000 (VR)	–	–	–	–	–	–
Mean Time Between Failures (MTBF) (hrs)	–	–	–	–	–	–	–	–	–
Bearing Life (hrs)	–	–	–	75 000	–	20 000	20 000	15 000	–
Manufacturer's Guarantee Period	–	–	2 years	1 year	–	1 year	1 year	1 year	–
'Power to Weight' Ratio (kW/kg)	–	.101	.055	.062	.07	.052	.077	.071	–

Notes: (a) The Soviet crane motors are for application in conditions of excess vibration, dust content & high humidity, including export markets. (b) The Soviet VSO type motors are for use as gearless drives on ventilators of water-cooling towers. (c) The Soviet Series 4A are intended for export markets. (d) Both Soviet V & VR series motors are explosion-proof and are designed for export markets. The VR series is for use in mining environments. (e) A hyphen denotes that the parameter is not quoted by the source.

Table 4.3 Operational characteristics for squirrel cage motors (45-160 kW Rated Output)

Index or operational parameter	GOST 5.618-73 Motor Type AB2-101-8YS	NEMA 100HP Design B 50HZ	GEC "Flowpak" Range Motor Type D135S	LEROY-SOMER 'N' Series Type N315M	BCPM Type 7-D316S (Hollow Rib Steel)	GOST 5.4-67 Motors Series A2-101-8	GOST 5.618-73 Motor Type AB3-315M-6Y3	GOST 23131-78 Motor A3 Series Type A3-315M-6Y3	GEC Flowpak Range Type D315MX
Rated Output (kW)	75.0	74.6	75.0	75.0	75.0	75.0	132.0	132.0	132.0
Synch. Speed (RPM)	750	750	750	750	750	750	1000	1000	1000
Efficiency (%)	92.1	–	93.0	94.5	93.0	92.1	93.5	93.5	94.5
Power Factor	0.85	–	0.78	0.8	0.80	0.85	0.90	0.90	0.86
Ratio Start Torque/Rated Torque	1.0	1.25	2.0	1.4	1.5	1.0	1.0	1.2	1.3
Ratio Max. Torque/Rated Torque	2.0	2.0	2.4	2.2	–	2.0	2.0	2.2	2.3
Ratio Start Current/Rated Current	5.0	5.15	6.0	5.3	7.7	5.0	6.0	6.0	6.0
Slip (%)	–	5	1.6	2.0	2.0	–	–	2.5	1.2
Weight (kg)	480	–	990	840	815	–	530	785	1225
Factor of Fault Free Operation	0.9	–	–	–	–	0.9	0.82	0.91	–
Period of Service	18 years	–	–	–	–	18 years	18 years	18 years	–
Mean Time Between Failures(MTBF)(hrs)	–	–	–	–	–	–	–	–	–
Bearing Life (hrs)	–	–	75 000	15 000	20 000	–	–	–	75 000
Manufacturer's Guarantee Period	3.5 years	–	1 year	1 year	1 year	2 years	3.5 years	3.5 years	1 year
'Power to Weight' Ratio (kW/kg)	0.156	–	0.076	0.089	0.092	.109	0.25	0.17	0.108

Manufacturer or GOST no. (USSR) and type of motor

Index or operational parameter	GOST 5.4-67 Motor Series A2-102-6	LEROY-SOMER LSP Series Type LSP315M	NEMA 200HP Design B 50HZ	GOST 23131-78 Motor Type A3-315S2-4	GOST 5.6-67 Motor Series A2-101-41	GEC Flowpak Range Type D315MX	NEMA 200HP Design B 50HZ
Rated Output (kW)	125	132.0	149	160	160	160	149
Synch. Speed (RPM)	1000	1000	1000	1500	1500	1500	1500
Efficiency (%)	93.5	94.0	91.5	93.4	93.4	95.0	–
Power Factor	0.90	0.83	0.92	0.9	0.9	0.88	–
Ratio Start Torque/Rated Torque	1.0	1.2	1.25	1.1	0.9	0.45	1.0
Ratio Max. Torque/Rated Torque	2.0	2.1	2.0	2.2	2.0	3.3	2.0
Ratio Start Current/Rated Current	6.0	5.0	5.6	6.0	6.0	3.0	5.0
Slip(%)	–	2.0	2.5	2.0	–	0.8	5
Weight(kg)	–	1050	–	755	–	1225	–
Factor of Fault Free Operation	0.9	–	–	0.91	0.9	–	–
Period of Service	18 years	–	–	18 years	18 years	–	–
Mean Time Between Failures (MTBF) (hrs)	–	–	–	–	–	–	–
Bearing Life (hrs)	–	15 000	–	–	–	75 000	–
Manufacturer's Guarantee Period	2 years	1 year	–	3.5 years	2 years	1 year	–
'Power to Weight' Ratio (kW/kg)	0.18	0.126	–	0.21	0.23	0.13	–

Notes: (a) The Soviet motor series AB2 has received the 'Mark of Quality' Award. (b) The initials B.C.P.M. are those of the Brook Crompton Parkinson Motor Co. (c) The Soviet series AB3 motor has received the 'Mark of Quality' Award. (d) The A3 series of Soviet motor (GOST 23131-78) replaced the series A2 motors, which in 1967 were the first industrial products to be awarded the 'Mark of Quality' (See GOST 5.4-67). (e) The average weight of motors to GOST 5.4-67 was 690 kg (see McKay (1984); p.1). This average weight was used as a basis to calculate 'power to weight'. (f) A hyphen denotes that the parameter is not quoted by the source.

Table 4.4 Operational characteristics for squirrel cage motors (200 – 1100 kW rated output)

Index or operational parameter	Manufacturer or GOST no. (USSR) and type of motor							
	GOST 16311-75 series VOA type VOA450S-8	BCPM TYPE 7-D355l (hollow rib steel)	LEROY-SOMER LSP series type LSP 355M	GOST 19523-81 series S4A type 4A355M2Y3	BCPM type 7-D355m (hollow rib steel frame)	LEROY-SOMER LSP series type LSP355S	GOST 19488-74 series ATD2type 2AZM	GEC 'Impax' range style C450-3B
Rated Output (kW)	200	200	200	315	315	315	1000	1100
Synch. Speed (RPM)	750	750	750	1500	1500	1500	3000	3000
Efficiency (%)	94.0	94.0	95.0	93.0	94.7	94.5	95.8	95.5
Power Factor	0.85	0.84	0.84	0.91	0.94	0.88	0.89	0.88
Ratio Start Torque/Rated Torque	1.5	1.25	1.2	1.0	1.3	1.1	1.1	0.6
Ratio Max. Torque/Rated Torque	2.2	–	2.0	1.9	–	2.0	1.9	2.0
Ratio Start Current/Rated Current	6.0	8.2	4.6	7.0	9.0	5.65	5.0	6.1

Slip(%)	0.6	2.0	1.3	2.0	1.0	1.0	1.0	0.9
Weight(kg)	2000	1830	1560	1570	1650	1360	4300	4100
Factor of Fault Free Operation	0.75	–	–	0.9	–	–	0.85	–
Period of Service	20 years	–	–	15 years	–	–	20 years	–
Mean Time Between Failures (MTBF) (hrs)	–	–	–	–	–	–	–	–
Bearing Life (hrs)	–	20 000	15 000	–	20 000	15 000	–	up to 40 000
Manufacturer's Guarantee Period	2 years	1 year	1 year	2 years	1 year	1 year	2 years	1 year
'Power to Weight' Ratio (kW/kg)	0.1	0.11	0.128	0.21	0.19	0.23	0.23	0.27

Notes: (a) The Soviet VOA Series of flameproof motor is designed for use in hazardous working environments such as those encountered in mining. (b) The Soviet series 4A range of motor is designed for export markets. (c) The Soviet ATD2 series of motor is rated at 6000 volts whereas the GEC 'Impak' range is rated at 6600 volts. In both cases additional weight is added for other forms of cooling. (d) A hyphen denotes that the parameter is not quoted by the source.

ratio of 'power' to 'weight';
rated (or full load) slip;
ratio of starting current to rated current;
ratio of maximum torque to rated torque;
ratio of starting torque to rated torque.

A comparative assessment of these indices is shown in graphical form in Figure 4.1.

There was also a general reluctance, on the part of Western firms, to commit themselves fully on motor reliability information. In addition to the normal twelve months guarantee from the date of delivery, most companies were only prepared to provide the number of operation hours of the motors that consisted of a) the bearing life expectancy; b) the inter servicing period of bearings; and/or c) the period of time between replacement and lubrication of bearings. Explaining this, a Western company representative stated that as bearings were the only moving part of squirrel-cage motors subjected to constant wear and tear, it was only necessary to issue reliability data on these components. The Soviet standards on the other hand were generally more consistent in their content on motor reliability. The indices which appeared in the Soviet state standards on rotating electrical machinery were as follows:

service life (up to first overhaul);
probability factor of fault-free operation;
mean time between failures (MTBF);
manufacturer's guaranteed period of operation.

The numerical values of these parameters are shown in Tables 4.1 to 4.4

To complete the overall study, technical requirements specified for rotating electrical machinery in general[4] were compared, and these are shown in Table A.13 in the Appendix. The technical requirements which have been covered include limits of temperature rise for windings, high voltage tests and tolerances for various motor characteristics. In addition, a study was made of certain characteristics of specialised small-powered squirrel cage motors.

'Squirrel Cage' Electrical Motors

Figure 4.1 Comparative motor parameters

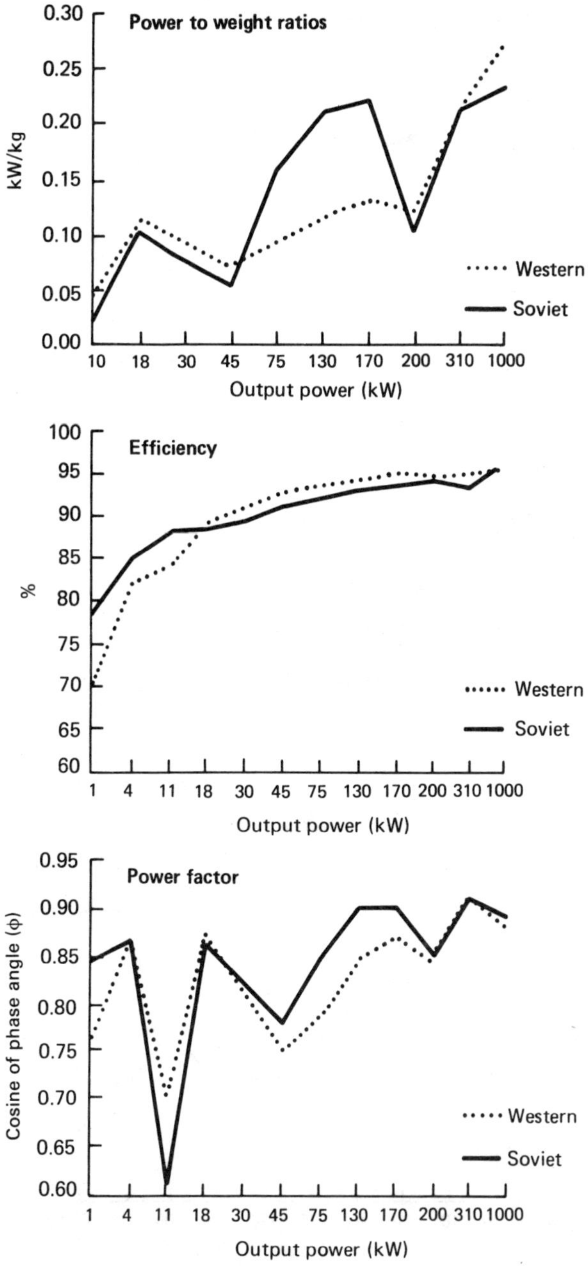

continued on p. 64

Figure 4.1 continued

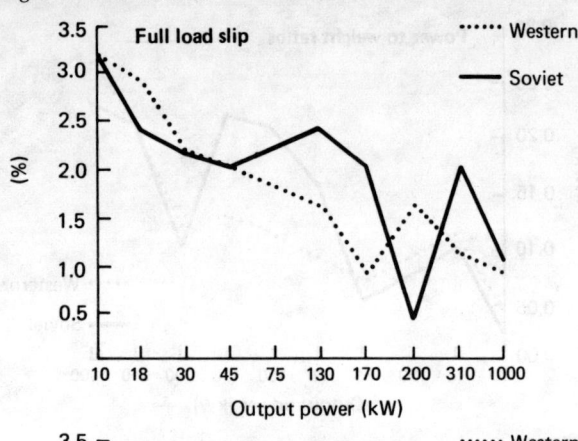

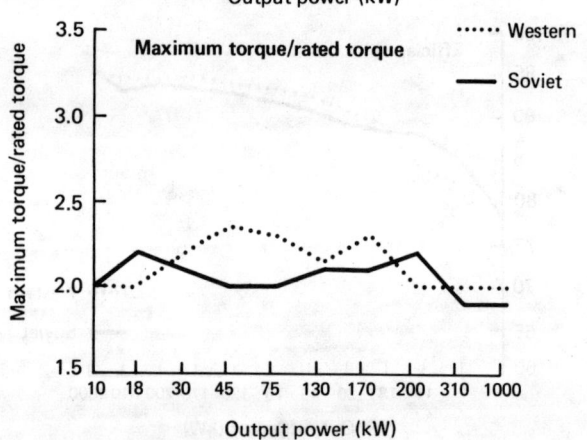

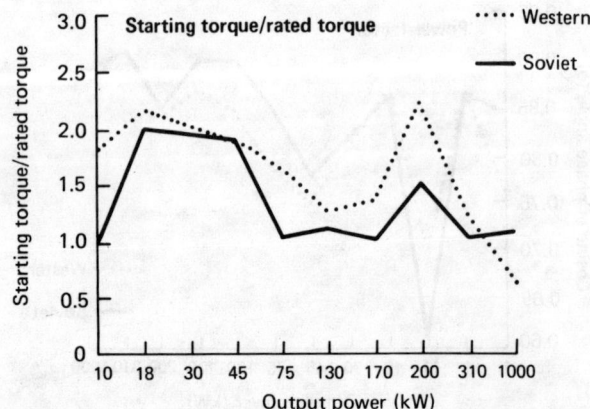

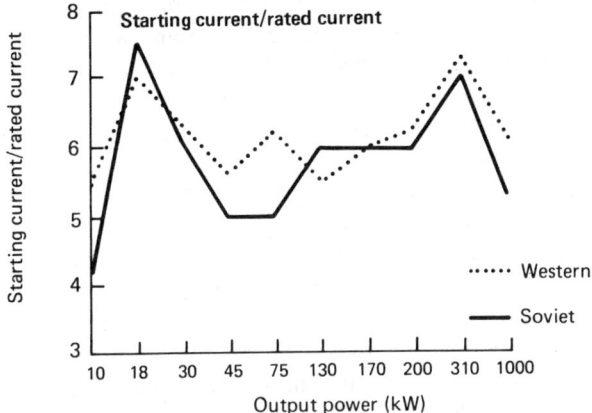

Note: In some cases, average values for the parameter shown on the vertical axis have been calculated for a range of Soviet or Western machines, at a defined value of output-power. The small number of Polish machines were considered as 'non-Soviet', and their parameters included in the larger sample of Western products.

COMMENTS AND CONCLUSIONS

Throughout the whole range of results presented in Tables 4.1 to 4.4, no consistent pattern emerges to suggest that either Western or Soviet manufactured machines are technologically better. It could be argued that, as far as 'power-to-weight' ratios are concerned, motors of Western origin possess a slight advantage in the upper and lower power groupings whereas Soviet built machines in the mid-range groupings appear to show better results; but care should be exercised before reaching any definite conclusions. For example, the results obtained for the 75kW and 132kW groupings indicate that the Soviet AB2 and 3 series are technically better than their Western counterparts, although further reading into the contents of the standard[5] concerned suggests otherwise. This reveals that no obligations are placed with the manufacturer to equip the motors with damp-proof, oil-resistant or chemically-protective insulation and also that the machines are not expected to be of 'explosion-proof' construction. These two factors obviously limit the practical applications of the machines to non-hazardous working environments and temperate climates and this is confirmed by the relevant specifications[6] stipulated for these motors in GOST 15150–69.[7] Any modifications or design changes aimed at rectifying these limitations are certain to have an adverse effect on any 'power-to-weight' advantage that the motors possess at present. Most of what has just been said applies to the Series A2 motor range of the 'Vladimir Il'ich' factory, and thus the apparent Soviet advantage in this mid-range of the power groupings may need to be qualified.

In respect to the other major parameters, some differences are seen to exist but, generally, the large variations in values that do occur tend to be in a small number of cases. The close similarity in the results appears to be a recurrent theme throughout the whole range of power groupings (see Figure 4.1) and is even more in evidence when comparing the technical requirements for rotating electrical machinery in general. The specified limits for temperature rise of machine windings, voltage tests for various windings and exciters, and a wide range of tolerances for various electrical characteristics, are almost identical for Soviet and British motors manufactured to either GOST 183–74 or BS 4999 Parts 32, 60 and 69 (see Table A.13 in the Appendix). The major differences occur in the limiting values of high voltage tests for insulating materials, where the two sets of standards specify different ranges for the threshold power-rating for which the requisite voltage limit is set. The differences in insulation requirements may be worthy of further research, particular at threshold output values of 1kW and 1000kW, and voltage values of 100V.

As far as specialised low-powered motors[8] were concerned, similarities existed for the values in the ratios of starting torque to rated torque and of starting current to rated torque. These ratios are found in tables 1 and 2 of GOST 10799-77 and part 11 of BS 5000, which caters for small-powered electric motors and generators.

From a theoretical point of view at least, it appears that very similar demands and stringencies are placed on both Soviet and Western motor manufacturers in their design, construction and testing of squirrel cage machines; and that to make a deeper assessment of the specific capabilities of individual motors, closer scrutiny of the relevant standards and specifications are necessary. In practice though, perhaps the best yardstick by which to judge the quality of a motor is its ability consistently to maintain its rated values of performance. In this respect, much depends on the working environment within which the motor is placed and whether it is properly equipped to cope with the prevailing conditions of operation. In the Soviet Union incorrect application of asynchronous motors accounts for between 15 per cent and 35 per cent of their failures[9] which, according to the same source, was approximately two to three times the number of failures which resulted from the natural causes of ageing and fair 'wear-and-tear'. Deficiencies in design and production were another major source of failures (30–35 per cent) of Soviet asynchronous motors, as were operational deficiencies and poor quality of repair (35–50 per cent). Under the heading 'operational deficiencies' we should also include those points highlighted in a recent article by Cooper,[10] namely the inconsistency of voltage regulation and inferior quality of power supplies.

An interesting point on which to conclude this chapter appears in the book by Ermolin and Zherikhim,[11] where mention is made that the degree of airgap evenness between rotor and stator represented an important reliability indicator for asynchronous motors. It was also admitted that state standards make no provision for the checking of this gap due to the practical difficulties involved. Indirectly, it seems that these statements justify the importance given by Western manufacturers to the reliability of bearings and also hint to the possibility that responsibility for overall motor reliability and quality of production lies to a certain extent, within other branches of engineering, which are beyond the terms of reference of the study presented in this chapter.

This view is further supported by evidence from the Soviet standard (GOST 185–70) providing data on both MTBF and bearing life. The former parameter was specified as being greater than the latter, and presumably applies to electrical failure only; although motor reliability will obviously be greatly influenced by bearing life. Consequently, a detailed study of the quality level of Soviet bearings, and their effect on overall product reliability is a subject worthy of further research.

5 Automotive Products and Components

INTRODUCTION

This chapter is an assessment of the quality level of the Soviet motor industry, using data available from both Soviet and Western published sources, and Soviet state standards. Particular attention is paid to three distinctive groups of products manufactured by the industry, namely passenger cars, trucks and engine components.

It is clearly difficult to quantify and standardise many of the characteristics of on-the-road vehicles which influence their general performance and suitability for purpose. This is particularly true for passenger cars, where their quality is influenced by such features as style and handling which are difficult to quantify. Nevertheless, some characteristics relating to product safety can be quantified, and reference is made to appropriate Soviet state standards. In addition, reference is also made to Soviet 'mark of quality' standards for particular widely-used trucks (no Soviet passenger car has yet been awarded the 'mark of quality'), since the specifications for these vehicles are useful bases for comparison.

A final point which it is important to make relates to the selectivity of data presented in this chapter. As a result of the range of descriptive technical detail in standards relating to products and components manufactured by the motor industry, it has been necessary to select those characteristics which are considered to be the most crucial and which can be readily quantified. Furthermore, in view of the large quantity of standards that exist, particularly for automotive components, it has been necessary to take a small sample of standards, in the interests of economy of research effort. Consequently, some selectivity has been apparent in terms of the quantity of standards selected and the parameters compared in these documents. Nevertheless, it is considered that this sampling has been carried out in an objective manner, and that the approach followed in this chapter serves as a basis for further discussions on the quality level of the Soviet motor industry.

PASSENGER CARS

Soviet 'Type Standards' for Passenger Cars

Soviet state 'type standards' for passenger cars are similar to their Western counterparts in terms of the range of topics covered (e.g.: safety belt fastenings, passenger compartment strength, car lighting, etc.), although the quantity of these standards appears to be lower than their British counterparts in the automobile category (BS AU standards). It is possible, however that the Soviet state standards are supplemented by a range of 'industry standards' published by the Ministry of the Automobile Industry of the USSR for use in its own research, development and production organisations.

It is difficult to use these state standards to assess the quality of Soviet passenger cars, since they mostly define general requirements relating to visibility and safety, but a possible exception is car body strength. Table 5.1 shows some specific requirements relating to car safety, namely the collision resistance of car body shells, introduced in 1976. From the information shown in this Table, it appears that Soviet practice was similar to that followed in Western countries,[1] but this standard was subsequently withdrawn from use in 1984, probably for reasons of further development and improvement.

In order to obtain a wider picture of passenger car quality, therefore, it was decided to use various Soviet and Western studies of the characteristics of Soviet models of passenger car. The models chosen for particular study have been the Moskvich 412, which was assimilated into production during the late 1960s, and the Zhiguli (or Lada) range assimilated during the early 1970s. The former model has been produced at the rate of some 450 000 per year in two factories (Lenin Komsomol Factory, Moscow, and the Izhevsk Automobile Factory), whilst the latter has been produced at the rate of 660 000 per year at the Volga Automobile Factory, Tol'yatti.[2] The total production of these two models having an engine size within the 1.5 litre range, accounted for more than 80 per cent of total Soviet car output[3] for several years, therefore. Although the Zhiguli has been subsequently modified by its manufacturers there has been no substantial change in the car's basic design, and a study of the characteristics of this model consequently provides an accurate indication of the quality characteristics of Soviet passenger cars.

Table 5.1 Soviet passenger car collision resistance

Frontal Collision – to GOST 21936–76
Rear Collision – to GOST 21959–76
Side Collision – to GOST 21961–76

Test Conditions
Vehicle to include all items affecting kerbside weight
90% of full fuel capacity to be carried
Luggage compartment to contain tools and a 20 kg canister filled with water

Testing Speed 48.3 – 53 km/hr (Frontal collision)
　　　　　　　35 – 38 km/hr (Side and rear collision)
Doors to remain closed

Test Results

Parameters measured after collision	Limiting distance after collision
Distance between instrument panel and front seat	450mm
Distance between brake pedal and front seat	650mm
Distance between brake pedal and side panel	250mm
Floor to roof compression	10%
Rear seat movement	75mm
Side Deformation	350mm

Quality Characteristics of the Moskvich and Zhiguli (Lada) Models

The 'Moskvich'
In a short discussion on the technical characteristics of Soviet passenger cars, included in their book on motor industry economics, published in 1971, Vlasov et al.[4] noted that 'when assessing the technical level of [automobiles], it is necessary to realise that each national manufacturer designs automobiles primarily for its own country's road and climatic conditions and demands in use.' Paying particular attention to Soviet passenger cars, they continued by noting that 'nationally [i.e.: Soviet] produced automobiles designed for our [i.e.: Soviet] demands in use, have, as a rule, a higher intrinsic weight and road clearance, and a lower maximum speed and brake horse power per litre of engine capacity; they are also less demanding with regard to the quality of fuels and lubricating oils.' As well as Soviet vehicle

Table 5.2 Comparative technical data for passenger cars

	Moskvich 412	Vauxhall Victor 1600	Opel Rekord	Fiat 125
Engine capacity (cc)	1478	1599	1432	1608
Maximum power (hp)	75	72	58	90
Maximum speed (km/hr)	145	150	133	160
Time to accelerate from rest to 100 km/hr (sec)	18.8	n.a.	20.5	14.8
Wheel base (mm)	2400	2590	2670	2506
Minimum road clearance (mm)	178	150	130	120
Number of lubrication points	14	4	none	none
Fuel consumption (litres/100 km)	9.1	10.0	9.9	11.2
Horse power per litre	50.9	45	38.8	56
Specific weight (ratio of the total weight of the car to the maximum power) (kg/hp)	17.9	19.4	23.9	14.9
Service interval to first major overhaul (km)	125	n.a.	n.a.	100

Source: Vlasov (1971) p.45

specifications having to meet the requirements of Soviet environmental conditions, however, Vlasov *et al.* also mentioned a general tendency towards contemporariness of Soviet-designed vehicles with their Western counterparts, stating that 'the latest models of [Soviet] passenger cars correspond, in terms of technical characteristics, to the best [international] models, as shown [in Table 5.2] in which basic parameters of the Moskvich 412 are compared with equivalent foreign models. Attention has also been given to the demands of export markets for improved internal and external finish and other requirements.'

The Moskvich range of vehicles were Soviet-designed[5] although manufacturing expertise was purchased from Renault during the mid-1960s.[6] It is useful therefore, to consider qualified assessment of this vehicle as a means of initially estimating the capabilities of the Soviet passenger car industry in terms of design and manufacture to specification during the late 1960s. A well documented *Motor*[7] road test consisted of an examination of the car's overall features and its various performance and handling characteristics. The report was favourable in terms of the car's acceleration, tractability and top speed, compared with Western-built cars of similar engine capacity, and particularly with cars sold for the same price as the Moskvich 412, since the sales price of this car was roughly equivalent to that charged for 'economy' cars such as the Renault 4, Hillman Imp and BLMC Mini, and some 30 per cent cheaper than Western-manufactured cars of similar engine capacity. A further advantageous feature of the car was its passenger accommodation and luggage space when compared with similar cars in the same price range, but this was to be expected in view of the car's engine capacity. The road test pointed to poor braking, however, and poor road-holding and imprecise steering, particularly at higher speeds. The fittings and finish were considered average, but this combined assessment was obtained as a compromise between 'well equipped for such a cheap car . . . surely the most comprehensive standard tool kit in the world', and, on the other hand, 'the paint-work of our L-registered test car was already bubbling and badly pitted . . . Inside we can only describe the decor as cheap and rather nasty.' A final, rather surprising point, was the poor ventilation and heating in the car, in view of the severe Russian climate.

Hence an overall assessment of the car from *Motor*'s road test points towards a 1.5 litre car capable of adequate performance, with large passenger space, well equipped for driver maintenance, but lacking in good finish. These characteristics would point well towards Soviet requirements for a car intended for public transport and some private use by drivers trained in car maintenance, although poor ventilation and bodywork finish may lead to shortcomings in use in the Russian climate. Furthermore, because of the large Soviet demand for passenger cars, it would have been natural for Soviet policy to concentrate on the immediate expansion of production of an adequate model for Soviet conditions, particularly in terms of ruggedness, rather than delay production to remove design imperfections viewed from the Western marketing standpoint, especially as its low selling price in the West would compensate for many of these. The ruggedness of the Moskvich 412 was also demonstrated by its successes in two rallies, namely the London–Sydney rally in 1968, run over a distance of some 16 000 kilometres in difficult terrain, and the London–Mexico rally in 1970, run over a distance of some 26 000 kilometres through 25 countries of Europe, South America and Central America. All four of the Moskvich cars completed the London–Sydney course, and the Soviet team was one of four to complete the course, from twelve contestants. In the London–Mexico rally, three Moskvich 412s were amongst the 22 competitors

Table 5.3 'Moskvich 412' – test results

Location of defect	Type of defect			
	Potential defect requiring remedial action	Defect to be put right at owner's convenience	Extreme defect requiring urgent attention	Extreme defect requiring immediate attention
Engine and cooling systems	2	8	0	2
Fuel and exhaust	1	1	2	0
Transmission	2	2	2	2
Braking system	0	1	3	15
Steering mechanism	0	15	3	11
Suspension and wheels	3	11	3	4
Body	14	4	1	0
Miscellaneous	6	3	0	1
Total	28	45	14	35

Note: 35 extreme defects were observed in the 9 cars tested, 2 in the engine and cooling system, 0 in the fuel and exhaust system, etc.
Source: Tests conducted by Consumers' Association, 1973 (unpublished)

completing the course from 96 entrants. The three Soviet cars were placed second, third and fourth in their class.[8]

Tests on the Moskvich range were also carried out by the Consumers' Association (CA) during the autumn of 1973. A sample of eleven cars were selected ranging from one car as purchased, to another having 30 000 miles recorded on the odometer. With nine of these cars tested by Consumers' Association inspectors, the unpublished results of this survey, approached mainly from the viewpoint of driver safety, are summarised in Table 5.3. The general picture that emerged from this study was that of lack of attention to safety features in both design and manufacture of this passenger car, caused, in many cases, by lack of attention to detail during assembly. The main areas of concern were steering and braking, most of the cars tested having serious brake defects requiring immediate attention, usually as a result of leaks in the hydraulic system or poor fitting of cylinders. Hence, although one Soviet source considered the Moskvich 412 to be equivalent to the Vauxhall Victor 1600 in terms of several technical characteristics (see Table 5.2 above), CA tests suggested that it was far below this 1962 British-designed model in terms of general safety.[9] One of the present authors was informed that the British distributors of this vehicle subsequently attempted to correct these faults by the establishment of a well equipped centre for checking and testing of vehicles prior to their release to local distributors.

It is important to note, however, that in spite of the design and manufacturing faults detected in the sample of Moskvich 412s tested by the Consumer's Association in 1973, the safety record of the 20 000 cars of this model sold in the UK was defended publicly by the Managing Director of the importing company,[10] while a London correspondent of *Izvestiya* recorded reports of satisfactory service from other British Moskvich owners.[11] This model of passenger vehicle is also reported to have been awarded a certificate of safety in Paris in 1970,[12] and several of the improvements to the braking system of this model recorded in the Soviet technical press in 1974[13] may have removed some of the previous design-based causes of the model's shortcomings. For example a Soviet journal records that following the introduction of an amplifier and pressure regulator in the rear brake hydraulic system, and the installation of separate brake activation and fault signalling, the Moskvich fully met international market demands, including those operating in Sweden. For further improvement of effectiveness and reliability, disc brakes with four piston pot calipers on the front wheels and separate hydraulic brake activation, guaranteeing not less than 60 per cent of full effectiveness from one of the hydraulic circuits only, have been introduced. Further reports indicate that a vacuum amplifier, separate circuits, front disc brakes, and force regulated rear brakes were introduced into the new model of Moskvich 2140 (a modernised version of the Moskvich 412) from the end of 1975.[14] Furthermore, the safety test technique at the Lenin Komsomol Factory (Moscow) has been substantially improved since 1974 with special attention being paid to improvement of body impact resistance and interior safety, in order that the Moskvich meet West European market requirements.[15]

The 'Zhiguli' (Lada)
As a result of the purchase of product technology from Fiat for the manufacture of the Zhiguli (Lada) at the Volga Automobile Factory (VAZ) Tol'yatti, the quality mix of Soviet passenger cars was substantially improved during the early 1970s. The Fiat 124 was selected as the prototype for this range (VAZ 2101 and VAZ 2102) and subsequently modified to suit Soviet operating and manufacturing

conditions.[16] These modifications included the use of heavier gauge metal for the floor pan, heavy duty springs and shock absorbers, a different braking system, a larger clutch, and a more powerful starter motor. Furthermore, a Soviet-designed 1198 cc engine was substituted for the 1197 cc Fiat push-rod unit.[17] This purchase of product technology was supplemented by the purchase of associated manufacturing expertise from Fiat chiefly related to process planning, and equipment selection;[18] and the purchase of manufacturing equipment from Western companies to enable the requirements of the purchased product and manufacturing technology to be met, and to overcome capacity constraints in the Soviet capital goods industries.[19]

In addition, product technology was purchased for various types of automotive components[20] which chiefly fell outside the boundaries of the final product technology referred to above. These have included product technology for electrical components, clutches and braking components. This purchase of product component technology was also supplemented by the purchase of manufacturing technology for the production of these same components.[21] It is these present authors' view, therefore, that the impact of these technology purchases on the Soviet passenger car industry was considerable.

The exported model of the Zhiguli (Lada) has been a substantial improvement on the Moskvich, as revealed from the following test comments on the Lada 1200 model. The motoring correspondent of *The Guardian*[22] newspaper reported that:

> The Lada has its faults which are primarily heavy steering, excessive engine noise and poor steering lock. But compared to all previous Russian cars it is a paragon . . . It handles safely and undramatically, appears to be quite strongly built, and in general is good basic transport . . . Apart from the inherent design faults in the steering and sound-proofing areas . . . the only obvious faults were minor. The door locks in particular appear to be somewhat inferior. In addition, there were early signs of surface rust, which is surprising considering the rigorous climate which the car has to cope with at home . . . Like its predecessors, the Lada shows the age of the basic design . . . But unlike its predecessors, the Lada is safe and apparently good value.

The road test reported in the *Autocar* magazine[23] compared the performance of the Lada, in terms of top speed, acceleration and fuel consumption, with four then contemporary UK manufactured cars of 1300 cc engine capacity (Ford Escort 1300 XL, Hillman Avenger

1300 GL, Morris Marina 1.3 and Vauxhall Viva DL). It was found to have the highest top speed of the four models tested, and was ranked in third place for economy of fuel consumption. Its rate of acceleration was found to be lower than the majority of the models tested, but not substantially lower to prevent *Autocar* from rating the Lada's performance as 'perfectly satisfactory'.

The handling of the car was described as 'traditional' in view of the modified ('beefed up') suspension system used on this car compared with that used on the Fiat prototype model. This modification was, no doubt, carried out to adapt the car for use in Soviet road conditions, since *Autocar* noted that 'on ordinary smooth roads the ride is good and well damped, but we found that the Lada really came into its own on rough unmade roads where it could cope with almost anything. There was little pitch or roll, and the Lada felt extraordinarily stable.' This good performance under rugged conditions, however, was obtained at the expense of lightness of handling under normal road conditions. The performance of the brakes was also found to be satisfactory, although their lack of sensitivity to feel ('totally dead feel') was considered to be a disadvantageous characteristic which could have been corrected by the fitting of a vacuum servo.

This model was also praised for the manner in which the engine was laid out under the bonnet. This layout, combined with the toolkit and maintenance manual supplied with the car ensured that the owner should be capable of servicing the car in a professional manner, this feature reflecting the higher degree of owner maintenance likely to be practised in the Soviet Union.

The main criticism of the car, in addition to those of heavy steering and insensitive braking referred to above, were aimed at the lack of driver support provided by the front seats, and the poor performance of the light bulbs provided with the car. It was also noted that although the car performed admirably under rugged conditions, inadequate protection of the handbrake central lever caused the rear brakes of the test car to be locked on when travelling over rough roads.

The magazine concluded its road test with the comment that 'we must congratulate the Russians on catching up so quickly (albeit with Italian advice and assistance) with the rest of the world's motor industry. The Lada 1200 is a thoroughly sound car, let down perhaps by sticking steering and dead brakes. But these are matters which can

Automotive Products and Components 77

Table 5.4 Soviet 'type standards' for goods vehicles

GOST 3163–76	Trailers and semi-trailers. General technical requirements
GOST 7593–80	Technical requirements for truck paint.
GOST 9218–80E	Tankers for edible fluids. Technical conditions.
GOST 1205–74	Tractor units and semi-trailers. Coupling dimensions.
GOST 13326–67	Truck anti-skid chains
GOST 19173–80	Container semi-trailers. Basic parameters and sizes. Technical requirements.
GOST 202288–74	Hydraulic transformers. Basic parameters.
GOST 21398–76	General truck requirements.
GOST 21561–76	Tankers for transporting liquefied gases up to 18kg/cm^2 pressure. General technical requirements.
GOST 24098–80	Container semi-trailers. Types, basic parameters and dimensions.

Source: Ukazatel' gosudarstvennykh standartov, 1982.

be rectified with a minimum of cost.' Similar reports were also received for the 1300 and 1600 models produced subsequently.

Since this range accounted for almost 50 per cent of total annual Soviet passenger car output by 1975[24] it can be concluded that the Soviet passenger car industry, although not in the vanguard of passenger car design technology, has become capable of producing a large production of its total output to design requirements demanded by the international market for average priced saloon cars of 1.2–1.5 litres engine capacity. This model has subsequently been modified externally and internally, with a broader range of options introduced. This has enabled the car to remain competitive within the price range in which it is located.

TRUCKS

Soviet Type Standards for Trucks

The list of type standards which are currently operational for Soviet goods vehicles is shown in Table 5.4. From this list it can be seen that the majority of standards relate to general technical requirements for trucks, such as overall dimensional size parameters and axle load bearing capacities; and also the definitions of those parameters which influence interchangeability in practice, such as coupling dimensions. It is apparent, however, that although the content of these standards are important from the viewpoint of basic practical capabilities, they say little about the quality and performance characteristics of commercial vehicles.

As in the case of passenger cars, the quantity of these standards appears to be smaller than that usually found in advanced Western industrial countries, but this list of state standards may be supplemented by a list of 'industrial branch' standards developed and approved for its own use by the Ministry of the Automobile Industry of the USSR.

In order to obtain a better estimate of the quality and performance characteristics of Soviet goods vehicles, therefore, it was decided to study certain aspects of the product mix of the industry, and the quality characteristics of those products which have been awarded the state 'mark of quality'. These studies are contained in the following sections of this chapter.

Technical Characteristics of Soviet Goods Vehicles

Product Mix and Payload

During the late 1950s and early 1960s, several authorities in the USSR had observed that the majority of the stock of Soviet commercial vehicles consisted of 2.5–4 ton payload trucks, with more than 70 per cent of trucks having a 'drop-side platform' construction. Less than 20 per cent of the stock consisted of tipper types required mainly for the construction and agricultural industries, while vans and tankers accounted for an even smaller percentage of the total stock.[25] As a consequence of that study, a perspective product range was developed by Soviet research institutes and factories for assimilation during the 1966–1970 Five Year Plan. That range would appear to have been adequate by the then international practices making use of the expedients of increasing the payload of a particular vehicle by means of trailer units towed by a conventional platform truck, or the design of tractor unit variants for use with semi-trailers.

A further aspect of product mix considered was that of structure, in terms of the absolute and proportional quantities of output of certain truck types classified by payload. From 1958–65, there had been an extremely low rate of expansion in total goods vehicle output (less than 1 per cent), although figures published by Vlasov[26] suggest that the output of lightweight goods vehicles of less than 2 tons payload increased by more than 900 per cent, and medium to heavy vehicles of greater than 5 tons payload increased by some 120 per cent. The total output of these vehicles in 1965 (70 000 vehicles approximately) however, appeared to be far lower than for those vehicles in the 2–5 tons payload range (310 000 vehicles in 1965) for which there was a contraction in output from 1958 to 1965. Similar, although less extreme, patterns in product mix output could be observed during the 1966–70 planning period with over 200 per cent increase in the output of trucks of up to 2 tons payload, and a smaller increase in output (60 per cent) of trucks of greater than 5 tons payload. The total output of these lighter vehicles, however, still remained far lower than for vehicles in the 2–5 tons payload range (160 000 vehicles compared with 408 000).[27]

In view of these changes in Soviet output proportions apparent from 1958 to 1970, and the availability of truck output statistics from certain Western countries (USA, UK, France, FRG) it is useful to compare Soviet goods vehicle output proportions for 1970 with those of the selected Western countries, although certain assumptions are necessary to allow for the differences in classifications between the different sets of statistics (see Table 5.5), particularly the use of 'payload' classification in Soviet statistics, and 'gross vehicle weight', in their Western counterparts. In general, a factor of two has been assumed to convert 'payload' to 'gross vehicle weight'.

It is apparent from the data shown in this table that the output product mix of Soviet goods vehicles at the end of the 1966–1970 Five Year Plan was different from that of the selected Western countries in many respects. In the first place the output from the USA, UK, France and FRG was dominated by light vehicles (less than 4 tons gross vehicle weight), the proportion ranging from 55 per cent for FRG to 83 per cent for France. The Soviet output for this category of vehicle, (0–2 tons payload), however, was less than the selected Western countries in terms of absolute values of output, but also far lower in terms of output proportion (8 per cent). On the other hand, the USSR was by far the largest producer in the assumed 4–10 tons GVW range (2–5 tons payload range) producing some estimated 408 000 goods vehicles of this type annually in 1970, which accounted for approximately 78 per cent of total Soviet goods vehicle output during that year. Hence, considering the '10 tons and less' gross vehicle weight category in total, it is reasonable to suggest, in spite of somewhat arbitrary selection of classification categories, that although the proportion of total output within this category was not

Table 5.5 Comparative output of trucks, by weight, USSR and selected western countries, 1970 (all output figures in thousands of units)

USSR Group	Output	Proportion
0–2 tons payload	43.3	8%
2–5 tons payload	408	78%
5–10 tons payload	27.3	5%
10 tons and greater payload	45.5	9%
Total	525	100%
Tractor Units	23	

USA Group	Output	Proportion
0–10 000 lbs (GVW)	1,351.8	80%
0–19 500 lbs (GVW)	76.5	4%
19 500–33,000 lbs (GVW)	162.9	10%
33 000 lbs & greater (GVW)	101.1	6%
Total	1,692.4	100%

FRG Group	Output	Proportion
0–4 tons (GVW)	157.2	55%
4–10 tons (GVW)	65.0	23%
10–16 tons (GVW)	40.8	14%
16 ton & greater (GVW)	22.2	8%
Total	285.2	100%
Tractor Units	14.4	

UK Group	Output	Proportion
0–3 tons (GVW)	175.6	73%
3–10 tons (GVW)	35.4	15%
10–20 tons (GVW)	27.8	11%
20 tons & greater (GVW)	3.6	1%
Total	237.4	100%
Tractor units	13.6	

France Group	Output	Proportion
0–4 tons (GVW)	233.3	75%
4–9 tons (GVW)	18.5	6%
9–20 tons (GVW)	25.4	8%
20 tons & greater (GVW)	3.5	1%
Total	310.7	100%
Tractor Units	7.1	

Notes: (a) The above categories were selected for comparison in view of the Soviet data being classified by payload and the Western data being classified according to Gross Vehicle Weight or Gross Laden Weight. The relationship between the categories was obtained from four Soviet 'Mark of Quality' state standards relating to four models of truck as follows:

Truck Model	Standard	Payload in tons (Metric)	Gross vehicle weight in tons (metric)
GAZ 66	GOST 5.340–70	2	3.47
ZIL 130	GOST 5.979–71	5	9.52
MAZ 500A	GOST 5.965–71	8	15
BelAZ 540A	GOST 5.21–72	27	48

(b) USA data includes buses; (c) Soviet data for output of 2–5 ton payload trucks estimated by a subtraction of output figures for 0–2 tons payload, 5–10 tons payload and 10 tons and greater payload, from total goods vehicle output figures.

Sources: (a) USSR data: Vlasov, B.V., *Ekonomicheskie problemy proizvodstva avtomobilei* (Mashinostroenie, Moscow, 1971) p. 17;
(b) Western data: Society of Motor Manufactures and Traders Ltd, *The Motor Industry of Great Britain 1972* (SMMT, London)
    (i) UK data; pp. 16, 17, based on statistics abstracted from Business Monitor; published by DTI
    (ii) French data; p. 40, based on statistics from Chambre Syndicated des Constructeurs d'Automobile
    (iii) FRG data; p. 40, based on statistics from Verband der Automobilindustrie.

dissimilar for the USSR and the selected Western countries (86 per cent for USSR; 79.5 per cent–89.5 per cent for the selected Western countries), the Western output was biased towards the lighter end of this range, while the Soviet output was biased towards the heavier end. For the '10 tons and greater' GVW category, it is likely that Soviet output was approximately equal to that of UK and FRG, but lower than that of USA. Differences between Soviet and Western output proportions could be identified since the majority of Western output was concentrated in the 10–20 tons and greater GVW range, while the majority of Soviet output was concentrated in the 20 tons and greater GVW range (i.e. 10 tons payload and greater). Within the lighter range of this 10–20 tons GVW category, Soviet output was lower than that of USA and UK; but in the heavier range of this category, the USSR was second only to the USA in terms of total output.

The most significant change likely to have occurred in the output product mix of Soviet goods vehicles since 1970 has been the proportionate increase in annual output of 8–11 ton payload vehicles, as a consequence of establishing a new factory to produce these vehicles at Kama (Kam AZ). The production capacity of this factory has been 150 000 vehicles per year, which will have substantially changed current Soviet goods vehicle output product mix compared with 1970, to bring the heavy vehicles product mix more into line with Western countries. This similarity in product mix should now become apparent as the KamAZ range is becoming assimilated into the national economy, supplemented by output of the ZIL 130 variants described in a subsequent part of this section.

Use of Diesel Engines

During the late 1960s and the early 1970s, it appears that the degree of application of diesel engines in Soviet goods vehicles was quite low, certainly when compared with the USA, but particularly so when compared with Western Europe. In 1971, Vlasov[28] claimed that only 10 per cent of Soviet goods vehicle stock was diesel-powered, and that the majority of applications were in the heavy goods range (ie: 14 tons and greater GVW). The use of diesel engines in the heavy payload category was quite extensive in Western countries at that time with 65 per cent of American vehicles over 11.5 tons GVW being diesel powered in 1968,[29] and for Western Europe the proportion was probably larger.

In the 6–11.5 ton GVW group, however, it appeared that there were also similarities between the USSR and the USA, and differences with Western Europe. In the USSR, it is probable that only a few of the Soviet vehicles in this range were diesel-powered, and only 10 per cent of vehicles produced in the USA in this range were

Table 5.6 'Mark of Quality' standard for Soviet Trucks (1982)

GOST 5.21–72	BelAZ 540A and BelAZ 540 tipper trucks and modifications
GOST 5.340–70	GAZ 66 high clearance trucks
GOST 5.979–71	ZIL–130 tractor unit and modifications
GOST 5.2098–73	TSV–6 fuel tanker
GOST 5.964–71	YaMZ 238 truck engine
GOST 5.1702–72	SMD-14B four-stroke water-cooled diesel engine

Source: *Ukazatel' gosudarstvennykh standartov, 1982.*

diesel-powered. In the United Kingdom, however, the proportion was of the order of 90 per cent. Changes within the engine output structure were implemented in both the US and the USSR during the mid to late 1970s. The American target was one of 35 per cent of output in this range by 1975,[30] and the Soviet target would appear to be close to this for the early 1980s as a consequence of development of capacity at the Yaroslavl' Engine Factory, and the establishment of a diesel engine production facility at the Kama River factory (KamAZ). This facility is capable of producing 250 000 truck diesel engines per year, 150 000 of which are used in KamAZ trucks whilst the remaining 100 000 are distributed to other factories.[31] According to the 'Draft Basic Guidelines of Economic and Social Development of the USSR for 1986–90' published by *Pravda* on 9 November 1985, output of diesel-powered trucks is to be increased to 45 per cent of total truck output by 1990.

'Mark of Quality' Approval

Several products manufactured by the Soviet truck industry have been awarded a 'Mark of Quality' by the quality attestation commission of the State Committee of Standards (see Table 5.6). As outlined in previous chapters of this book (see chapters 1 and 3), the 'Mark of Quality' is awarded to those products which are considered to meet contemporary international requirements for product quality, and which are produced under modern conditions.

The most widely used of the products listed in Table 5.6 is probably the ZIL 130 range, which are used extensively throughout the USSR for freight haulage in trailer and semi-trailer configurations. A detailed listing of the major parameters of this product is shown in Table 5.7 from which it can be seen that this vehicle does not compare particularly unfavourably with similar vehicles of the same vintage in use in Western countries. It is important to note, however, that no new truck has been designated as the highest category of

Table 5.7 Technical specifications of the ZIL 130 truck range (to GOST 5.979 – 71)

Parameter	ZIL 130	ZIL 130 V1	ZIL 130G	ZIL 130 D1
Full load (kg)				
platform	5000	—	5000	4500
chassis	5600	—	5700	5485
Load on saddle (kg)				
Class 1	—	5400	—	—
All roads	—	—	—	—
Trailer or semi-trailer laden weight (kg)	8000	12 400	8000	3690
Truck kerbside weight (kg)	4300	3860	4575	—
Fully laden weight (kg)				
without trailer	9529	—	9800	9400
with trailer	17 525	16 485	17 800	—
Track: Front wheels (mm)		1800		
Rear wheels (mm)		1790		
Wheelbase (mm)	3800	3300	4500	3300
Angle of overhang, fully laden				
front°	27	38	22	47
rear°		47		
Front truck overhang, (mm)		1075		
Overall dimensions, (mm)				
Length	6675	5280	7610	5280
Width	2500	2360	2500	2360

Cabin Height		2400	
Internal platform dimensions			
Length (mm)	3752	—	4686
Width (mm)	2326	—	2326
Dropside height (mm)	575	—	575
Maximum speed (fully laden) km/hr			
without trailer	90	—	90
with semi-trailer	—	80	—
Minimum turning circle (m)	8.9	8.0	10.1
Fuel consumption (litres/100km)			
without trailer	28	—	28
with semi-trailer	—	35	—
Oil consumption as % of fuel consumption		0.5	
Fuel tank capacity (litres)	170	250	170
Nominal engine power (min HP)		150	
Engine RPM at nominal power		3200	
Maximum engine turning moment (kg-m), minimum		41	

Notes: Braking System: Pneumatically powered brake shoes with hand-brakes connected to the transmission; Steering System: Hydraulic powered; Hand brake: Must hold fully laden truck on a 20% incline (Time of test – 5 minutes); Braking System: 11m braking distance at 30 km/hr for truck fully laden without trailer. 13m braking distance at 30km/hr for ZIL–130VI tractor unit pulling a 12 400 kg trailer unit; Generator: Must charge battery at 30km/hr sufficient for headlamps, rear lamps and heater motor; Starting: Pre-starting heater must guarantee engine starting after not longer than 30 minutes at –40°C; Oil Changes: Engine oil, every 8400–9200 km. Transmission, every 50–55 000km.

quality since the early 1970s, suggesting that the momentum of quality attestation in the 1970s may have been subsequently lost. Truck design and development in the West, however, has contined unabated in view of the pressures of increased efficiency requirements in distribution.

The manufacturer's guarantee extends from 12 months of commissioning into service, or 13 months of receipt by the customer, or for 25 000 km. Batteries and tyres are covered by suppliers' guarantees.

ENGINE COMPONENTS

The quantity of components used in contemporary passenger and goods vehicles is extremely large, and standards exist for these components in both the USSR and UK. In order to obtain a rapid assessment of product quality, therefore, it was decided to select two types of critical engine component for which information was really available, namely crankshafts and gudgeon pins. The technical requirements for these components are shown in Tables 5.8 and 5.9.

Table 5.8 shows various parameters for Soviet steel crankshafts, including material composition, material structure, hardness, and pin and journal geometric form and surface finish tolerances. It is impossible to compare these requirements with British standard practice, since no such document has been approved by the British Standards Institution. It is possible, however to compare the geometric accuracy and surface finish requirements with a sample of crankshafts which were observed being finish-ground in British factories in the early 1970s.[32] The Soviet standard, for example, quotes an out-of-roundness tolerance of 0.005 mm, which is also the usual tolerance observed by British crankshaft manufacturers.[33] There is a difference, however, in surface finish specification, with the Soviet standard specifying a tolerance of 0.160 mkm CLA, compared with normal British practice of 0.4–0.5 mkm CLA.[34] This difference is accounted for by the normal Soviet practice of lapping crankshaft pins and journals after grinding,[35] whereas it is normal British practice to consider the grinding process as the final stage of production.[36] It is difficult to establish the reason for the Soviet practice of crankshaft lapping, unless it is expected to lead to enhanced crankshaft fatigue resistance.

Table 5.9 shows various parameters for steel gudgeon pins including material composition and hardness, and geometric tolerance and

Table 5.8 Steel crankshafts (Requirements to GOST 4669–68, Material Composition to GOST 14959–79)

Symbol	Type	Element content%					
		C	Si	Mn	Cr	Ni	Other
45	Light alloy	0.42–0.49	0.17–0.37	0.50–0.80	—	—	—
40Kh	Chrome Steel	0.37–0.45	0.17–0.37	0.50–0.80	0.80–1.10	<0.25	
40KhN	Chrome Nickel Steel	0.37–0.45	0.17–0.37	0.50–0.80	0.45–0.75	1.00–1.40	
40KhNMA	Chrome-Nickel Molybdenum Steel	0.37–0.44	0.17–0.37	0.50–0.80	0.60–0.90	1.25–1.65	Mo 0.15–
50G	Manganese Steel	0.47–0.55	0.17–0.37	0.70–1.00	—	—	
50KhLFA	Chrome-Vanadium Steel	0.47	0.17	0.50	0.80	<0.20	Va 0.10
		0.54	0.37	0.80	1.10		–0.20

Notes: Forging hardness after heat treatment 163–269 Brinell (Variation must not exceed 50 Brinell); journal and pin hardness to be 52–62 Rockwell 'C'; journal and pin microstructure to be fine or medium acicular martensite, changing to troosto-martensite; Depth of heat-treated surface to be greater than 1mm after grinding.

Accuracy and Surface Finish
Out of roundness = 0.005mm
Parallelism of pin and journal axes = 0.03mm per 100mm
Surface finish (journals and pins) = 0.160 mkm CLA
Surface finish (fillets) = 0.25 mkm CLA

surface finish. It is possible to compare these latter requirements with similar British parameters, however, since a British standard has published on this topic (BS 3537: 1979: *Gudgeon pins up to 200 mm diameter*).

Comparing core hardnesses first, it can be seen that there are certain similarities between the two sets of documents. In the Soviet case, however, the permissible range depends upon the material selected, whereas the British standard is more specific in terms of maximum piston pressure (ie: 20 HRC for cylinder maximum pressure less than 7MN/M^2, 25 HRC for cylinder pressure between 7 and 12 MN/M^2, and 37 HRC for cylinder pressures greater than 12MN/M^2).[37] In a similar fashion, the Soviet standard specifies a pin external surface hardness range of 56–65 Rockwell 'C', whereas the British Standard range is slightly higher and more specific in terms of material and type of surface hardening (58 for carburized plain carbon steel, 56 for carburized alloy steel, 69 for nitriding steel containing aluminum, and 64 for aluminum-free nitriding steel). Furthermore, the British Standard is more exacting for depth of hardened case. Regarding geometric tolerance, it can be seen that the Soviet standard specifies a geometric tolerance of 0.00125 mm for bending and waviness and 0.0025 mm for other geometric irregularities. The tolerance specified in the British Standard, however, varies with the diameter and length of the gudgeon pin (see Table 5.10). Comparing the figures presented in Tables 5.9 and 5.10 therefore, it appears that the British Standard is more demanding for the smaller-sized components having diameters of less than 50 mm, whilst the Soviet standard is more demanding for the larger sized components having a diameter of greater than 120 mm. The surface finish requirements for these components is specified as 0.16 mkm CLA, whereas the British Standard requirements varies with the size of the pin from 0.1 mkm for diameters less than 80 mm, to 0.2 mkm for pin diameters varying between 80 and 140 mm, to 0.4 mkm for pin diameter greater than 140 mm. As previously, therefore, it appears that the British Standard is more demanding for the smaller-sized components. Finally, with regard to concentricity tolerances, both sets of standards appear to be equally demanding.

Table 5.9 Gudgeon pins – requirements to GOST 776–66; material composition to GOST 4543-71

(a) For gudgeon pins undergoing cementation and hardening

Symbol	Type	C	Si	Element content % Mn	Cr	Ni	Other
15Kh & 15KhA	Chrome Steel	0.12–0.18	0.17–0.37	0.40–0.70	0.70–1.00	<0.25	—
15KhM	Chrome Molybdenum Steel	0.12 — 0.18	0.17 — 0.37	0.40 — 0.70	0.80 — 1.10	<0.25	Mo 0.40–0.55
12KhN3A 12Kh2N4A		not available		not available			

(b) For gudgeon pins undergoing case hardening to GOST 1050-74

45	Light Alloy	0.42–0.49	0.17–0.37	0.50–0.80	—	—	—

Notes: Hardness of pin external surface, 56–65 Rockwell 'C' (differences along the pin must not exceed 5 Rockwell 'C').
Core Hardness: 20–35 Rockwell 'C' for carbon steels
20–40 Rockwell 'C' for medium steels
25–35 Rockwell 'C' for case-hardened components

Martensitic treatment to produce a matrix of medium-acicular structure; case hardening to produce a low-acicular structure; surface finish of external surface = 0.16 mkm CLA; tapering, bulging, waisting and ovality of external surface = 0.0025 mm; bending and waviness = 0.00125 mm; internal surface of the pin to be concentric with the external surface:
   10% of wall thickness, for pins up to 3.5 mm thick
   0.5 mm for wall thickness greater than 3.5 mm.

Table 5.10 Gudgeon Pin Tolerances to BS 3537: 1979

Pin length	O.D (d_1) (mm)	Tolerances on longitudinal form 'Z' and Roundness 'K' (mm)
<185	<50	0.0015
	>50 <80	0.002
>185	<50	0.0025
	>50 <80	0.0025
All	>80 <100	
	>100 <120	0.0025
	>120 <180	
	>180 <200	0.004

CONCLUSIONS

This study has served as an introductory investigation into the quality levels of the Soviet motor industry, demonstrating that both state standards and published specialised reports can be used as relevant infomation sources. The results of the research can be criticised for the smallness of the samples chosen for comparison, but the authors' main concern was one of obtaining an assessment across a broad range of topics rather than detailed study in any one area. The topics of passenger cars, goods vehicles and components have been surveyed in some detail, and a basis established for further research into each.

Certain difficulties are encountered when attempting to compare the quality features of the products manufactured by this industry. In the first place, the Western car industry has been established for many years as a heavily consumer oriented volume industry, operating in a highly competitive environment with a large multinational presence. Furthermore, the product has an image which is very much part of Western culture. These commercial pressures are almost completely absent in the tightly planned Soviet economy, and the USSR's industry appears to compete in Western markets on the basis of 'adequacy' and 'price competitiveness' rather than product sophistication. Consequently, it would be expected that cultural pressures alone would create a quality gap between Western and Soviet products, but it appears that Soviet policy makers have made efforts to close this gap through policies of the purchasing and assimilation of Western product and manufacturing technology. Finally, the commercial pressures surrounding motor sport in Western societies lead eventually to improved performance in Western automotive products, particularly in the area of components. To date, the USSR has generally only participated in rallies, but no top level international races.

Furthermore, it is also interesting to note that no Soviet model of passenger car has been awarded the 'Mark of Quality', although this may change if technological innovation becomes more widespread in the industry. The monitoring of such technological innovation is worthy of further research, particularly with regard to electrical and electronic components which have not been included in the present research. In addition, it is interesting to note that the USSR has been a comparatively late entrant into the large scale manufacture of front wheel drive vehicles. It is anticipated, however, that front wheel drive configuration cars will soon come into large-scale production at the Zaporozhets Automobile Factory, (the ZAZ 'Oka' mini-car),[38] the Moscow 'Lenin Komsomol' Factory (Moskvich 2141),[39] and the Volga Automobile Factory, Tol'yatti (VAZ 2108).[40] The performance of these cars should be watched with interest, particularly as the VAZ model is also equipped with electronic ignition and a five-speed gearbox.[41]

More research is also required on the Soviet truck industry, which has been more consistently favoured by Soviet policy-makers than the passenger car sector. It was found that several products had been awarded the 'Mark of Quality' although most of these dated from the early 1970s and some have now been withdrawn as obsolete. Clearly these should be studied, and more information sought on practical performance and servicing requirements. Furthermore, it is interesting to note that the KamAZ factory has not been awarded a 'Mark of Quality' even though its product is advanced. Perhaps it is not Soviet policy to award this prize to factories receiving large amounts of Western technology, but this should be investigated. The performance of diesel engines may also be a topic for further research, particularly as the use of these power units are to become more widely used in Soviet trucks,[42] and there are plans to also commence production of diesel-powered cars.[43]

Finally, component standards appear to be similar in both the UK and the USSR although Soviet standards may include a broad range of requirements whereas the British documents appear to be more specific. This practice should be investigated further.

6 Domestic Refrigerators

INTRODUCTION

This chapter is a preliminary investigation into the levels of technology and quality of the Soviet domestic goods industry. Refrigerators have been selected for special study, since two surveys[1] of consumer acquisition patterns for domestic appliances, show quite clearly that a domestic refrigerator is invariably the first and most essential of the household appliances acquired by the average family in industrial societies. Other surveys, analysing the technical merits and other features of a whole range of refrigerators, made reference to the importance attached to the ownership of a refrigerator.[2] They also included evidence to show that of all the domestic electrical appliances in common use, the refrigerator is usually the most reliable.[3]

This chapter contains four main sections. The first of these is a technical description of the basic operating principles of a refrigerator, followed by general information related to the growth and development of the Soviet domestic refrigerator industry. The third section of the chapter contains an account of the quality characteristics of the 'Biryusa' range of refrigerators, which are probably the best known of all Soviet models to appear on the domestic and international markets in the last two decades. This study of Soviet refrigerators is complemented by a similar survey of refrigerators of West European manufacture followed by a comparative assessment of the Soviet and West European models.

THE DOMESTIC REFRIGERATOR

The refrigeration cycle makes use of refrigerant pressure, temperature and latent heat of vaporisation, in order to create a heat transfer process which provides a temperature reduction in the cooling compartment of the refrigerator. The two major types of refrigeration cycle encountered in practice are known as the 'absorption' and the 'compression' cycles.

In absorption refrigerators, a gas or electrical heater is used to provide the necessary heat transfer to vaporise the refrigerant in the evaporator; the refrigerant then cools to a liquid as it passes through the system extracting heat from the surrounding cooling compartment as it travels.

In compression refrigerators, on the other hand, a liquid refrigerant is evaporated in a container, taking sufficient heat from the surrounding cooling compartment to provide the necessary latent heat of vaporisation. The refrigerant is then transferred in its gaseous state to a compressor, where it is condensed at a temperature much higher than that of the evaporating liquid.

In addition to the major evaporating, compressing and heating components described above, a refrigerator also requires a thermostat to control the temperature of the system, and a valve to control the flow of refrigerant.

THE SOVIET DOMESTIC REFRIGERATOR INDUSTRY

The Soviet domestic refrigerator industry was originally established in the early 1950s and sales of domestic refrigerators subsequently grew by approximately 35 per cent each year to reach annual sales of nearly 5 million by 1973. During the mid 1970s the industry was producing over 5.8 million refrigerators each year, which did not compare unfavourably with the industrially developed nations of USA, Japan and Italy.[4] The result of this Soviet production effort was that by early 1978, 77 per cent of Soviet families were in possession of a refrigerator, which subsequently increased to 90 per cent by 1984.[5] In spite of this impressive growth in output, however, there is evidence to suggest that Soviet consumer requirements were not fully satisfied, as a result of a shift in demand to larger capacity refrigerators which occurred in the mid-1970s. It was estimated at one stage that between 60 per cent and 70 per cent of overall demand (measured by orders placed) was for refrigerators with storage capacities of 200 litres and above, whilst only 23.7 per cent of the industry's production capacity had been allocated for this purpose. The situation in large Soviet towns and cities was such that over half the demand for large capacity refrigerators was not being satisfied; and in rural and outlying districts there were reports which indicated that nearly 80 per cent of the demand was not being met, in spite of a large number of product models being manufactured.[6] Consequently, the yearly growth rate of stocks during the ninth five-year plan was almost five times the yearly increase in sales, compared with an approximately equal balance in growth of sales and stocks during the previous planning period. Efforts were subsequently made to rectify this situation, changing production capacity during the first half of the 1970s from smaller to larger sized refrigerators;[7] and these efforts have been continued into the 1980s.[8]

QUALITY LEVELS OF SOVIET REFRIGERATORS

General Features

The drawbacks and shortcomings of the Soviet refrigerator industry have not been confined just to matters of demand and supply imbalance. According to accounts of poor design and inferior performance of refrigerators which appear regularly in the Soviet technical and national press, the post-inspection rejection of refrigerators is still a commonplace occurrence.[9] Some of the more common faults have included the following:

> high levels of energy consumption;
> excessively noisy operation;
> cumbersome and weighty construction;
> faulty temperature control and regulation;
> flimsy and badly-fitting doors and other fixtures.[10]

The non-availability or shortages of some essential raw materials has also been a major reason for many production problems. Two most notable examples of this are poor quality finishes resulting from the use of sub-standard paints and pigments and the low values of food-storage efficiency caused by inferior-graded insulation material.

In addition to these problems it appears that the working environment within which Soviet refrigerators are expected to operate is not conducive to efficient and reliable operation. This is caused by the poor quality of existing power supplies in the Soviet Union, restricting the size and electrical safety of most household appliances to a 5 amp two-core cable with no earthing facilities.[11] Furthermore, urban 'peak-period' voltage variations, reported to occur at values three times the specified limit, have caused a substantial deterioration in the overall performance of most electrical appliances. In rural or outlying districts, the situation is reported to be even more serious with reports of complete failure of a number of refrigerators on account of these power supply deficiencies.

Quality Levels of the 'Biryusa' Refrigerator

The 'Biryusa' model of refrigerator manufactured by the Krasnoyarsk Engineering Factory is reported to be the best Soviet model in production, with almost 100 per cent of the range attested to meet the requirements of the 'mark of quality' procedure.[12] The model is also reported to have accounted for a significant proportion of Soviet deliveries to the home market, and also of Soviet output to the export market. Finally, it is also claimed that the best manufacturing techniques in the Soviet refrigerator industry are being used by the Krasnoyarsk factory. The export of these refrigerators to many Western European countries means that more information is available regarding their design, construction and performance, than for other Soviet models.

Production of the 'Biryusa' range was commenced in 1964, with annual output varying between 100 000 and 150 000 units per annum during the remainder of the 1960s. In 1970, new methods of production were introduced into the Krasnoyarsk factory and production increased to 580 000 units per year, reaching more than 700 000 per year by the late 1970s. During this same time interval, exports were increased from 12 500 in 1970 to 63 100 in 1977.

Increases in the levels of output of this refrigerator were also paralleled by improvements in the product's design features. These have included:

the use of improved insulation materials such as polyurethane foam, enabling the thickness of the layers of insulation to be reduced from 60 to 35 mm;
an increase in the net volume of food-storage space available;
a reduction in overall weight;
savings in the consumption of electrical energy;
an improvement in the frozen-food compartment temperature from $-6°C$, for the earliest models, to $-12°C$.

The 'Biryusa – 1' model was the first Soviet refrigerator to be accredited with the 'Mark of Quality' award in 1970; and three other models (the Biryusa 5, 6 and 8) were later designated as 'products of the highest category of quality'.

'Biryusa' refrigerators were also one of the first consignments of Soviet-made electrical goods to be exported to Britain, Holland, Belgium, and Ireland. Imports to Britain began with an order for 20 000 units and it is claimed that they eventually occupied second place in terms of volumes of refrigerators imported in competition with other leading refrigerator manufacturers from the United States, Japan and countries of Western Europe.[13] According to the same source, 'Biryusa' refrigerators (under the UK trade name of 'Snowcap') have successfully completed tests in accordance with the relevant British standards and, in the process were awarded a certificate of worthiness from the national test centre concerned. Subsequent investigations by the present authors have revealed, however, that the refrigerator had not received the approval of the British Electrotechnical Approvals Board (BEAB), the organisation which usually carries out this national approval task for domestic electrical appliances in the UK. It would appear, therefore, that the testing for the UK market was carried out in *a* British testing centre, not *the* British testing centre. The absence of BEAB approval could partly be explained by the Board's insistence that the methods of manufacture of an approved product be observed by a team of the Board's inspectors. It is not normal Soviet practice to welcome such tours of inspection by non-Soviet citizens, particularly if the factory concerned is in the defence sector. It is also claimed that similar recognition has been achieved in West Germany (where recent imports of 'Biryusa' totalled 20 000) and Austria.[14]

Finally, claims are also made that steps have been taken at the Krasnoyarsk factory to bring quality standards of production in line with those of other overseas countries. In the mid-1970s an advanced system of quality control employing computerised monitoring techniques was put into operation enabling a complete and all-round quality control check of a refrigerator to be accomplished within two hours.[15]

COMPARATIVE ASSESSMENT OF THE QUALITY INDICATORS OF SOVIET REFRIGERATORS

This study consists of a comparative assessment of some eighteen parameters, related to the design, construction and performance of individual refrigerators. The parameters selected are as follows:

external compactness (the height of the worktop and the floor area to be occupied);
internal capacity (the effective space available in the main food compartment and the frozen food compartment);
convenience in use (the type of storage facilities available and the accessibility of compartments, shelves and trays);

Domestic Refrigerators 97

type of defrosting (manual, semi-automatic or fully- automatic);

noise during operation and adjustment facilities incorporated to compensate for uneven surfaces;

refrigerating capability (the 'star rating' of the frozen food compartment);

running costs based on the quarterly consumption of electricity at the unit cost of 5p per kilowatt-hour of energy. These theoretical estimates can be influenced in practice by:

the thermostat setting,

the temperature of the external environment, and the refrigerator's location within that environment,

the use of the refrigerator (frequencies of door opening, location of hot food and defrosting),

price (the retail price of the refrigerator in the high street shops. These prices depend to a certain extent on the time of purchase. Most of the prices quoted in this comparative study are taken from 1984 sales and advertising literature. Where that is not the case, an alternative date has been given);

Safety and reliability (safety standards, 'after sales' guarantees, back-up service and repair facilities).

Data has been collected on four categories of 'Biryusa' refrigerator (the KSH280, KSH240, KSH160 and KSH150) from two main data sources, namely Soviet state standards, and technical sales data provided by the Soviet seller. Details on at least three similarly rated models of West European manufacture have been included for comparison, using data collected from a series of British Standards and manufacturers' catalogues. Overall, the study has provided a reasonable range of examination, and this has been further broadened by the inclusion of both 'larder' and 'absorption' types of refrigerators,[16] since their design, construction and performance differ slightly[17] from those of the remaining refrigerators. The results of this comparative study are shown in Tables 6.1 to 6.4.

Both Soviet and British refrigerator manufacturers have to ensure that they maintain certain minimum levels of technology. These previously determined levels are officially laid down in technical documentation[18] published by national standards organisation specifically for this purpose. To complete the comparative study it was decided to scrutinise the relevant sections of this documentation and establish where some of the coincidences occurred in the test and inspection procedures for both sets of refrigerators. These were recorded and are listed in Table 6.5.

Table 6.1 Comparison study results, small to medium capacity refrigerators

Design features and performance specifications	Refrigerator make and model number				
	Soviet KSH150 or Snowcap 150 DI	Frigidaire RJ510	Zanussi Z1142 TRM (Italy)	LEC Cameo R141 CM (UK)	Electrolux RA513 (Absorption Type)(UK)
Height(cm)	85	86	85	88	91.5
Width(cm)	57	57	50	51	50.2
Depth(cm)	60	60	60	57	57.5
Gross internal volume (litres)	150	151	140	146	143
Net internal volume (litres)	—	106	120	104	133
Low temperature compartment volume (litres)	14	18	Not stated	9	Not stated
Defrosting	SA	SA (main) M (frozen food compartment)	FA	M (main) M (frozen food compartment)	FA M (frozen food compartment)
No. of adjustable feet (for levelling purposes)	4	Non-adjustable	∨	1	Non-adjustable
No. of shelves	3	3	3	3	3

No. of salad crispers, salad or fruit drawers	2 (half width)	2 (half width)	1 (full width)	1 (full width)	1 (half width)
Drip tray and cleaning facilities	√	√	√	√	√
Defrosting evaporator tray	√	√	√	√	√
Interior light	√	√	√	Not fitted	
Positions of door hinges	RHS (LHS on request)	RHS	Reversible door	RHS (LHS on request)	RHS (LHS on request)
Food storage temperature rating	2 star	2 star	2 star	2 star	3 star (suitable for long term food storage)
Running costs (based on 5p/kWhr)	£3.50 per quarter	£3.65 per quarter	£3.85 per quarter	£4–£4.50 per quarter	£9.00 per quarter
Retail price	£75 (1985)	£80 (1982)	£102 (1985)	£95 (1984) £80 (1982)	£154 (1985)
Manufacturer's guarantee	1 year	1 year	1 year	1 year	1 year
Electrical safety, service reliability or repair back-up facilities	3 years	Not stated	5 year cover plan available	Not stated but BEAB approved	4 year cover scheme available

Notes: (i) √ indicates that the facility is included; (ii) For defrosting, the following symbols have been used: M = manual, FA = fully automatic, SA = semi-automatic.

Table 6.2 Comparison study results; medium capacity refrigerators

Design features and performance specifications	Refrigerator make and model number				
	Soviet KSH160 or Snowcap 160DL	Zanussi Z1162M (Italy)	Gram KF 197 (Denmark)	Miele KA 818/2 (FRG)	Tricity 65.37882 (UK)
Height (cm)	119	85	107	86	114
Width (cm)	56	56	55	60	51
Depth (cm)	60	60	62	50	60
Gross internal volume (litres)	160	160	194	175	180
Net internal volume (litres)	140	140	142	118	140
Low temperature compartment volume (litres)	15	Not given	32	19	14
Defrosting	M	FA	SA (main) M (frozen food compartment)	FA (main) M (frozen food compartment)	FA (main) M (frozen food compartment)
No. of adjustable feet (for levelling purposes)	4	∨	4	Non-adjustable	Non-adjustable

No. of shelves	4	3	4	4
No. of salad crispers, salad or fruit drawers	1	2	Not fitted	1
Drip tray and cleaning facilities	√	Not stated	√	√
Defrosting evaporator tray	Not fitted	Not stated	√	√
Interior light	√	√	√	√
Positions of door hinges	RHS (LHS on request)	Reversible door	RHS or LHS	RHS or LHS	RHS or LHS
Food storage temperature rating	2 star	2 star	3 star	4 star
Running costs (based on 5p/kWhr)	£4.25 per quarter	£4.25 per quarter	£6.35 per quarter	£5.45 per quarter	£6.35 per quarter
Retail price	£70-£85 (1985)	£115 (1985)	£150 (1982)	£270 (1982)	£155 (1982)
Manufacturer's guarantee	1 year	1 year	1 year	1 year	Not stated
Electrical safety, service reliability or repair back-up facilities	3 years	5 year cover scheme	Not stated	Not stated	Not stated but BEAB approval

Notes: (i) √ indicates that the facility is included; (ii) For defrosting, the following symbols have been used: M = manual, FA = fully automatic, SA = semi-automatic.

Table 6.3 Comparison study results; medium to large capacity refrigerators

Design features and performance specifications	Soviet KSH 240 Model 62 GOST 5.1517	Soviet KW 240	Philco RN240 (Italy)	Indesit 011A00 (Italy)	Super-Ser Model GL225 (Spain)	Zanussi ZB2406R Larder-type (Italy)
Height(cm)	141	121	120	128	118	128.5
Width(cm)	59	57	55	55	56	52.5
Depth(cm)	68.5	60	61	61	70	60
Gross internal volume (litres)	240	240	230	249	210	248
Net internal volume (litres)	214		191	192	156	228
Low temperature compartment volume (litres)	26	26	17	19	21	Not applicable
Defrosting	SA	SA	SA	SA (main compartment) M (frozen food compartment)	SA	FA
No. of adjustable feet (for levelling purposes)	4	4	✓	1	✓	✓

No. of shelves	4	4	4	4	3	5
No. of crispers, salad or fruit drawers	2	2	2	1		1
Drip tray and cleaning facilities	✓	✓	✓	Not stated		✓
Defrosting evaporator tray	✓	Not stated	Not stated	Not stated	✓	✓
Interior light	✓	✓	✓	✓	✓	✓
Positions of door hinges	RHS (LHS on request)	RHS (LHS on request)	Either side	Either side	RHS	Reversible door
Food storage temperature rating	2 star	2 star	2 star	2 star	Not stated	Not applicable
Running costs (based on 5p/kWhr)	£9.45 per quarter	£4.50 per quarter	£4.70 per quarter	£5.45 per quarter	£3.90 per quarter	£3.60 per quarter
Retail price	Not presently on sale in UK	Not presently on sale in UK	£159 (1982)	£150 (1982)	£150 (1985)	£200 (1985)
Manufacturer's guarantee	Not stated	1 year	1 year	1 year	1 year	1 year
Electrical safety, service reliability or repair back-up facilities	20 years expected service life	3 years	Not stated but BEAB approved	Not stated but BEAB approved	Not stated	5 year cover scheme available

Notes: (i) ✓ indicates that the facility is included; (ii) For defrosting, the following symbols have been used: M = manual, FA = fully automatic, SA = semi-automatic; (iii) UK importers of these models stated that import of Soviet KW240 refrigerators into Britain had been discontinued.

Table 6.4 Comparison study results, large capacity refrigerators

Design features and performance specifications	Refrigerator make and model number			
	Soviet KSH 280 Snowcap Model 280	Indesit 2204 (Italy)	Fagor FM7405 (Spain)	Husqvarna QR121P (Larder refrigerator) (Sweden)
Height(cm)	144	144	149	155
Width(cm)	57	60	61	60
Depth(cm)	60	63	60	61
Gross internal volume (litres)	280	317	285	343
Net internal volume (litres)		269	217	328
Low temperature compartment volume (litres)	26	23	21	Not applicable
Defrosting	SA	SA	SA(main)M (frozen food compartment)	FA

No. of adjustable feet (for levelling purposes)	4	√	2	√
No. of shelves	5	5	5	6
No. of salad crispers, salad or fruit drawers	2	2	1	2
Drip tray and cleaning facilities	√	√	Not stated	√
Defrosting evaporator tray	√	√	Not stated	√
Interior light	√	√	√	√
Positions of door hinges	RHS (LHS on request)	Either side	RHS	Either side
Food storage temperature rating	2 star	2 star	2 star	Not appicable
Running costs (based on 5p/kWhr)	£6.00 per quarter	£8.40 per quarter	£5.45 per quarter	£4.30 per quarter
Retail price	£110 (1985)	£180 (1985)	£170 (1984)	£299 (1985)
Manufacturer's guarantee	1 year	1 year	1 year	1 year
Electrical safety, service reliability or repair back-up facilities	3 years	5 year guarantee scheme	Not given (BEAB approval)	Not given (BEAB approval)

Notes: (i) √ indicates that the facility is included; (ii) For defrosting, the following symbols have been used: M = manual, FA = fully automatic, SA = semi-automatic.

Table 6.5 General technical conditions for Soviet and British domestic refrigerators

Test and Inspection Procedure	Soviet Requirement	U K Requirement
Classification of frozen food storage compartment (star markings)	* −6°C ** −12°C *** −18°C (To GOST 16317–76, Section 6.1)	* −6°C ** −12°C *** −18°C (To B.S. 3739:1964)
	Similar tests are carried out for the verification of these markings, although the GOST standard is slightly more demanding for the average cabinet temperature during tests at ambient temperature of 32°C (0°C to 5°C) and 43°C (0°C to 7°C). BS 3739:1964 specified a range of 0°C to 8°C for both 32°C and 43°C ambient temperatures.	
Size, weight and composition of test packages	(To GOST 16317–76, p. 12) 250g 500g 1000g Composition per 1000g 230g : oxy-ethyl-methyl cellulose	(To BS 6291:1983, p. 11) 125g 500g 1000g

	764.2g : water 5.0g : sodium chloride 0.8g : parachlorometacresol (To GOST 16317–76, pp. 19, 20)	
Compressor motor locked rotor test	15 day test, polarity reversed every 24 hours, external temperature not to exceed 150°C 30A earthed fuse in parallel (to GOST 16317–76, p. 21)	(To BS 3456: Part 3: Section 3.18:1980: App.D) 10A earthed fuse in parallel (To BS 3456, Part 3, Section 3.18, 1980, p. 10)
Motor starting	Tests carried out between 32°C and 40°C at a voltage between 0.85 and 1.1 times the rated voltage. Refrigerators switched on ten times at each voltage. (to GOST 16317–76, pp. 5, 6)	(To BS 6291:1983, Appendices B, C, & D.)
Doors, shelves and other elements	15–70N force for door opening 100 000 cycles for door opening (To GOST 16317–76, p. 7)	70N for door opening
External condensation	12 hours duration	(To BS 922 & 1691:1959 Clause 40) 12 hours duration

A final aspect of refrigerator design and construction which provides a valuable insight into the state of the art of the respective manufacturing industries is the weight to cubic capacity ratio of individual refrigerators. This parameter acts as a guide to the level of technology involved, particularly the types of materials used, and the overall design configuration.

Unlike their Soviet counterparts, Western manufacturers did not include refrigerator weights in their technical sales literature, and enquiries to the distributors of the Zanussi refrigerators were necessary before the following data on comparative weights could be compiled for Soviet and Western refrigerators of three different sizes. From this data it can be seen that the Soviet refrigerator has a weight/cubic capacity which is some 25 to 35 per cent heavier than its selected Western counterpart.

Table 6.6 Comparative weights of Soviet and Western refrigerators

Refrigerator cubic capacity (litres)	Refrigerator weight (kg)		Refrigerator weight/cubic capacity (kg/litre)	
	'Biryusa'	'Zanussi'	'Biryusa'	'Zanussi'
240	60	46	0.25	0.19
160	55	38	0.34	0.23
150	53	33	0.35	0.22

COMMENTS AND CONCLUSIONS

The objective of this chapter has been to provide an insight into the levels of product quality achieved by the Soviet domestic goods industry, using domestic refrigerators as representative products of that industry. From a comparative assessment, it appears that the Soviet refrigerators selected for comparison were apparently similar in specification, and quality to analogous Western products (see Tables 6.1 to 6.4). In addition, there are also many similarities for the general technical conditions for both sets of refrigerators, showing that during test and inspection procedures, similar technical demands are placed on both Soviet and Western designers and manufacturers of domestic refrigerators. (see Table 6.5).

There are certain factors present, however, which may have given rise to a high quality level for the 'Biryusa' refrigerator, compared with the broad range of appliances produced in the USSR. In the first place, the Soviet appliance chosen for comparison is an export model. The manufacturer of 'Biryusa' refrigerators in Krasnoyarsk also appears to use the best and most up-to-date techniques in production and quality control of the industry concerned; possibly because the factory is responsible to an industrial ministry in the defence sector.[19] The acknowledged privileged position of the defence industries, with regard to resource allocation invariably means that the attainment of high standards of production is a less difficult task than for enterprises making similar products in the civilian sector.

Before closing this chapter, a few more comments will be made about 'Biryusa' refrigerators, particularly those models which are on sale in Britain under the trade name of 'Snowcap'. At a retail distributor, located near to the authors' university, both Soviet and Western models of refrigerator were displayed side-by-side, and a practical method of comparison was possible. After a brief examination it became apparent that the Soviet models were lacking in some finer points of cabinet design (paint finish quality, and tolerances for fitting doors and other fixtures). The higher priced Western models also included a greater number of shelf positions, as well as catering for a wider variety of drinks, dairy products and perishable foodstuffs. An assistant of the distributor in question assured one of the present authors that despite these shortcomings, 'Snowcap' refrigerators still presented a sturdy and reliable unit within the lower price range of the market and, collectively, these characteristics were proving a very effective selling point. On the question of their reputation within the retail market, discussions with a multiple retailer in the Midlands area revealed that for over eleven years 'Snowcap' refrigerators had maintained a reputable market position and created an atmosphere conducive to good customer relations. This position was also due in part to the existence of an efficient and well established after-sales service within the English Midlands area. These claims, however, can only be validated by extensive consumer research amongst refrigerator owners themselves, which was considered to be beyond the terms of reference of this current research.

As a further point for discussion, it is evident that the Soviet range of refrigerators were far heavier than their selected Western counterparts for defined values of storage capacity, although the sample chosen for comparison was extremely small. Nevertheless, this result would appear to conform with the frequently cited view that Soviet-produced articles are bulky and heavy, particularly those manufactured for consumer use.

This chapter can be concluded, therefore, with the comment that the methodology used here to assess the quality characteristics of Soviet domestic refrigerators can also be used for further research on other types of Soviet domestic appliances. These could include vacuum cleaners, electric irons, electric shavers and fans, since Soviet state standards have been published for many of these products, and their distribution is now being commenced in Western markets.[20]

7 Cameras

INTRODUCTION

A camera is a light-tight box incorporating three basic components to achieve good photography, namely: a reliable lens, an adjustable aperture and a fast moving shutter. All the components work together and permit the use of the camera in the varying circumstances of lighting and speed in which a picture may be taken. Cameras also require a viewing system, or viewfinder, through which a picture can be composed, and cameras are most clearly distinguishable by the type of viewfinding arrangements as follows:

a) 'direct vision viewfinder' which use a viewing window (e.g. the Soviet 'Cosmic Symbol').
b) 'single lens reflex' (SLR) where the subject is viewed through the 'taking' lens (e.g. the Soviet 'Zenith "E"' range).
c) 'twin lens reflex' (TLR) which have a separate viewing lens (e.g. the Soviet 'Lubitel 166B' model).
d) Medium Format SLR (e.g. the Soviet 'Zenith 80').

Russian photography is reported to date back to the 1830s,[1] although camera production in pre-Revolutionary years was small.[2] Measures were taken from 1919 onwards to promote photographic development on a national scale,[3] although it was not until around 1930 that a semblance of a Soviet national photographic industry began to take shape. There was a steady increase in camera production from that date except for a break due to the Second World War, but increases in camera production became more marked after 1965 when the civilian production of cameras became the responsibility of certain industrial ministries within the Soviet defence sector.[4]

A similar pattern of development was apparent for the production of photographic film, but by the mid-1960s, film production in the Soviet Union had reached levels which placed the USSR second only to the United States. In a closely related area of the industry, involving the production of sensitised materials, significant progress was also made before and immediately following the Second World War.

This chapter assesses the quality levels of cameras manufactured by the Soviet photographic equipment industry. The methodology adopted is, in many respects, similar to that of earlier chapters in which the various strengths and weaknesses in the design, construction and performance of selected components and assemblies have been highlighted. The assessment has been carried out using Soviet and British national standards, and also using published reports by experts working for photographic journals. The results of this assessment are presented in the next section of this chapter.

TECHNICAL APPRAISAL OF SOVIET CAMERAS

Comparative State Standards

Previous chapters of this book have included comparisons between Soviet and British approved technical standards for the components, assemblies and finished products under investigation. Because of the very small number of remaining British Standards on photographic equipment, however, it has been necessary in this present chapter to include standards from the closely related science of optics. These standards, although primarily concerned with the technical requirements of spectacles and magnifiers, also provide information about aspects of photography crucial to the performance and design of cameras, namely: effective lens power, focal length, and field of view. In addition, several of the photographic standards referred to have recently been withdrawn from the officially-approved list of standards. It was considered to be useful to use this information, however, to provide a broader scope for the investigation.

From the similarities in the technical requirements themselves, shown in Table 7.1, it can be seen that, except for one or two slight differences in tolerance levels (see requirement 6(a), Table 7.1), both Soviet and Western-made camera, projector and film equipment are manufactured to similar physical dimensions, as stated in requirements 1 to 6 listed in Table 7.1. The same can be said of the minimum bearing surfaces provided for the push-on lens attachments of both Soviet and Western cameras (see requirement 9). Only a small difference in pull-out force is required for the only mechanical test (requirement 1 (c)) to be performed on both sets of 135 mm size film cartridge: and the photographic flash equipment, used in conjunction with both sets of cameras, is expected to have similar electrical insulation qualities (specified in requirement 3(b)).

For camera shutters, the allowable deviations from the stipulated exposure time (requirement 7a) shows the Soviet standard to be more stringent on the longer exposure times (above 1/250 second), whereas BS 1592:1958 requires less variation from the expected norm for some exposure times of 1/250 and shorter. The efficiency values (requirement 7(b)) reveal a similar pattern to this, with stricter Soviet requirements for the longer exposure time, although this time the dividing line is drawn at 1/500 second.

Not surprisingly, the temperature range within which Soviet camera shutters are required to maintain their rated values begins at a much lower point (minus 15° C) than the Western equivalent. This applies to both the operating temperature and relative humidity acceptance checks. (requirements 7c(i) and 7c (ii) respectively).

The general technical specifications laid down for photoelectric exposure meters (requirements 8(a) and (b)) show that, according to BS 1383, calibration calculations and temperature error corrections are to be made within slightly narrower limits than those expected in GOST 9851–79. This holds true even for the more accurate Soviet Class A meters which are manufactured to Soviet export requirements.

The final set of srtandards investigated in this current research relate to optical equipment of two types, namely:

supplementary (or close-up) lenses for use in spectacles;
and low-power magnifiers rated up to a linear magnification value of 16.

In the case of supplementary lenses, both sets of 'Back Vertex Power' and 'Cylindrical Axis' are accompanied by insignificant differences in the tolerance deviations permitted at each of their values, although there is some mismatch in the range values selected for each level of 'lens' and 'cylinder' power which has caused consistency problems for making comparisons. A similar problem occurred in the case of requirement 11 (a) which also made an accurate assessment of the 'focal length' and 'field of view' qualities of magnifiers more difficult; although the tolerance levels for deviation from these parameters were smaller for the Soviet model than for 'Class C Low-Power Magnifiers' of Western manufacture.

In the case of linear magnification, however identical values are used to categorise the three groups of Soviet 'pocket folding' and 'measuring' magnifiers as well as the 'low-power' types 'A', 'B', and 'C' Western magnifiers. The 'working distance' (or focal length) qualities in two of these groups were expected to be of similar value but in the third group, the type 'C' low-power magnifier of Western make would be accepted with a slightly inferior 'focal length' than its Soviet counterpart.

The 'field of view' qualities demanded of all three categories of magnifier varied but this was not unexpected, depending a great deal on the purpose for which the magnifier is designed, (i.e.: whether a concentrated 'field of vision' is required or not). Once again, the allowable limits within which Soviet magnifiers could deviate from the stated norms of 'focal length' and 'field of view' were slightly more stringent.

In conclusion, therefore, it is apparent that of the twenty three groups of comparative tests considered for cameras and related photographic and optical equipment, as listed in Table 7.1, approximately 50 per cent of the tests and specifications are equivalent, whilst the remaining 50 per cent are divided almost equally between more demanding requirements for Soviet and British Standards respectively.

Soviet Cameras in the UK Market – Expert Assessments

A June 1982 publication of a Soviet monthly information bulletin on consumer goods[5] contained a list of all the photographic cameras produced in the Soviet Union at that time. Thirty-one models of camera were listed, and details were given on the main constructional and operational features of their design. The cameras were categorised into four groups, according to their types of control. Of these four groups, three were, 'Scale',[6] 'Rangefinder'; and 'Reflex'. For each individual model, reference was also made to the accessories and attachments which could be used in conjunction with the basic design.[7] This section concentrates on the technical parameters of a small selection of these cameras which have been sold in Britain since the 1960s outlining the observations and criticisms made about these cameras when they were introduced into this country. In addition, attention will be drawn to various attributes of their design, performance and construction.

In this respect, the most useful sources of information have been the comparative studies and technical appraisals published in photographic periodicals and magazines such as *The Amateur Photographer*, *Which* and the *British Journal of Photography*. Useful contributions to the study were also found in a 1980 'Equipment Survey', carried out with the help of the membership of the Royal

Table 7.1 Comparison of Soviet and British standards requirements for photographic equipment

Requirement	Soviet State (GOST) standard and specifications	British Standard (BS) and specifications	Soviet standard more demanding	Equivalent requirements	British standard more demanding
1. Specifications for 135mm film cartridge for 35mm camera	GOST 3453–80	BS 1879–81			
(a) dimensions and tolerances of cartridge construction and design				√	
(b) dimensions and weight of gauge block used in the measurement of pull-out force				√	
(c) maximum pull out force for the first 100mm of film				(2.45N (GOST) 2.5N (BS)) √	
2. Specifications for camera tripod connections (dimensional)	GOST 3362-75	BS 5855-80		√	
3. Photographic Flash Equipment (a) dimensions for plugs and sockets	GOST 10312-74	BS 5841 Pt.3		√	
(b) minimum allowable value of insulation resistance (10ohms)				√	
4. Image area and picture frame sizes for cameras using 35mm film	GOST 18053-73	BS 1487 Pt.2		√	
5. Specifications for dimensions (120 photographic film spool)	GOST 3458-79	BS 1491-80		√	

Table 7.1 continued on p. 116

Table 7.1 continued

Requirement	Soviet State (GOST) standard and specifications	British Standard (BS) and specifcations	Soviet standard more demanding	Equivalent requirements	British standard more demanding
6. Specifications of cameras for 8mm Film					
(a) location and dimensions of formed and projected image (type S film)	GOST 1693-71	BS 5550 Sect. 1-2			∨
(b) rate of projection and position of film claw				∨	
7. Still camera shutters, general technical requirements	GOST 19821-83	BS1592-58			
(a) effective exposure time:					
above 1/250th second	(±0.15 & ±0.25)	(±0.25)	∨		
below 1/250th second	(±0.35 & ±0.25)	(±0.33)			
(b) efficiency					
above 1/500 second	(65%)	(60%)	∨		
below 1/500 second	(55%)	(60%)			∨
(c) temperature & humidity					
(i) operating temperature limits	(-15°C to +45°C)	(0°C to 40°C) 12 hrs. at each temperature	∨		
(ii) relative humidity limits	-15°C to 0°C @ 50±5% humidity, 0°C	20°C @ 85% humidity 12 hours at this			

		to 46°C @ 80±5% humidity	humidity	
8. Photoelectric exposure meters calibration deviation (single scale)		GOST 9851-79	BS 1383-66	✓
		±0.5 Steps (Class A) (±0.7 Steps (Class B)	±0.333 steps	✓
(multi scale)		(±0.25 Steps (Class A) ±0.35 Steps (Class B)	±0.167 steps	✓
9. Dimensions for camera lenses and lens attachments		GOST 3933-75	BS 1618-61	✓
10. Spectacle lenses		GOST 23265-78	BS 2738-62	✓
(a) back vertex power		±0.06 to 0.25 (Class A) ±0.06 to 0.35 (Class B)	±0.06 to 0.50	
		range: less than 0.5	range: up to 4 dioptres to	

continued on p. 118

Table 7.1 continued

Requirement	Soviet State (GOST) standard and specifications	British Standard (BS) and specifications	Soviet standard more demanding	Equivalent requirements	British standard more demanding
(b) cylindrical axis	dioptres to above 15 dioptres ±5% to ±2% range: less than 0.5 dioptres to above 3 dioptres GOST 18504-73	above 20 dioptres ±5% to ±1.25% range: up to 0.25 dioptres to above 1.25 dioptres BS165-74		√	
11. magnifiers					
(a) for viewing 35mm film (Soviet specification) or low-power magnifier for visual inspection (British specification)	±5% tolerance on focal length	10% max. tolerance on focal length	√		
(b) pocket folding magnifiers (Soviet specification) or low power magnifier for visual inspection (British specification)	GOST 7594-75 & GOST 8309-75 ±5% tolerance on focal length	BS 5165-74 10% max tolerance on focal length	√		

Photographic Society of Great Britain. The product ranges and individual models which have been considered are the Zenith, Kiev, Lubitel, Cosmic Symbol and Zorki.

Zenith-80

Prior to its introduction in the late 1960s, the model 80 had already been the target of rumour and speculation. Apparently, it was not a completely new Soviet camera as very similar looking models had previously been seen in Moscow.[8] In addition, its overall design was virtually the same as the more expensive Hasselblad 1000F and 1600F models, both of which had previously been removed from production.[9] A true roll-film SLR camera, the Model 80 had a large 6 × 6 cm format and an 80 mm standard focal length lens. Priced at over £150, it was considered an attractive proposition for the British buyer. It is possible that the Model 80 constituted a serious Soviet attempt to break into the more lucrative market of professional photography since one photo-critic stated in 1969, 'The Zenith 80 looks every inch a professional camera. Mainly finished in polished stainless steel with hard-wearing black panelling, the appearance is most impressive . . . the distributors have an excellent testing set-up: all cameras are thoroughly checked before being sent out and if anything does eventually go wrong there are no difficulties in obtaining spare parts or making repairs. They recognise that the purchaser of such a camera may well depend on it financially and it is reassuring to know this view is held'.[10]

In another review,[11] published two months later, one leading critic commented, 'One of the nice things about Soviet cameras is, like Soviet cars, they come supplied as a ready-to-use outfit. The Zenith 80 is no exception.'

The Zenith models are arguably the best known and most popular cameras imported into Britain from the USSR and there is no doubting that above everything else, price is the main attraction to buyers in Britain. In articles and reviews, published during the course of the last 18 years, the sentiments expressed about their price provide ample evidence to this effect.[12]

Another common attraction of Zenith cameras is that they help to form the basis of a good camera budget system and thus 'offer the beginner to photography an inexpensive way in'.[13] The Royal Photographic Society's survey of minor brands of camera[14] also revealed that, in a very high proportion (92 per cent) of cases, a Zenith was the first SLR camera to be owned by its purchasers. Wilmott similarly points this out in his review[15] of the 11 and 12XP models of Zenith, as follows

> these Russian cameras have introduced thousands of newcomers to SLR photography...because you have to do everything manually yourself before taking a picture, the camera offers a lesson in using aperture, shutter speed and such like.

In the above quotation, Wilmott is also pointing to a third feature of Soviet cameras, namely that they provide the starter with a good teacher. This feature is similarly attributed to two other Zenith models in test reports performed by the same periodical, namely the Zenith Model 19 ('it should gain a comfortable niche among first-time SLR buyers seeking a budget camera without too many frills and complicated extras'[16] and 'but at the price it can still be recommended. For the beginner it could be a good bet. You have to do everything yourself, so you'll learn all about apertures, shutter speeds and exposures in the process'.[17]

Three other positive attributes, regarding the make-up of Zeniths, can be grouped under the general heading of 'overall performance'. These are good picture definition, quality of lens and reliability of operation. As previously, the statements made in equipment surveys and test reports testify to the creditable standard attained by the range of Zenith models.[18]

A 'Servicing and Reliability' test, based on the records of nearly 25 000 cameras and projectors from four different countries, was published in the May 1981 edition of *Which*. In a sample of 142 Zenith 35 mm SLR cameras, bought during the previous five years, the test revealed that nearly three quarters of them required no repair or servicing during their working life. A similar proportion (75 per cent) of Zenith owners in the 1980 'Equipment Survey' of the Royal Photographic Society[19] stated they were satisfied with distributor repair services for their cameras, hence endorsing the earlier observation made by Maud regarding the Zenith 80 back-up service.[20]

Turning now to take a look at negative attributes associated with the design, construction and performance of Zeniths we find that a repeated criticism levelled at them is their outmoded design and appearance, sometimes expressed as a time lag behind Western or Japanese counterparts. The type of criticism varies from the relatively mild 'just a little tank-like. Everything about it appears basic and functional rather than "designed" and "streamlined"',[21] to the much more pointed 'by Western or Japanese standards the Russian cameras are primitive (about 20 years out-of-date) badly designed and poorly manufactured and finished'.[22] A similar time lag was said of the Zenith models 11 and 12XP designs when 'compared with Japanese and German cameras',[23] the ET and TTL models fared only slightly better, lagging behind Western equivalents by an estimated fifteen years.[24]

The cumbersome nature of Zenith camera construction and the awkwardness of some of their controls are other common faults. The range of Zenith models have been described as big, heavy, tank-like, and rugged. Their controls have been referred to as fiddly, misleading, and sluggish. In one particular model the major drawback was the number of operations required prior to shutter release.[25]

Zenith shutters and film winding mechanism also present problems for the user.[26] Proneness to flare when shooting into light appears to be another deficiency of Zeniths[27] and, as far as the Model 19 is concerned, the film speed range is somewhat limited.[28]

If a similar exercise is performed with other lesser known makes of Soviet camera, it soon becomes apparent that they too are accredited with similar features of design and performance as the Zeniths, namely; advantages of price, an ideal beginner's camera, excellent lens and picture definition; and disadvantages of weight, bulkiness, and outdated design. The camera ranges referred to are the Lubitel, Cosmic, Kiev and Zorki, as outlined below.

The Lubitel
This camera will be discussed first, as it is the only roll-film camera of the group – the Lubitel 166B – which was once referred to as 'probably the strangest camera on the medium format market'.[29] It follows the twin-lens reflex principle, which means that both viewing and taking lenses are coupled. Hence its focusing, although very accurate, does tend to be a prolonged operation. Better quality pictures are possible than from most 35 mm cameras, however, because its negatives (or slides) are that much bigger, and so 'the lesser magnification required to print the 6 × 6 cm negative doesn't show up imperfections like whiskers and drying marks nearly so blatantly as 35 mm negatives'.[30]

Based on a camera of pre-war design,[31] the Lubitel has earned, according to its distributors, a reputation with some people as a camera 'of astonishing quality and performance for its price',[32] although there is a drawback of comparatively slow shutter speed.[33]

Furthermore, the construction and design has been reviewed as 'primitive', although the lens is considered as 'not too bad', and results 'not all that much inferior to Japanese TLR cameras at many times the price'.[34]

It is interesting to note that the basic design of the Lubitel TLR lends itself to improvisational design changes. This is exemplified by the ways in which both Soviet and British camera enthusiasts incorporated their ideas and modifications to the basic body of the camera.[35]

The Cosmic Symbol and Cosmic 35
The Cosmic range of cameras are all produced at the well-known Leningrad Optical-Mechanical Association (LOMO), as is the 'Lubitel' described above. The comments published on 'Cosmic Symbol' have been mixed, but generally favourable with regard to lens and shutter quality and consistency, but critical over the convenience in use of these cameras.[36]

Another model in the LOMO 'Cosmic' range is the Cosmic 35, which has received particularly good reports for its ability to photograph outdoor scenes, although it has also been criticised for its inconvenience in use.[37]

The model 35 was subsequently updated to the model 35M. In July 1973, Ronald Spillman, of *Amateur Photographer* published a test report on the new model, and some of his observations provide a useful assessment:

> Now the Russians have updated the Cosmic 35, their low-priced but efficient 35 mm camera for novices . . . all changes are for the good. There are no frills on the Cosmic 35M . . . the lens is of excellent quality . . . the shutter is a Russian compound type, placed behind the lens and, checked out on our chronometer was suprisingly accurate – within ± 15 per cent at all speeds [see technical requirement no 7 in Table 7.1]. It's an admirable instrument for the novice.

Just over a year later, however, in December 1974, *Which* published another article on 'Cheap Cameras', in which the 35M came in for some harsh criticism, as illustrated by the following statement:

> the Cosmic 35M was much more fiddly to use . . . settings not clear, no automatic block to prevent you taking double exposures . . . some shutter problems.

The Kiev Range

An assessment of the Kiev 4 range of Single Lens Reflex cameras (including the Kiev 4A which has a built-in exposure meter), was reported by the *British Journal of Photography* in April 1974. This assessment first of all pointed to the camera's apparent similarity to the Zeiss 'Contax', but then followed by a criticism that the lens mountings are not compatible. The shutter was found to be fairly consistent, although not always totally accurate. Furthermore, rangefinding was found to be accurate, although the lens was not considered to be up to professional quality.[38]

A further assessment of the Kiev range of cameras was carried out by *Which* in 1979 as part of a test on 31 non-reflex cameras. As was the case with Cosmic 35M previously, the Kiev models were severely criticised, as follows: 'Kiev cameras were found particularly awkward to use . . . and though the cheapest cameras tested . . . would be among the least suitable for a beginner . . . not very good performance and very difficult to use. Very large and very heavy'.[39]

In the light of such criticism it is not surprising to discover that both models of Kiev cameras were removed from the British market in 1981 'because of poor sales'.[40]

Zorki

The final camera models on which material has been gathered are the Zorki 4 and 4K, using reports given in the *Amateur Photographer*. Although these reports were published several years ago, they point to several similarities with the other ranges of Soviet cameras, such as economic price, heavy construction, and a good lens. In conclusion, the assessors considered the Zorki 4 and Zorki 4K to be good beginners' cameras.[41]

CONCLUSIONS

The salient features of Soviet camera design and performance are well covered in the second part of the previous section of this chapter. These can be summarised as: low price, ideal beginner's camera, good lens, and picture definition on the positive side; and weighty, bulky construction, awkward controls, and outmoded design on the negative side. From the comparative study of Soviet and British national standards, it is apparent that there are similarities and close approximations in the eleven technical requirements selected for comparison. Nevertheless, it is important to highlight two major sets of factors which may influence this comparison.

The first of these sets of factors concerns the shutter speed test results, which are mentioned in several of the camera reviews and surveys mentioned throughout this chapter, with varying viewpoints expressed. It should be kept in mind, however, that some of the Soviet cameras chosen for the reviews had already been in service for an appreciable period of time, which meant that the amount of deterioration of shutter accuracy would not be known. Secondly, in the vast majority of the reviews carried out on Soviet cameras, the test sample involved was very small; it is not surprising, therefore, that no consistent pattern of shutter accuracy emerged from the published results. It could possibly be concluded that the shutter accuracy of the smaller models of camera (the Zorki, Kiev and Cosmic) came within the deviation limits allowed more often than did the accuracy of most Zenith models, particularly at higher shutter speeds; although such a conclusion would need to be tempered with caution because of the small sample from which the information was taken.

The second set of factors relate to the involvement of photographic industries in overseas markets leading to the general standardisation of photographic equipment on an international scale. As has already been mentioned many British Standards have been withdrawn and conformance is now made to ISO recommendations. Further research should consequently attempt to comapare the ISO recommendations with Soviet practice, and an extension of the terms of reference of the research to include other types of optical equipment (e.g. binoculars, microscopes and telescopes, etc.) would also add to a better understanding of the production quality levels in the industries concerned.

For the present, it is considered that the use made of the published camera reviews and surveys in the second part of the previous section constituted an adequate substitute for the reduced number of British Standards which could be used. The result has been an insight into the level of technical proficiency which is incorporated into the design and construction of Soviet cameras; and the quality of their manufacture.

As a final point in this concluding section, it is important to note that none of the Soviet cameras covered in this survey could be considered to be at the leading edge of camera design and technology, compared with many models produced in Europe, USA and Japan. Many of the contemporary features of cameras produced in the Western industrially developed economies, however, are related to the application of electronic devices to provide faster operation and tighter control; and these features are almost completely absent from the Soviet-made models, as they are from many other products of Soviet manufacture. The comparative study can conclude, therefore, that Soviet-made cameras can compare satisfactorily in most aspects of mechanical and optical construction and robustness with their Western counterparts, although there may be room for improvement in reliability and lightness of construction. If 'automaticity' in control and operation is considered a virtue, as appears to be the case with most Western cameras, it is apparent that Soviet camera design and construction is clearly seen to lag behind the Western market leaders. If simplicity and operator discretion in setting and control is considered a virtue, however, the Soviet camera industry can be considered to be manufacturing products of adequate quality.

8 Comments, Conclusions and Further Research

GENERAL COMMENTS AND CONCLUSIONS

The research described in this book was initially commenced as a consequence of the various published Western perceptions that Soviet product quality was generally lower than that encountered in the West (see Chapter 1), although much of the evidence advanced for such perceptions was itself largely based on secondary information in published reports rather than primary data on product specification and performance. The causes of these perceived views of the 'quality gap' existing between Soviet and Western products has been ascribed to a number of factors operating in the Soviet economy such as the strong seller's market created by tight central planning, skill shortages, and management styles caused by the output-related incentive scheme originally introduced for rapid economic growth in the 1930s. This mix of economic, technical, social and political factors which have historically influenced Soviet industry are supposed to have exerted a generally negative effect on product quality when compared with Western systemic factors, in the civilian sector at least. The aims of this research, therefore, have been threefold, namely to seek to identify whether a Soviet product 'quality gap' exists, and if so, how it can be measured; and thirdly to survey the major programmes and procedures used in the USSR for quality stabilisation and improvement to determine those systemic factors which may be strengthening product quality in the USSR.

In order to meet these aims of the research it was decided to use Soviet state standards as a data base in view of the scope of these documents; the possibility of access to this data base in the UK through the library of the British Standards Institution; the legal status of these documents in the USSR; and the possibility of comparing the requirements of these documents with those of their British counterparts, as typical examples of standards published by an advanced industrialised Western country. Because of the large number of these documents, however, and the wide range of the products to which they relate, it was necessary to select a product sample considered to be generally representative for Soviet industry.

For the first part of this research, it was decided to select a sample of two industrial products for study, namely general purpose machine tools as typical mechanical engineering products on which some work had previously been carried out by one of the present authors; and asynchronous electrical motors as typical electrical engineering products. From a comparative study of the state standards for these two groups of products it became apparent that the tests and tolerances specified in these documents for machine tools and asynchronous squirrel cage electric motors were generally equivalent to those specified in their British counterparts. In view of these results, therefore, it was seen to be appropriate to reconsider some of the generally held Western views of Soviet product quality, since some of the criticism of Soviet industrial quality may have been overstated. It could be justifiably argued, on the other hand, that the selection of machine tools and squirrel cage motors were small, and perhaps biased samples, since machine tool manufacture and electrical engineering have been priority civilian industries in the USSR since the early 1930s. To counteract such a criticism, therefore, the research methodology was extended to cover the comparative study of other product groups in the industrial and consumer sectors, namely automobiles and their components, refrigerators and photographic equipment. The results from the comparative study of a sample of Soviet state standards for this mix of products was similar to that obtained for the previously-studied industrial products, namely that the tests and tolerances specified in these documents were generally neither better nor worse than those specified by their British counterparts.

In view of these results, therefore, it appears that the claim by the Head of the Administration for State Supervision (B. Ya. Belobragin) of the State Committee of Standards that 'sixty to seventy standards out of every hundred contain requirements of international organisations for standardisation'[1] has some justification. What is important in this context, however, is the proportion of standardised tests and tolerances which meet those of the International Standards Organisation (ISO), rather than those of the Council for Mutual Economic Assistance alone, and further research is necessary to establish this proportion. Furthermore, whilst discussing this topic of comparability it is important to note that the technical requirements of these documents should be thoroughly checked by Western companies when they form part of a contract between themselves and a Soviet foreign trade organisation. If this is not done, undetected differences in tests and tolerances which become apparent later at product inspection, testing, or performance stages may lead to protracted delays in the fulfilment of contractual conditions.[2]

It is apparent from the results discussed in the third paragraph of this chapter that the development and implementation of a standardisation policy in the USSR have served to counteract some of the factors which are claimed to have led to poor product quality during the rapid Soviet industrialisation drive. It is also apparent that for many years, the leading Soviet industrial policy makers have attempted to use standardisation procedures in the context of an industrialising and expanding planned economy, to contribute towards the stabilisation and improvement of Soviet product quality; and that these procedures have been made more rigorous since 1965. Furthermore, it also seems that the methodology of standardisation has lent itself well to 'plan fulfilment' conditions prevailing in a planned economy, since standardisation quantifies a product's major parameters and tolerances as a basis for assessment. In other words a 'pass/fail' decision on product quality, with its associated consequences for plan fulfilment and factory receipts, can be based on objective tests and quantifiable data for defined parameters. Such an approach is likely to have had an intrinsic attraction to policy-makers, planners and administrators in the Soviet economy where factory success is usually judged according to a range of quantifiable indicators.

It is clear, however, that the degree to which the Soviet state standardisation system acts as a means of quality control, is dependent upon the extent to which products actually embody all of the requirements of the relevant standards. Furthermore, the methodology of using state standards as a data base for the assessment of Soviet industrial quality also depends upon product conformity to the demands of these documents.

The legal status of state standards in the Soviet economy has been an important factor favouring the observation of these documents, together with the existence of a network of local inspection organisations throughout the USSR having the right to verify factories' conformance to standards (see Chapter 1). These favourable factors may be negated, however, by those systemic factors also discussed in Chapter 1 which have been operating in the Soviet economy for many years, and acting as a hindrance to product quality and innovation.

These negative factors, in their turn, have led to the careful and 'creative' presentation of production information by enterprise personnel, in order that favourable bonus payments be received.[3] Since the fulfilment of product quality requirements has become an increasingly important factor in enterprise success, there remains the strong possibility that 'creative' presentation of data has also been extended to quality control activities.[4] This viewpoint is strongly supported by the recently quoted statement by Belobragin that 'if our inspector visits a factory, then in fifty to seventy cases out of a hundred he will detect breaches of these [standards] requirements'.[5]

In spite of the strong possibility of some manipulation of inspection data at Soviet enterprises, the present authors are inclined to the view that state standards still represent an important data source for the assessment of Soviet product quality in a rapid and cost effective manner. Furthermore, these documents represent a minimum legal requirement for a wide range of products; and penalties for significant breaches of these requirements are probably large enough to act as a deterrent to blatant and widespread falsification of important quality control results. This topic is clearly worthy of further research, since it is difficult to estimate from Belobragin's statement whether the breaches to which he refers were serious, and whether 'cases' related to factories, individual standards or tests.

In addition it is important to note that Soviet enterprise management is not alone in its practice of 'creative' reporting; the business pressures which exist in Western manufacturing and commercial environments have been known to cause similar practices in Western companies also.[6] It is the experience of one of the present authors that these practices are less likely to happen over inspection reports than financial and delivery information in Western companies and vendor assessment programmes have probably reduced this practice even further. Since these latter pressures are absent in the Soviet economy, however, the state supervision function has taken on added importance; and on two visits to Soviet factories and standards organisations in 1969 and 1985, one of the present authors gained the impression that although the state supervision system was not entirely foolproof, it was being steadily improved. As a final point on this topic, a sample of British businessmen interviewed in the late 1970s found the accuracy of Soviet general purpose machine tools to be acceptable, as defined by the relevant state standards and delivered to their factories.[7] It is also the experience of one of the present authors that Soviet inspectors and engineers engaged in acceptance and installation of machine tools are inclined to meticulously observe the relevant requirements of Soviet state standards.

The methodology of using standards alone may also be criticised for concentrating almost exclusively on a product's major parameters, whereas the total performance of a product in service may also be influenced by other, more minor, parameters. Many of these latter parameters are frequently difficult to standardise, and some are often discretionary; but the aggregate effect of these minor parameters can have a significant effect on product performance. These criticisms of 'type standardisation' methodology, in which only the 'major parameters' of a defined 'product type', 'group' or 'range' are considered, must also reflect on the limitations of using such an approach to regulate product quality in the Soviet centrally planned economy, particularly as increasing technological sophistication is viewed as a national-economic objective. In spite of these criticisms, however, it still remains the view of the present authors that 'type standardisation' has proved generally to be a convenient, economic and effective procedure for regulating product quality in the USSR, particularly in terms of setting 'minimum' or 'threshold' values for a limited range of important parameters. Furthermore, the methodology of comparing the requirements of state standards for defined product groups has proved to be economic and effective for assessing the 'minimum' or 'threshold' values for major parameters, for these same defined product groups manufactured in the USSR.

It is apparent, however, that even though 'type standardisation' is a convenient procedure for product quality regulation and assessment, it can still only give a partial account of a product's total quality and performance. Since the late 1960s, therefore, Soviet policy-makers have supplemented 'type standardisation' procedures with 'quality attestation', which is aimed at quality improvement of individual product models manufactured in series (or batch) production at particular factories. These product models, submitted for approval by their manufacturers, are assessed on a far broader basis than 'major parameter fulfilment' alone, with account being taken of the product's design configuration, the materials and methods used in its manufacture, and anticipated performance in service.

According to the results presented in Chapters 3 and 4 of this present book, these 'quality attestation' policies and procedures appear to have been successful in the machine tool and electrical motor industrial sectors at least, and at least moderately successful for motor vehicles and domestic refrigerators. Further research should test whether the same is true for a broader range of product groups, and should also attempt to monitor the recently introduced system of quality attestation,[8] and a new procedure in which it is intended to monitor more closely the stages of new product design and manufacture with approval being necessary at each stage prior to full-scale production.[9] An added reason for further study of the implementation of these new quality assurance procedures is their anticipated impact on the retained profits of industrial enterprises under the modified system of industrial incentives announced during the early part of 1985.[10] Finally, it is necessary to investigate further whether the apparent momentum of 'quality attestation' in the early 1970s has been maintained into the 1980s.

It is also interesting to speculate whether type standardisation and quality attestation may also be supplemented by 'certification', a policy followed in some Western countries where individual factories are certified as capable of achieving specific quality levels for defined product types.[11] This would represent a move from 'product-based' approval to 'enterprise-based' approval, across a broader range of products than those considered in individual 'Mark of Quality' standards; but it may be an appropriate procedure for the Soviet economy as its growth towards technical sophistication continues.

In addition to published standards as data sources, this present research programme has also used the 'expert assessment' of Soviet-produced articles carried out by consumers', professional, and 'informed amateurs' associations and published in their respective magazines, journals or newspapers. Clearly the use of such reports carries the risk of being unduly influenced by the prejudices or whims of the expert assessor, but these risks are outweighed by the advantages associated with the technical and professional competence of these reporters. Furthermore, the conclusions from the assessment are reported in great detail for a technically appreciative audience, and any inordinate prejudice is usually readily seen. This latter point of wealth of technical detail is also important when comparing the information contained in such assessments with that contained in the reports of Western economic and political specialists of the Soviet economy as summarised in Chapter 1, where specific technical information is virtually absent.

The majority of such assessments are limited to consumer products, and they are chiefly concerned with such factors as operational efficiency, style, convenience of use, reliability, and the capability to meet the contemporary demands of the Western consumer market.

Most of the expert assessors were of the view that the Soviet products were generally satisfactory in terms of mechanical construction and operation, and were also robust, simple in construction, and convenient to service and repair. There was no overt criticism of those parameters which were defined by state standards, which would therefore appear to support some of the conclusions stated in the earlier paragraphs of this present chapter. As also outlined in earlier paragraphs, however, the parameters defined by these standards may be quite small in number and narrow in range, and have probably been considered as taken for granted. Furthermore, there may be some standards which may affect a component's service of which the assessor of the end-product is totally unaware: the surface finish of a gudgeon pin (see Chapter 5) in an automobile engine is probably a good example.

Although Soviet products were considered to be adequate in terms of mechanical construction and praiseworthy in terms of robustness, there was also a general view that these were achieved at the expense of lightness in construction. Furthermore, although the simplicity of the product's design led to ease in service and maintainability, there were frequent criticisms that the lack of sophistication in design led to inconvenient operation. This was particularly the case for those product groups where the increased application of electronic components to provide faster setting and more accurate control has become generally accepted by Western manufacturers. Criticisms were sometimes made about the product's reliability, although this could be balanced by ease of service; and also about the general out-of-date design of many products. In summary, most of the Western assessors viewed Soviet consumer products as mechanically adequate, simple in construction and to service, and robust; but heavy, sometimes unreliable and inconvenient to use, lacking contemporary control devices, and generally dated and unsophisticated in design and appearance. At the prices for which these products were sold on Western markets, however, the balance of their advantages and disadvantages led to the conclusion that they were usually value for money.

It is apparent, therefore, that the British expert assessors were looking at far more criteria than conformance to type standards (which were usually taken for granted) and far more 'marketing' than 'construction' factors, far more 'subjective' than 'objective' factors, and far more 'non-quantifiable' than 'quantifiable' factors. As a result of these perspectives, the expert assessors appear to confirm several of the quality criticisms ascribed to Soviet products by the Western specialists referred to in Chapter 1.

It is important to note, however, that the technical specifications and product performance for these items need to be seen in the context of market conditions within the Soviet economy itself, particularly for consumer products. In the first place, the average consumer spending power per head is far lower in the USSR than in most industrially developed Western nations; and probably less easily segmented. This has led to Soviet industry manufacturing relatively narrow ranges of comparatively unsophisticated, but robust, consumer products, which are capable of providing a broad range of the population with the basic features required in an economy where services are poorly developed and the physical environment is harsh for much of the year. This product design philosophy is also reinforced by a small concern for internationally competitive overseas markets since the bulk of production is sold domestically, or to export markets in other socialist countries; and by the lack of a developed consumer-oriented electronics sector. It is arguable, therefore, that Soviet-designed products meet the total range of requirements of these market conditions better than would their Western counterparts, which are highly dependent upon a developed consumer product oriented electronics sector, and an advanced service sector for after-sales and maintenance activities. As a final point, when considering the appropriateness of Soviet products for Western markets, it is apparent that these products appear to meet a particular niche in the market where low price, simplicity, serviceability, and robustness are valued more highly than sophistication, lightness and elegance. In other words, the overall balance of quality characteristics are adequate for products at the mature stage of the product life cycle, where a combination of certain minimum technical standards combined with a highly competitive price are probably more important than advanced technological sophistication.

This is not to dismiss the fact, however, that there is substantial room for improvements in quality and technical sophistication for Soviet products, both to meet the contemporary demands of the Soviet economy itself, and also to increase market shares abroad. It is suggested, however, that many modifications will consist of 'non-quantifiable' design changes, and the increased use of control components. It is recommended, therefore, that these modifications be closely monitored. In the industrial field, particular attention should be paid to the areas of manufacturing equipment, particularly 'advanced manufacturing technology' machinery such as CNC machine tools and industrial robots. Although such modifications may be viewed as falling within the category of 'product innovation' rather than 'quality improvements' it is apparent that large quantities of contemporary control units and interface components will be required by Soviet equipment makers if industrial productivity within the USSR is to be substantially increased. To achieve the requisite quality and reliability for such units, it is likely that new state standards will be required to regulate quality conformance for these products.

To conclude, therefore, it is likely that state standardisation procedures are going to play more of an important role in the Soviet economy and not less, by paying more attention to the requirements of products at the growth stage of the product life cycle, rather than the mature and declining stages. This in its turn will require attention to be paid to the development of appropriate testing and approval procedures for products and factories alike; and the development of appropriate quality regulatory documentation for advanced technology products, particularly those manufactured in the civilian sector. Such changes will be necessary for Soviet standardisation procedures to support further product innovation in the Soviet economy.

The quality changes and product innovations likely to occur in Soviet industry, therefore, still remain a promising area for further study, and this research programme has demonstrated that an adequate data base exists. It is the view of the present researchers, however, that 'advanced manufacturing technology' equipment should be the focus of any further study, in view of its importance to the Soviet national economy, and the necessity of using the scarce available Western research resources in this field in the most effective manner. Some work is already in progress in this area,[12] which should be extended to cover the technical characteristics, features and performance parameters of Soviet CNC machines, robots, flexible manufacturing systems, and CAD/CAM systems; and the capability of these systems to link, or integrate, with production management information systems. Such research would certainly extend research currently in progress on the Soviet computer and micro-electronics industries,[13] but with the specific focus on advanced manufacturing technology. In addition, studies in this field would also provide a basis for a more informed debate on Western governments' policies in the area of export trade controls,[14] with particular reference to those related to advanced manufacturing technology products. The

Comments, Conclusions and Further Research

remaining paragraphs of this chapter, therefore, consist of a discussion of the features of advanced manufacturing technology equipment, and future possible research activities in this area.

FURTHER RESEARCH ON SOVIET ADVANCED MANUFACTURING TECHNOLOGY

Computerised Numerical Control and Flexible Manufacturing

Since the mid-1960s, the technology of medium-batch production, and also production of small batches repeatedly manufactured at subsequent intervals, has been radically changed by the development of numerically controlled equipment. This machinery provides for the programming of machine cycles either on or off the machine, for a defined range of components, with increased on-machine editing capability being provided by computerised numerical control (CNC). Although the pre-production time for the first component is probably longer than when universal machinery is used, it is usually smaller for subsequent identical components and repeat batches once the programme has been proven. Furthermore, the machine cycle itself, once proven, will usually be shorter than that consistently achieved by a human operator.

Numerically controlled machine tools do not usually operate as intensively as special-purpose or dedicated equipment in large-batch or high-volume production conditions since time is spent on tool change between operations and it is usual to carry out single-tool cutting. They do have the advantage of shorter change-over times however, and it has become the case that numerically controlled machinery is the most economic type to use in medium-batch production conditions; and even in large-batch production conditions where there is a likelihood of product change, since they can combine high productivity with high flexibility.

In addition, due to developments in robotics and vehicle guidance, a range of components may now be automatically loaded and unloaded to and from these machines by manipulators which can be more easily reprogrammed than dedicated workhandling devices used in high volume production. The linking of machines, handling mechanisms, transfer devices and associated computerised control systems into a 'flexible manufacturing system' provides the possibility of a faster total throughput time for components as in the case of dedicated link lines and transfer machines; but flexible manufacturing systems can manufacture a wider spectrum of components.

A discussion on numerically controlled machinery by Soviet engineers and managers was reported in 1982 in a leading Soviet industrial-economic journal. The major points arising from this discussion relating to Soviet numerically controlled machine tools can be summarised as follows:

a) the mechanical design and construction of the machines were generally satisfactory although problems still occurred over the production of necessary 'interface' mechanical units such as recirculating ball leadscrews, particularly for spares.[15]
b) there was room for improvement in the design and supply of machine control interface units such as measurement units.[16]
c) there was a limited range of electric motor drive units available for machine tools in the USSR compared with Western sources.[17] Furthermore, the feedback circuitry of some motors was insufficient to enable certain machines to retain their ex- works accuracy after some three to four months.[18]
d) there were serious shortcomings in the design and supply of numerical control systems. These arose from:
   i) shortages and deficiencies in the supplies of the individual components;[19]
   ii) deficiencies in the systems assembled from these components[20] whilst these systems were still becoming more expensive;[21]
   iii) a lack of close contact between the makers of control systems and machine tool factories. This lack of contact prevents special-purpose control equipment from being designed for particular machine models, and also prevents machine tool designers from becoming fully conversant with the capabilities of various control systems.[22] This problem however is a reflection of the tradition of autarky which still prevails in various Soviet industrial ministries.
e) there have been problems in the reliability of Soviet numerically controlled machines, although problems in the reliability of this equipment are not peculiar to the USSR alone. The problem appears to be aggravated in the USSR however as a consequence of the imperfections in the control systems and the lack of after-sales service provided by machine tool suppliers. This latter problem, in its turn, is aggravated by the Soviet planning system which

is product rather than service-oriented; and the lack of provision of after-sales service is even found in those factories delivering to the export market.[23]

f) there is room for improvement in the design, working speeds and working life of tooling.[24] This, however, is caused partly by bottlenecks in the supply of specialised tooling.

g) there is a need for the development of programming systems which are convenient to programme, using microprocessor technology, and the provision of adequate programming facilities.[25]

The USSR is clearly a large producer of numerically-controlled machine tools,[26] and their proportion in the machine tool stock is also increasing[27] but it is obviously important to assess the quality of these machines in order to assess their impact on productivity of Soviet industry. This is quite possible using data published in Soviet books and technical journals such as *Stanki i Instrument*, where a methodology similar to that outlined in chapters 2 and 3 of this book could be used to assess the machines' accuracy and repeatability, using either Western national standards or selected models of Western machine tools as benchmarks. For example a Soviet book published in 1977[28] provided a comprehensive account of the major performance parameters of several types of machine tool, and their associated control systems.

The available data on a range of turning machines, milling machines, drilling and boring machines and machining centres in that publication suggests that their ex-works accuracy capability, as measured by machined workpiece accuracy,[29] is not dissimilar from that for their manually operated counterparts. These latter machines, in their turn, have been shown in Chapters 2 and 3 above not to differ substantially in accuracy from their British counterparts. Positional accuracy for machine assemblies is of the order of 0.05mm per 500mm for milling machines, and ±0.01 mm for drilling and boring machines; whilst bore centre distances can be held to 0.01–0.03mm on machining centres, and 0.05–0.07mm on horizontal boring machines.[30] It is not altogether clear, however, whether this measure of accuracy is the same as the 'repeatability' measure used in British national standards. It is also important to note that all of the technical data available in the above-cited 1977 publication relates to open-loop numerical control systems only, using stepping motors. There is no data available on Soviet closed loop systems, with Soviet machine tools appearing to use a French 'Alcatel' system when increased machine accuracy is required.

In addition, attention should also be paid to the tooling supplied for use with numerically-controlled machinery, since this has a significant effect on the machine's operation. Finally, and perhaps most importantly of all, particular attention should be paid to the control systems used in these machines, since the accuracy and repeatability of these machines are influenced more by the capability of the control systems than any other single factor. Furthermore, the machines' reliability is also significantly influenced by the reliability of the control systems themselves, and also the level of diagnostic skills and training of service engineers combined with the level of support provided by suppliers. As a final point, it is also important to assess the ease with which the Soviet systems can be programmed, since this will greatly influence their efficiency, and their capability to be linked to computer-aided design systems, and thereby reduce pre-production lead-times even further.

The USSR also has ambitious plans for the development of flexible manufacturing, claiming to have 60 FMS systems operating at present[31] (compared with 30 in the UK)[32] and aiming for 1800 installations by 1990. Experience in the West has shown that successful development, manufacture and implementation of FMS systems, however, requires machines, tooling, robots, and automatic guided vehicles of high quality and reliability; and the demands on both computer hardware and software are immense. In addition, their successful utilisation depends on careful selection of components to be manufactured, extremely close contact between suppliers and purchasers, good after-sales service support, and high levels of machining, programming and diagnostic skills within the workforce. Finally, most of the systems appear to have been selected for market-driven reasons to reduce throughput times for critical components.[33] Clearly, therefore, it is important to assess the Soviet-produced equipment from the viewpoint of capability, and also to clearly assess those factors which have contributed to its selection and implementation.

CAD/CAM Systems

Computer-aided design (CAD) systems provide the capability of reducing the design lead time of a new product in several ways. For example, computers may be used to carry out design calculations and

Comments, Conclusions and Further Research 139

hence rapidly reduce the time required to carry out numerical data manipulation which is frequently repetitive. This becomes particularly important when it is necessary to attempt to optimise a product's specification under conditions of varying external parameters. Such applications, however, may be seen merely as an extension of a computer's power as an extremely rapid calculating machine, harnessed to the requirement of numerical solutions to design problems.

There is room for research on the scale of diffusion of such methods throughout the Soviet engineering industry, however, bearing in mind the apparent shortage of computer equipment throughout the USSR as a consequence of manufacturing difficulties in the past.[34] Shortfalls in the supply of disc-driven mini and microcomputers would be particularly noticed in this area, since these types of hardware lend themselves to applications in engineering design calculation; and shortages of software packages could also act as barriers to the diffusion of computer aids in design calculation. Although such shortages have been apparent across the broad spectrum of computer applications in the Soviet economy, they should have been less serious in the area of engineering design calculations than in other areas of application, as a consequence of the strong mathematical traditions[35] and the network of scientific-research institutes[36] that have been established in the USSR.

Computer aids can also be used at the design stage to generate the requisite data on quantities of assemblies, components and materials for a product to be manufactured. These 'bills of materials' usually consist of lists of alpha-numeric data, and are linked to management information systems used for scheduling and stock-control to facilitate timely production according to delivery requirements and capacity availability. There is evidence to suggest that the design and implementation of management information systems in the USSR have met with difficulties. Some of these have been caused by the size and scope of the systems, particularly at the level of the industrial ministry[37] and were not too different from those encountered when implementing over-ambitious systems in the West. These problems have been further compounded, however, by shortcomings in the supply of the requisite equipment from the Soviet computer industry, particularly peripherals and associated service support.[38] It is also likely that there may have been certain systemic features hindering the implementation and diffusion of such management information systems in the production management area in the USSR, since

Soviet industry is arguably less concerned than its Western counterparts with the efficient use of fixed and circulating assets, which is the main objective of most computer-aided production management systems. Savings from anticipated stock reductions are frequently used in the West as a source of financial justification for the purchase of the computerised system.[39]

The most contemporary field of application of computers to the engineering design process, however, is in the area of design and draughting (CADD). This application is a significant advance in information technology as the data has to be presented and manipulated primarily in graphical form, supplemented by the other capabilities previously referred to of engineering design mathematical calculation, and the generation of alpha-numerical data on parts lists. The Soviet engineering industry clearly has experience in the use of these systems as evidenced by literature on the topic,[40] but it is doubtful whether the equipment in use is as advanced as that used by its Western counterparts in terms of computing power and consequent response speed, and graphical display and drawing plotter quality.[41] This view is based on the generally held opinion that computer-aided design and draughting systems require even more sophisticated software and peripherals than conventional management information systems, with which Soviet industry has already been shown to have experienced difficulty during implementation. The demands for this equipment are similar to those encountered in the West, namely shorter design lead times, faster drawing modification, and more effective use of trained manpower;[42] but it is to be seriously questioned whether the Soviet computer industry is capable of meeting these requirements. It would be extremely useful, therefore, to carry out a study on the capabilities of Soviet CADD systems, similar to those carried out by Cave on mainframe management information systems.[43] Particular attention should be paid to computer power, quality of peripherals, and supplier support.

Finally, it is being found in Western industry that new product development lead times can be even further reduced if CAD systems can be linked to CNC machine tool programming systems to enable the requisite machine programme to be generated directly from the graphical display of a component. The underlying assumption is that as the shape of the component can be defined in co-ordinate terms, and a machine programme in its turn defines a series of co-ordinate positions for a cutting tool relative to a workpiece, then time can be saved by using a system capable of translating the graphical data for the product, to co-ordinate data for the tool position, with associated feeds and speeds.

The difficulties in implementing these computer-aided design and manufacturing systems (CAD/CAM) can be even more difficult than CAD or NC systems alone, however; and few Western companies have mastered these techniques fully. It is questionable, therefore, whether the Soviet engineering industry is anywhere near as advanced as its Western counterparts, in view of the general historical problems in development in the Soviet computer industry. This topic, however, is clearly worthy of further research.

Appendix

Table A.1 Comparative lathe accuracies (all tolerances in microns)

Test	'P' Class lathes GOST 18097–72	Precision lathes BS 4656 Pt. 1	'N' Class lathes GOST 18097–72	Other lathes BS 4656 Pt. 1
A. GEOMETRIC TESTS				
Straightness of carriage movement in a horizontal plane with reference to the axis of centres (Test 1.1 and G2)	12 (800–1250mm centre distance)	15 (500–1000mm centre distance)	20 (800–1250mm centre distance)	20 (500–1000mm centre distance)
Difference in height between headstock and tailstock centres (Test 1.3 and G11)	20 (up to 400mm swing) 25 (400–800mm swing)	20 (up to 500mm swing)	30 (up to 400mm swing) 40 (400–800mm swing) 60 (800–1600mm swing)	40 (up to 800mm swing) 60 (800–1600mm swing)
Parallelism of tailstock guides to carriage movement:				
a) vertically	25	30	40	30
b) horizontally (Test 1.4 and G3)	16 (500–2000mm centre distance)	20 (up to 500mm centre distance)	25 (500–2000mm centre distance)	30
Spindle nose run-out (Test 1.5 and G5)	7 (250–800mm swing)	7 (up to 500mm swing)	10 (250–800mm swing) 16 (800–1600mm swing)	10 (up to 800mm swing) 15 (800–1600mm swing)

Test	Tolerance values
Spindle axial slip (Test 1.6 and G4(a))	5 (up to 400mm swing); 7 (400–800mm swing); 5 (up to 500mm swing); 8 (up to 400mm swing); 10 (400–800mm swing); 16 (800–1600mm swing); 10 (up to 800mm swing); 15 (800–1600mm swing)
Camming of spindle face plate (Test 1.7 and G4(b))	10 (up to 400mm swing); 12 (400–800mm swing); 10 (up to 500mm swing); 16 (up to 400mm swing); 20 (400–800mm swing); 25 (800–1600mm swing); 20 (up to 800mm swing); 20 (800–1600mm swing)
Run-out of axis of work spindle taper a) at face	7 (up to 400mm swing); 7 (400–800mm swing); 5 (up to 500mm swing); 10 (up to 400mm swing); 12 (400–800mm swing); 16 (800–1600mm swing); 10 (up to 800mm swing); 15 (800–1600mm swing)
b) at length 'L' from face	10, L = 200mm (up to 400mm swing); 12, L = 300mm (400–800mm swing); 10, L = 200mm (up to 500mm swing); 15, L = 300mm; 16, L = 200mm (up to 400mm swing); 20, L = 300mm (400–800mm swing); 30, L = 300mm (800–1600mm swing); 20, L = 300mm (up to 800mm swing); 50, L = 500mm (800–1600mm swing)

continued on p. 144

Table A.1 continued

Test	'P' Class lathes GOST 18097-72	Precision lathes BS 4656 Pt. 1	'N' Class lathes GOST 18097-72	Other lathes BS 4656 Pt. 1
(Test 1.8 and G6) Parallelism of spindle axis to carriage longitudinal movement				
a) in a vertical plane (all measurements taken over length 'L')	10 L = 200mm (up to 400mm swing) 12 L = 300mm (400–800mm swing)	20 L = 300mm (up to 500mm swing)	16 L = 200mm (up to 400mm swing) 20 L = 300mm (400–800mm swing) 35 L = 300mm (800–1600mm swing)	20 L = 300mm (up to 800mm swing) 40 L = 500mm (800–1600mm swing)
b) in a horizontal plane (all measurements taken over length 'L')	5 L = 200mm (up to 400mm swing) 8 L = 300mm (400–800mm swing)	10 L = 300mm (up to 800mm swing)	8 L = 200mm (up to 400mm swing) 12 L = 300mm (400–800mm swing) 16 L = 300mm (800–1600mm swing)	15 L = 300mm (up to 800mm swing) 30 L = 300mm (800–1600mm swing)
(Test 1.9 and G7) Parallelism of longitudinal movement of top slide to spindle axis (Test 1.10 and G12)	16 (over 150mm length)	15 (over 150mm length)	35 (over 150mm length)	40 (over 150mm length)

Test				
Squareness of movement of top slide to spindle axis (measured over length 'L') (Test 1.11 and G13)	8 L = 200mm (up to 400mm swing) 12 L = 300mm (400–800mm swing)	10 L = 300mm (up to 500mm swing)	12 L = 200mm (up to 400mm swing) 20 L = 300mm (400–800mm swing) 30 L = 300 (800–1600mm swing)	20 L = 300mm (up to 800mm swing) 20 L = 300 (800–1600mm swing)
Parallelism of axis of tailstock sleeve to carriage movement a) in a vertical plane (all measurements taken over length 'L')	10 L = 50mm (up to 400mm swing) 20 L = 100mm (400–800mm swing)	15 L = 100mm (up to 800mm swing)	10 L = 50mm (up to 400mm swing) 20 L = 100mm (400–800mm swing) 30 L = 100mm (800–1600mm swing)	20 L = 100mm (up to 800mm swing) 30 L = 100mm (800–1600mm swing)
b) in a horizontal plane (all measurements taken over length 'L')	6 L = 50mm (up to 400mm swing) 6 L = 100mm	10 L = 100mm	8 L = 50mm (up to 400mm swing) 12 L = 100mm	15 L = 100mm

continued on p. 146

Table A.1 continued

Test	'P' Class lathes GOST 18097-72	Precision lathes BS 4656 Pt. 1	'N' Class lathes GOST 18097-72	Other lathes BS 4656 Pt. 1
(Test 1.12 and G9) Parallelism of taper box of sleeve to carriage movement in both vertical and horizontal planes (measurements taken over length 'L') (Test 1.13 and G10)	16 L = 200mm (up to 400mm swing) 20 L = 300mm (400–800mm swing)	(up to 800mm swing) 20 L = 300mm (up to 500mm swing)	(400–800mm swing) 16 L = 100mm (800–1600mm swing) 20 L = 200mm (up to 400mm swing) 30 L = 300mm (400–800mm swing) 40 L = 300mm (800–1600mm swing)	(up to 800mm swing) 20 L = 100mm (800–1600mm swing) 30 L = 300mm (up to 800mm swing) 50 L = 300mm (800–1600mm swing)
Accuracy of pitch generated by leadscrew (measured over length 'L') a) L = 50mm	10 (up to 400mm swing) 12 (400–800mm swing)	10 (up to 500mm swing)	16 (up to 400mm swing) 16 (400–800mm swing)	15 (400–800mm swing) 15 (800–1600mm swing)

b) L = 300mm
    20   35
 (up to 400mm swing)   (up to 400mm swing)
    25   30   40   40
(400–800mm swing) (up to 500mm swing) (400–800mm swing) (up to 800mm swing)
                       50   50
             (800–1600mm swing)   (800–1600mm swing)

(Test 1.14 and G15)

Axial displacement due to camming of end thrust bearing
    5   8
 (up to 400mm swing)   (up to 400mm swing)
    7   10   10   15
(400–800mm swing) (up to 500mm swing) (400–800mm swing) (up to 800mm swing)
                       16   20
             (800–1600mm swing)   (800–1600mm swing)

(Test 1.15 and G14)

B. Workpiece tests

Machining of cylindrical piece

a) roundness
  5   7   8   10

b) cylindricity (measured at length 'L')
  12   20   20   30   40
L = 200 L = 300 L = 300 L = 300
(up to (400– (400– (800–
400mm 800mm 800mm 1600mm
swg.) swg.) swg.) swg.)
    (up to 500mm swing)   16   25
                             (up to L = 300
                            800mm (up to 1600mm
                             swg.)   swing)

(Test 2.1 and P1)

Facing tests (measured over length 'L')
 10   15   20   25
L = 200 L = 300 L = 300 L = 300
(up to (up to (400– (up to 1600mm
400mm 500mm 800mm swing)
swg.) swing) swg.)
                         L = 300
                   (800–1600mm swg.)

(Test 2.2 and P2)

continued on p. 148

Table A.1 continued

Test	'P' Class lathes GOST 18097–72	Precision lathes BS 4656 Pt. 1	'N' Class lathes GOST 18097–72	Other lathes BS 4656 Pt. 1
Threading of a cylindrical piece (deviation over length 'L') (Test 2.3 and P3)	16 L = 50mm 30 L = 300mm	10 L = 50mm 30 L = 300mm	20 L = 50mm 40 L = 300mm	15 L = 50mm 40 L = 300mm
	16 (500mm–800mm measuring length)	15 (500mm–1000mm centre distance)	25 (500mm–800mm measuring length)	20 (500mm–1000mm centre distance)

Tests 1.2 and 1.16 have been omitted, since no comparable tests were specified in BS 4656 Part 1. The nearest comparison is probably "bed flatness" (Test G1) where similar tolerances are given for both tests:

Table A.2 Comparative milling machine accuracies (all tolerances in microns)

Test	Tolerances to GOST 17734-72		Tolerances to BS 4656 Part 3
	'P' Class millers	'N' Class millers	
Flatness of table surface, measured over 1000mm (Test 1 and G4)	25 (1000–1600mm measuring length) 20 (630–1000mm measuring length)	40 (1000–1600mm measuring length) 30 (630–1000mm measuring length)	40 (1000mm measuring length)
Squareness of the movement of the table transversely to its longitudinal movement (Test 2 and G11)	12 (300mm measuring length)	20 (300mm measuring length)	20 (300mm measuring length)
Parallelism of the table surface to its movement, longitudinally (Test 3 and G5(b))	30 (greater than 1000mm table travel) 20 (630–1000mm table travel)	40 (greater than 1000mm table travel) 30 (630–1000mm table travel)	50 max. and 25 per 300mm along table travel.
Parallelism of the table surface to its movement, transversely (Test 4 and G5(a))	16 (250–400mm table movement)	25 (250–400mm table movement)	25 (500mm measuring length)
Parallelism of reference T-slot face to longitudinal movement (Test 5 and G10)	16 (400–630mm table movement)	25 (400–630mm table movement)	15 per 300mm measuring length.

continued on p. 150

Table A.2 continued

Test	Tolerances to GOST 17734-72		Tolerances to BS 4656 Part 3
	'P' Class millers	'N' Class millers	
Periodic axial slip of spindle (Test 6 and G14(c))	20 (630–1000mm table movement)	30 (630–1000mm table movement)	40 max. over complete length.
Camming of spindle nose face (Test 7 and G14(b))	6	10	10
Radial run-out of spindle internal taper:	12	20	20
a) close to spindle	6	10	10
b) at a length of 300mm from spindle nose (Test 8 and G15)	12 (table width greater than 250mm)	20 (table width greater than 250mm)	20
Radial run-out of spindle nose external face (Test 9 and G14(a))	6	10	10
Squareness of spindle axis to table reference T-slot (300mm measuring distance) (Test 10 and G9)	12	20	20
Parallelism of spindle axis to table surface (300mm measuring distance) (Test 11 and G6)	16 (table width greater than 250mm)	25 (table width greater than 250mm)	25

Test			
Squareness of spindle axis to table surface (300mm measuring distance) (Test 12 and G16)	16 (table width greater than 250mm)	25 (table width greater than 250mm)	25
Squareness of table surface to column ways (300mm measuring distance) (Test 13 and G2)	16	25	25
Squareness of table surface to column ways for spindle head slide. (300mm measuring distance) (Test 14 and G3)	16	25	25
Parallelism of arbor support guide to spindle axis (300mm measuring distance) (Test 15 and G12)	12 (table width greater than 250mm)	20 (table width greater than 250mm)	20
Coincidence of the axis of the bore of the arbor support to the spindle axis (300mm measuring distance) (Test 16 and Test G13)	20 (table width greater than 160mm)	30 (table width greater than 160mm)	30
Workpiece test			
Flatness	16 (250–400mm measuring length)	25 (250–400mm measuring length)	20
Parallelism	16	25	30
	12 (250–400mm measuring length)		
Squareness	12 (100mm measuring length)	20 (100mm measuring length)	20 (100mm measuring length)

Table A.3 Comparative accuracies for vertical drilling machines (all tolerances in microns)

Test	Tolerances to GOST 370–76		Tolerances to BS 4656 Part 11 (1974)
	'P' Class Machines	'N' Class Machines	
Flatness of table surface (Test 1.1 & 1G.1)	16 per measuring length of 200–320mm	25 per measuring length of 200–320mm	30 per measuring length of 300 mm
Radial run-out of spindle axis (a) at spindle nose (b) at distance of 300 mm from the spindle nose (Test 1.2 & 1G.2)	12 20 (for machines greater than 18mm drill capacity)	20 30 (for machines greater than 18mm drill capacity)	25 50
Squareness of spindle axis to table (a) in a plane perpendicular to the plane of symmetry of the machine	25	40	50
(b) in a plane parallel to the axis of symmetry of the machine	30	50	50
Tolerances for a measuring length of 300mm (Test 1.3 & 1.G.3) Squareness of spindle movement to table surface (a) in a plane perpendicular	40	60	100

to the axis of symmetry of the machine (b) in a plane parallel to the axis of symmetry of the machine	60 measuring length of greater than 250mm	90 measuring length of greater than 250mm	100 measuring length of 300mm

Table A.4 Comparative accuracies for radial drilling machines (all tolerances in microns)

Test	Tolerances to GOST 98-71	Tolerances to BS 4656 Part 10 (1975)
Flatness of base plate (Test 1 & Test G1)	50 for measuring distances of 630–1000mm 65 for measuring distances of 1000–1600mm	100 for measuring length of 1000mm
Radial run-out of the internal taper of the spindle:		
(a) adjacent to the spindle nose;	20	25
(b) at a distance of 300mm from the spindle nose. (Test 2 & Test C4)	30	50

continued on p. 153

Table A.4 continued

Table A.4 Comparative accuracies for radial drilling machines (all tolerances in microns)

Test	Tolerances to GOST 98-71	Tolerances to BS 4656 Part 10 (1975)
Squareness of spindle axis to base plate:		
(a) in the longitudinal plane;	100 per 500mm measuring length	200 per 1000mm measuring length at 4 points of contact 90° apart
(b) in the transverse plane.	50 per 500mm measuring length	
(Test 3 & Test G5) Parallelism of saddle movement to base plate.	200 for measuring distances up to 1000mm	300 for any measuring length over 1000mm
(Test 4 & Test G1)	300 for measuring distances from 1000–1600mm	
Squareness of vertical movement of the spindle to the base plate:		
(a) in the longitudinal direction (ie in a plane parallel to the axis of symmetry of the machine;	100 for measuring distances up to 320mm	100 per measuring length of 300mm
(b) in the transverse direction (ie: in the plane perpendicular to the plane of the machine.	50 for measuring distances up to 320mm	50 per measuring length of 300mm
(Test 5 & Test C6)		

Table A.5 Comparative accuracies for surface grinding machines (all tolerances in microns)

Test	Tolerances to GOST 273-77		Tolerances to BS 4656 Part 7 (1971)
	'A' Class Machines	'V' Class Machines	
Flatness of table surface (Test 1.1 & G3)	5 630–1000mm measuring length 6 1000–1600mm measuring length	8 630–1000mm measuring length 10 1000–1600mm measuring length	10 up to 1000mm measuring length
Horizontal and vertical straightness for longitudinal and transverse table traverse (Test 1.2 & G4)	4 630–1000mm measuring length 5 1000–1600mm measuring length	6 630–1000mm measuring length 8 1000–1600mm measuring length	10 & 15 up to 1000mm measuring length
Parallelism of centre Tee-slot to table longitudinal movement (Test 1.4 & G5)	6 630–1000mm measuring length 8 1000mm–1600mm measuring length	10 630–1000mm measuring length 12 1000mm–1600mm measuring length	15 up to 1000mm measuring length
Radial run-out of spindle nose (Test 1.5 & G8)	3 200–320mm table width 4 320–500mm	4 200–320mm table width 5 320–500mm	10

continued on p. 156

TABLE A.5 continued

Test	Tolerances to GOST 273-77		Tolerances to BS 4656 Part (1971)
	'A' Class Machines	'V' Class Machines	
Spindle axial slip	table width 2.5	table width 4	10
	200–320mm table width 3	200–320mm table width 5	
(Test 1.6 & C9)	320–500mm table width 5	320–500mm table width 8	
Parallelism of spindle axis to table surface	200mm measuring distance	200mm measuring distance	25 300mm measuring distance
(Test 1.7 & G.10) (Different testing procedure).			
Squareness of spindle axis to table longitudinal surface	3 150mm measuring distance	5 150mm measuring distance	15 300mm measuring distance
(Test 1.8 & G11)			

Test			
Squareness of spindle sub-assembly movement to longitudinal table movement (Test 1.9 & G7)	6 200mm measuring distance	8 200mm measuring distance	40 per 300mm
Setting accuracy (a) vertically for spindle head	0.5 per 2 microns measuring length 2 per 10 microns measuring length	1 per 2 microns measuring length 3 per 10 microns measuring length	
(b) transversely for table	0.5 per 2 microns measuring length 2 per 10 microns measuring length	1 per 2 microns measuring length 3 per 10 microns measuring length	
(Test 1.10) Workpiece thickness test (Test 2.2 and p2)	3 250–400mm measuring distance	5 250–400mm measuring distance	5 per 300mm measuring distance

The Soviet standard also specifies tests for squareness of ground faces, and surface finish, which the British Standard does not.

Table A.6 Comparative accuracies for cylindrical grinding machines (all tolerances in microns)

Test	Tolerances to GOST 11654-72		Tolerances to BS 4656 Part 9 (1974)
	'V' Class Machines	'P' Class Machines	
Parallelisms of location surfaces for workhead and tailstock, to the longitudinal movement of the table (Test 3 & Test G3)	8 500–800mm table movement 10 800–1250mm table movement 12 1250–2000mm table movement	12 500–800mm table movement 16 800–1250mm table movement 20 1250–2000mm table movement	10 per 1000mm table movement
Run-out of axis of workhead spindle (a) at spindle nose (b) at 300mm from spindle nose (Test 4 & Test G5)	4 6 200–400mm max. workpiece diameter	6 10 200–400mm max. workpiece diameter (a) 10 (b) 12 400–800mm max. workpiece diameter	5 15
Run-out of external register of workhead spindle (Test 5 & Test G4(a))	4 200–400mm max. workpiece diameter	6 200–400mm max. workpiece diameter 8 400–800mm max. workpiece diameter	5

Test			
Periodic axial slip of workhead spindle (Test 6 & Test G4(b))	2.5 200–400mm max. workpiece diameter	4 200–400mm max. workpiece diameter	5
Camming of register face or workhead spindle (Test 7 & Test G4 (c))	5 200–400mm max. workpiece diameter	6 400–800mm max. workpiece diameter	10
		8 200–400mm max. workpiece diameter	
		10 400–800mm max. workpiece diameter	
Parallelism of spindle axis to table movement, over 300mm measuring length (a) = vertical plane (b) = horizontal plane			
(i) Dead spindle	(a) 12 (b) 6	(a) 20 (b) 10	(a) 25 (b) 25
(ii) Live spindle (Test 9 & Test G6)	(a) 12 (b) 6 200–400mm max. workpiece diameter	(a) 20 (b) 10 200–800mm max. workpiece diameter	(a) 10 (b) 10
Parallelism of tailstock taper bore to table movement over 300mm measuring length (a) = vertical plane	(a) 12	(a) 20	(a) 15

continued on p. 160

Table A.6 continued

Test	Tolerances to GOST 11654-72		Tolerances to BS 4656 Part 9 (1974)
	'V' Class Machines	'P' Class Machines	
(b) = horizontal plane (Test 10 & Test G7)	(b) 6 200–400mm max. workpiece diameter	(b) 10 200–800mm max. workpiece diameter	(b) 15
Parallelism of axis of centres to movement of table (vertical plane only) (Test 11 & Test G8)	10 Table movement less than 2000mm	10 Table movement less than 2000mm 20 Table movement between 2000mm and 8000mm	20
Parallelism of grinding wheel spindle axis to table movement, over a measuring length "L" (a) in vertical plane (b) in horizontal plane (Test 12 & G 10)	10 6 L = 100mm 200–400mm max. workpiece diameter	10 10 L = 100mm 200–800mm max. workpiece diameter	30 30 L = 100mm
Radial run-out of grinding wheel spindle mounting (Test 13 & G9(a))	4 200–400mm max. workpiece diameter	6 200–400mm max. workpiece diameter	5

Axial slip of grinding wheel spindle (Test 14 & G9(b))	4 200–400mm max. workpiece diameter	8 400–800mm max. workpiece diameter 6	10
Squareness of wheelhead feed to table longitudinal motion (Test 17 & G11)	5 200–400mm max. workpiece diameter	8 400–800mm max. workpiece diameter 8 200–400mm max. workpiece diameter 8 200–400mm max. workpiece diameter	20 per 300mm distance of wheelhead feed
Repeatability accuracy of wheel positioning	2 200–400mm max. workpiece diameter	10 400–800mm max. workpiece diameter 3 200–800mm max. workpiece diameter	2 less than 500mm workpiece diameter 4 greater than 500mm workpiece diameter
(Test 18b & G13) Grinding of a cylindrical test piece between centres: Cylindricity	5 200–400mm max.	8 200–400mm max.	8 for 630mm centre

continued on p. 162

Table A.6 continued

Test	Tolerances to GOST 11654-72		Tolerances to BS 4656 Part 9 (1974)
	'V' Class Machine	'P' Class Machine	
Circularity	workpiece diameter 1.6 200–400mm max.	workpiece diameter 10 400–800mm max. workpiece diameter 2.5 200–400mm max. workpiece diameter 3 400–800mm max. workpiece diameter	distance machine 10 for 1000mm centre distance machine 1.5 centre distance less than 630mm 2.5 machines having centre distance greater than 630mm
Grinding of a disc	Tolerances as above for circularity	Tolerances as above for circularity	5 for a 100mm diameter disc

Notes: 'A' Class tolerances are only given for machines having a maximum workpiece diameter of up to 200mm. In general, these tolerances are 60–70% of those given for "V" Class machines of the same maximum workpiece size category. The tolerances of cylindricity have been doubled for the British Standard, as they are based on changes in radius, and the Soviet tolerances are based on changes in diameter.

Table A.7 Comparative accuracies for internal grinding machines

Test	Tolerances to GOST 25-72		Tolerances to BS 4656 Part 8
	'V' Class	'P' Class	
Straightness of table movement			
(a) in the vertical plane	6 for a table travel from 200–320mm	10 for a table travel from 200–320mm	
(b) in the horizontal plane	4 for a table travel from 200–320mm	6 for a table travel from 200–320mm	8 per 300mm travel (in a horizontal plane only)
(Test 1.1 & 1G1)			
Axial run-out of work head spindle nose	3 for a maximum workpiece diameter of 200–400mm	5 for a maximum workpiece diameter of 200–400mm	5
(Test 1.2 & 1G2 b)	5 for a maximum workpiece diameter of 400–800mm	8 for a maximum workpiece diameter of 400–800mm	
Camming of spindle register	5 for a maximum workpiece diameter of 200–400mm	8 for a maximum workpiece diameter of 200–400mm	10
(Test 1.3 & 1G2 (c))	6 for a maximum workpiece diameter of 400–800mm	10 for a maximum workpiece diameter of 400–800mm	

continued on p. 164

Table A.7 continued

Test	Tolerances to GOST 25-72 — 'V' Class	Tolerances to GOST 25-72 — 'P' Class	Tolerances to BS 4656 Part 8
Radial run-out of the external register diameter of the spindle (Test 1.4 & 1G2 a)	4 for a maximum workpiece diameter of 200–400mm; 5 for a maximum workpiece diameter of 400–800mm	6 for a maximum workpiece diameter of 200–400mm; 8 for a maximum workpiece diameter of 400–800mm	5
Radial run-out of workhead spindle axis (a) at spindle face	200–400mm max. diameter: 4; 400–800mm max. diameter: 5	200–400mm max. diameter: 6; 400–800mm max. diameter: 8	
(b) at a distance 'L' from the spindle face (Test 1.5 & 1G3)	200–400mm max. diameter L=200mm: 5; 400–800mm max. diameter L=300mm: 6	200–400mm max. diameter L=200mm: 8; 400–800mm max. diameter L=300mm: 10	5; 15 for L=300mm
Parallelism of workhead spindle axis to table movement (a) in vertical plane	200–400mm max. diameter: 8; 400–800mm max. diameter: 10	200–400mm max. diameter: 12; 400–800mm max. diameter: 16	25
(b) in horizontal plane (Test 1.7 & 1G4)	200–400mm max. diameter L=200mm: 4; 400–800mm max. diameter L=300mm: 5	200–400mm max. diameter L=200mm: 6; 400–800mm max. diameter L=300mm: 8	10 L=300mm

Test			
Parallelism of grinding wheel spindle axis to table movement	8 per 100mm	10 per 100mm	30 per 300mm
Difference in height between axis of workhead and wheelhead spindles (Test 1.9 & 1G7)	10	16	25
Axial run-out of grinding wheel spindle nose (Test 1.10 & Test 3G1b)	12 for 400–800mm max. workpiece diameter 3 for 200–400mm max. diameter	20 for 400–800mm max. workpiece diameter 5 for 200–400mm max. diameter	5
Radial run-out of grinding wheel spindle (a) at spindle nose (b) at a distance 'L' from the spindle nose (Test 1.11 & 1G5)	4 for 400–800mm max. workpiece diameter 200–400mm max. diameter: 4, 400–800mm max. diameter: 5 6, 8 L = 75mm	6 for 400–800mm max. workpiece diameter 200–400mm max. diameter: 6, 400–800mm max. diameter: 8 10, 12 L = 75mm	10 20 L = 200mm

continued on p. 166

Table A.7 continued

Test	Tolerances to GOST 25-72		Tolerances to BS4656 Part 8
	'V' Class	'P' Class	
Repeatability Test (Test 1.14 & 1G9)	1.5 for 200-400 max. workpiece diameter	2.5 for 200-400 max. workpiece diameter	2
	2 for 400-800mm max. workpiece diameter	3 for 400-800mm max. workpiece diameter	
Workpiece Accuracy Circularity	3-4	5-6	7.5 for 150mm length
Cylindricity	3	3-4	2.5 for 150mm length

Table A.8 Comparative accuracies for semi-automatic vertical broaching machines (all tolerances in microns)

Test	Tolerances to GOST 16025–79 Class "N" with puller load 50–800 kN (Unified domestic & export requirement)	Tolerances to BS4656: Part 17: 1973
Table flatness (Test 1.1 & G.1)	up to 500 mm 20 greater than 500 mm 30	40 per 1,000 mm
Concentricity of puller axis with central hole of work table (Test 1.3 & G11)	40	50
Squareness of puller movement to work table (Test 1.4 & G10)	20 per 300 mm test length	25 per 300 mm
Alignment of puller and retriever axis (Test 1.6 & G.6)	40	125
Squareness of tool slide movement to work table (Test 1.8 & G.4)	30 per 300 mm test length (front to back) 20 per 300 mm test length (side to side)	25 per 300 mm test length (front to back & side to side)
Parallelism of slide surface to its movement (Test 1.9 & G.2)	50 per 1000 mm test length	25 per 1000 mm test length
Parallelism of vertical keyway to vertical movement of slide (Test 1.10 & G.3)	30 per 1000 mm	25 per 1000 mm test length
Parallelism of work table side to side keyway to the tool slide (Test 1.11 & G.8b)	20 per 300 mm	25 per 300 mm test length
Alignment of tool slide vertical keyway with work table front to back keyway (Test 1.12 & G.6)	30	25

Table A.9 Comparative accuracies for vertical gearhobbing machines (all tolerances in microns) (Unified domestic and export requirements)

Test	GOST 659–78 (Vertical Machine)		BS4656: Part 19: 1976	
	Normal Precision	Improved Precision	Normal Accuracy	High Accuracy
Table surface flatness (Test 1.1 & G.1)	20 (300 mm test length)	12	20 300 mm test length maximum permissible deviation of 40 mkm, concave only	
Work-spindle mounting bore run-out (Test 1.2 & G.4)	8 at spindle nose	5 at spindle nose		5 at spindle nose
	12 at 300 mm from spindle nose (these tolerances are for a 500mm max. workpiece diameter machine)	8 at 300 mm from spindle nose		15 at 300 mm from spindle nose
	10 at spindle nose	6 at spindle nose		
	16 at 300 mm from spindle nose (these tolerances are for 501– 800 mm max. workpiece dia. machines)	10 at 300 mm from spindle nose		
Table spindle axial run-out (Test 1.3 & G.2)	No tolerances given for normal precision machines	6 (for 320–500mm m/cs) 6 (for 500–800mm m/cs) 10 (for 800–1250mm m/cs)		6

Test			
Table surface run-out (Test 1.4 & G.3)	10 (for 200–320 mm max. workpiece dia.)	6	10 per 150 mm radius of table
Radial run-out of cutter spindle (Test 1.5 & G.7)	10 at spindle nose	6 at spindle nose	5 at spindle nose
Axial slip of cutter spindle (Test 1.6 & G.8)	16 at 300 mm from spindle nose	10 at 300 mm from spindle nose	20 at 300 mm from spindle nose
Co-axiality of cutter spindle & arbor mounting bore (Test 1.7 & G.9)	6 (for 320–800 mm max. workpiece dia.)	4	5
Parallelism of cutter saddle movement to table axis (Test 1.8 & G.5)	20 (for 320–800 mm max. workpiece dia.; no test length given)	16	10 (per 300 mm from the arbor mounting bore)
Parallelism of cutter axis to tangential slide movement (Test 1.9 & G.10)	20 (perpendicular to hob axis) 25 (parallel to hob axis) (250–400 mm. measuring length) 20 per 300 mm (320–800 mm. workpiece size m/cs)	12 (perpendicular to hob axis) 16 (parallel to hob axis) 16 per 300 mm	20 (perpendicular to hob axis) 10 (parallel to hob axis) (300 mm. measuring length) 15 per 300 mm
Co-axiality of work steady bore to work spindle bore (Test 1.10 & G.6)	16 (in the lower steady position) 20 (in the upper steady position)	12	20 per 300 mm 10
Accuracy of table mechanism (Test 1.11 & G.11)	50 (for 500–800 mm workpiece diameter)	32	25 per 300 mm 20 (for 600 mm workpiece diameter)

Table A.10 Comparative accuracies for horizontal gearhobbing machines (All tolerances in microns)

Test	GOST 18065-72 (Horizontal Machine)		BS4656: Part 19: 1976	
	Normal Precision	Improved Precision	Normal Accuracy	High Accuracy
Work spindle mounting bore run-out (Test 1.4 & G.4)	10 at spindle nose 20 at 300 mm from spindle nose (these tolerances are for a 500 mm max. workpiece diameter machine) 12 at spindle nose 30 at 300 mm from spindle nose (these tolerances are for a 500–800 mm max. workpiece dia. machine)	5 at spindle nose 10 at 300 mm from spindle nose 6 at spindle nose 12 at 300 mm from spindle nose		3 at spindle nose 15 at 300 mm from spindle nose
Table spindle axial run-out (Tables 1.5 & G.2)	10 (for 320–500 mm machines) 12 (for 500–800 mm machines) 16 (for 800–1250 mm machines)	6 8 10		6

Test		
Table surface run-out (Test 1.6 & G.3)	16 (for 200–320 mm max. workpiece dia.)	10 per 150 mm radius of table
Radial run-out of cutter spindle (Test 1.7 & G.7)	10 at spindle nose 6	5 at spindle nose
	20 at 300 mm from spindle nose 12	20 at 300 mm from spindle nose
Axial slip of cutter spindle (Test 1.8 & G.8)	8 5 (for 320–500 mm max. workpiece dia.) (for 320–800 mm from spindle nose)	5
Co-axiality of cutter spindle & arbor mounting (Test 1.9 & G.9)	20 16 (for 320–800 mm max. workpiece dia. machines; no test length given)	10 (per 300 mm from the arbor mounting bore)
Parallelism of cutter saddle movement to table axis (Test 1.10 & G.5)	20 (perpendicular to hob axis) 12	20 (perpendicular to hob axis) 10
	25 (parallel to hob axis) 16 (320–500 mm measuring length)	20 (parallel to hob axis) 10 (300 mm measuring length)
Co-axiality of work steady bore to work spindle bore (Test 1.13 & G.6)	20 16	20 per 300 mm 10

Appendix

Table A.11 'Mark of Quality' standards – selected turning machines

GOST 5.1347–72   Six-spindle horizontal bar auto, model number 1A225–6

1. Basic parameters and dimensions

Maximum dimensions of bar, diameter	25 mm
Maximum dimensions of bar, length	4000 mm
Maximum material feed	150 mm
Maximum toolpost travel	160 mm
Toolpost feed	0–70 mm
Number of toolboxes	6
Number of spindles	6
Range of spindle speeds	280–2560 rpm
Distance from spindle axis to toolpost face	52.5 mm
Maximum diameter of spindle collett bore	60 mm
Camshaft idle time	2.26 secs
Cycle time limits	6.4–166.3 secs
Dimensions of machine and bar	
Length	5700 mm
Width	1200 mm
Height	1700 mm
Machine Weight, including motor	5700 kg
Workpiece accuracy	
Dimensional accuracy, cross section	8 mkm
Dimensional accuracy, longitudinal section	12 mkm
Dimensional accuracy, batch, cross section	60 mkm
Dimensional accuracy, longitudinal, cross section	60 mkm

2. Technical requirements

2.1 The bar auto must be manufactured to the requirements of this present standard, GOST 7599–55, GOST 43–65 and technical documentation approved to established procedure.

2.2 Accuracy must be maintained for not less than:
  (a) 1.5 years for tolerances specified in section 1 above.
  (b) 4.5 years for tolerances specified by GOST 43–65, with user's observance of operating conditions.

2.3 The service life to first overhaul must not be less than 9 years, with user's observance of operating conditions.

2.4 The external appearance, finish and paintwork must correspond to the documentation approved to established procedure.

3. Completeness

3.1 The machine must be supplied complete with the following tooling and accessories in correspondence with the documentation approved by the established procedure:
  rapid drilling drive,
  screw cutting drive,

Appendix

spindle,
clamping collett,
release collett,
set of change gears,
set of fitter's hand tools,
set of rapid wear components.

4. Rules for acceptance and testing

4.1 The rules for acceptance and methods of testing are laid down by GOST 7599–55, GOST 8–71, GOST 43–65, and the technical documentation approved to established procedure.

5. Marking, packing, transport and storage

5.1 A 'Mark of Quality' to GOST 1.6–67 must be attached to the frame of the machine, and a table containing the following:

(a) manufacturer's trade mark,
(b) manufacturer's serial number,
(c) model,
(d) production year,
(e) present standard number.

5.2 Packing, storage and transport to GOST 7599–55, GOST 10198–62, GOST 13168–69, GOST 2991–69 and technical documentation approved to the established procedure.

5.3 The 'Mark of Quality' must be shown on operating documentation.

6. Manufacturer's guarantee

6.1 The manufacturer must guarantee that the machine corresponds with the requirements of this standard, with customer's observance of operating conditions.

6.2 The guaranteed time interval is 1.5 years from the time of introduction into service.

GOST 5.1012–71
Screwcutting Lathe, Model Number 1622

1. Basic parameters and dimensions

1.1 The basic parameters and dimensions must be as follows:

Range of workpiece diameters	20–85 mm
Maximum screwcut length	2,500 mm
Pitch of screw	
metric	3.–12 mm
inch	1/4in–1in
module	2–5 mm
Height of centres	225 mm

continued on p. 174

Appendix

Table A.11 'Mark of Quality' standards – selected turning machines

---

GOST 5.1347–72   Six-spindle horizontal bar auto, model number 1A225–6

Number of spindle speeds	
straight rotation	6
reverse rotation	6
Range of spindle speeds	
straight rotation	4–40 rpm
reverse rotation	8–80 rpm
Spindle diameter	22 mm
Normal working temperature	$20 \pm 1°C$
Machine size	$4420 \times 1340 \times 1250$ mm
Machine weight	3300 kg

2. Technical requirements

2.1 The machine must be manufactured to the requirements of this present standard, GOST 7599–55, TU2–024–2508–70, instruction number 6–1, ENIMS, and technical documentation approved to the established procedure.

2.2 Tolerances for machine accuracy. (*Authors' note.* This clause of the standard provides tolerances for more than 30 geometric tests. Those relating to workpiece accuracy are shown in Table 3.2. The majority of the geometric tolerances conform to requirements for 'V' Class or 'A' Class machines.)

2.3 The machine must be manufactured to the accuracy requirements specified in section 2.2 of the present standard, guaranteeing the tolerances specified in TU2–024–2508–70 for a five-year period with the customer observing the correct working conditions.

2.4 The service life to first overhaul is to be ten years, assuming customer's observance of rules for machine transport, packing and installation.

2.5 The quality of materials, appearance, finish and paintwork must correspond with existing standards, TU2–024–2508–70, and ENIMS Instruction Number 6–1.

Appendix

Table A.12   Translation of Soviet State Standard GOST 5.4–67 on Series A2 3 Phase Asynchronous Motors with Squirrel Cage Motors

Approved 3/8/1967   *Date of Introduction* 1/8/1967

The present standard is applicable for 3 phase asynchronous electric-motors with squirrel cage rotors for general use, continuously rated and with drip-proof construction. Electricity supply frequency is to be 50 Hertz.

The present standard is not applicable for electric motors of special design, for example motors with damp-proof, oil-resistant or chemical resistant insulation and with explosion-proof construction.

1. *Types, Basic Parameters and Dimensions*
1.1 The following types of electric-motors are to be manufactured:
    A2–100–4:
    A2–101–4:   A2–101–6:   A2–101–8:
    A2–102–4:   A2–102–6:   A2–102–8:
    In these designations the letter A denotes the protective design (or construction). The numeral after the letter is the index which specifies the new series. The numbers after the first hyphen represent the size of the electric motor. The number after the second hypen indicates the number of poles, which determine the synchronous speed of rotation in revs per minute.
1.2 The motors have to be manufactured with horizontal output shafts and a body housing with fixing lugs. The form of design construction M101 is in accordance with GOST 2475–65.
1.3 In agreement with the factory-supplier the motors may be made with vertical output shafts. The form of design construction M103 has built-in (or bedded-in) enclosure.
1.4 The motors have to be manufactured with a single salient cylindrical output shaft. The dimensions of the shaft are to be in accordance with GOST 12080–66. According to the requirements of the customer the motors may be manufactured with two salient output shafts.
1.5 The mounting dimensions of the motor should correspond to those shown in the diagram and are listed in Table 1 below.

Table 1

Type of Motor	Dimensions in Millimeters			
	L	L_1	L_6	$2C_2$
A2–100, A2–101	980	492	406	406
A2–102	1030	543	432	457

2. *Technical Requirements*
2.1 The rated values of the motor must correspond to Table 2. The permissible tolerances on efficiency; power factor (cos Ø); the ratios Start torque/Rated torque; Max. torque/Rated torque; and Start current/Rated current are to GOST 193–66.

continued on p. 176

TABLE A.12 continued

Table 2

Type of Motor	Power KW	Voltage	Eff. %	Cos Ø	Speed (RPM)	T Start / T Rated	T Max / T Rated	T Start / T Rated	T Min / T Rated
A2–100–4	125	220/380	92.8	0.89	1500	0.9	2.0	6.0	0.8
A2–101–4	160	380	93.4	0.90	1500	0.9	2.0	6.0	0.8
A2–102–4	200	380	94.3	0.91	1500	1.0	2.0	6.0	0.8
A2–101–6	100	220/380	92.4	0.89	1000	1.0	2.0	6.0	0.8
A2–102–6	125	220/380	93.3	0.90	1000	1.0	2.0	6.0	0.8
A2–101–8	75	220/380	92.1	0.85	750	1.0	2.0	5.0	0.8
A2–102–8	100	220/380	92.3	0.86	750	1.0	2.0	5.0	0.8

2.2 The enterprise manufacturer's guarantee is to correspond to GOST 183–66.

2.3 The following reliability and durability indices are to be established for the motors:
    a) Period of Service – no less than 18 years
    b) The probability of fault-free operation with the corresponding service life:
        0.99 – with 2 years' operation
        0.95 – with 10 years' operation
        0.90 – with 18 years' operation
    Notes: (i) The above indices are guaranteed with adherance to the manufacturer's operating conditions
        (ii) The average daily operating time is taken to be 14 hours.

2.4 The motor's external surface has to be covered with enamel after a preliminary coat of paint and filler according to technical documentation approved, in established procedure.

2.5 The 'frequency of use' coefficient has to be no less than 0.86.

2.6 The permissible residual imbalance of the rotor is according to GOST 12327–66.

2.7 The vibration of the motors has to correspond to the specification laid down in documentation, approved in established procedure.

2.8 Assembly and operation instruction must accompany each delivered motor unit.

2.9 The assembly and operation of the motors are to be carried out according to the operating instructions for '3 phase Asynchronous Electric-Motors, Standard Series of Power above 100 KWatts' and '3 Phase Asynchronous Electric Motor, Standard Series type A2–101–8B', (instructions which are delivered by the manufacturer.)

2.10 Lubrication changes done during operation are to take place with the dismantling of motors.

2.11 The motors are to correspond to all the requirements of the present standard, GOST 9352–60 and GOST 183–66.

3. *Testing Methods*

3.1 Every motor must undergo inspection tests according to GOST 183–66.

Appendix 177

3.2 The standard tests of the motor are to be carried out according to GOST 183–66. The frequency of these tests – no less than once every two years. The number of machines selected for tests – no less than 2.

3.3 The motor test method are to be according to GOST 183–66; GOST 11828–66; GOST 7217–66.

4. *Marking, Packing, Transportation & Storage*

4.1 On the casing of the motor is to be fixed a plate on which are indicated the following:

Manufacturer's Trade Mark.
The Mark of Quality to GOST 1.9.–67
Type of Motor and Factory Number
Type of Current
Frequency and No. of Phases
Power in Kilowatts
Rated Voltage in Volts
Rated Current in Amps
Synchronous Speed
Rated Efficiency & Power Factor
Class of Insulation
Rated Operating Mode
The weight in kilograms
Delivery Date
No. of Standard

4.2 The motor packing is to protect the motor during transportation and is to be made according to the technical documentation of the manufacturer.

4.3 The motors are to be stored in an enclosed and dry compartment.

Table A.13 Comparative assessment of electrical rotating machinery (to GOST 183–74 and BS 4999 (Part 32: 1972, Part 60: 1976 and Part 69: 1972))

Technical requirement	Item number to GOST 183–74	Number of specified limits or tolerances	Item number to BS 4999	Number of specified limits or tolerances	Number of identical limits or tolerances, in both Soviet and British standards
Limits of Temperature Rise for Machines:	to Table 1		to table 32.2.5		
AC, Windings of ac machines (500 kVA or greater)	1	10	1a	10	10
AC Windings of ac machines (less than 5000kVA)	2a	5	1b	5	5
Armature windings with commutators	2v	10	2	10	10
DC excited single layer field windings, with exposed metal surfaces	4	10	3c	10	10
DC excited low resistance field windings of more than one layer, and compensating windings	5	10	3b	10	10
Permanently short-circuited insulated windings	6	5	4	5	5
Metallic cores and other parts in contact with insulated windings (NB steel in the GOST standard and iron in the British Standard)	9	10	7	5	5
Commutators and slip rings	10	5	8	5	5
Sub-total		65		60	60

High voltage tests*	to Table 2		to Table 60.11.5	
Insulated parts of machines below 1kW and below 100V	1	1	1a	1
Insulated parts of machines more than 1kW, but below 100V	2	1	—	0
Insulated parts of machines up to 1000kW, but more than 100V	3a	1	—	0
Insulated parts of machines, 100kW and greater	3b	3	—	0
up to 3300V				
3300V to 6600V				
6600V to 17 000V				
Sub-total		6	1	1
High voltage tests cont.				
Separately excited field windings of dc machines	4	1	2	1
Field windings of synchronous windings:				
Generators	5a	1	3	1
Short Circuit Starting	5b	1	4a	1
Field winding connection starting	5v	1	4b	1
Asynchronous machines secondary windings	6	2	5	2
Exciters	7	1	6	1
Sub-total		7	7	7

continued on p. 180

Table A.13 continued

Technical requirement	Item number to GOST 183-74	Number of specified limits or tolerances	Item number to BS 4999	Number of specified limits or tolerances	Number of identical limits or tolerances, in both Soviet and British standards
Tolerances	To table 3		To table 69.2.1		
Efficiency	1	3	1	3	3
Total losses	2	1	2	1	1
Power factor (asynchronous machines)	3	1	3	1	1
DC motor speed	5 & 11	9	4	9	8
Slip (asynchronous machines)	6	1	5	2	1
Voltage regulator (generators)	7 & 8	2	10	2	1
Starting current	9	1	8	1	1
Locked rotor torque	12 & 14	1	6	1	0
Pull-out torque	13	1	7	1	1
Moment of inertia	15	1	13	1	1
Sub-total		21		22	18
Grand total		99		90	86

Note: For insulated parts of machines having output ratings of greater than 1kW, there are certain differences in thresholds in output and voltage values between Soviet and British Standards, for the same specified values of voltage limits. These are outlined below:

Motor Specification to GOST 183–74	Motor Specification to BS 4999	Limit to high voltage test for insulated parts of machines
up to 1 kW less than 100V	up to 1 kW greater than 100V	1000V + 2 × rated voltage
1 kW–1000 kW 100V and greater	1 kW–10 000 kW 100V and greater	1000V + 2 × rated voltage but less than 1500V
greater than 1000 kW up to 3300V	greater than 10 000 kW up to 2000V	1000V + 2 × rated voltage
greater than 1000 kW 3300–6000V	greater than 10 000 kW 2000–6000V	2.5 × rated voltage
greater than 1000 kW 6600–17 000V	greater than 10 000 kW 6000–17 000V	3000V + 2 × rated voltage

Notes and References

Preface

1. Berry, M. J., Hill, M. R., 'Technological Level and Quality of Machine Tools and Passenger Cars' in Amann, R., Cooper, J. M., Davies, R. W. (eds), *The Technological Level of Soviet Industry*, (New Haven and London: Yale University Press), 1977, pp. 523–63; Hill, M. R., 'The Contribution of Soviet State Standards to the Assessment of Soviet Product Quality', *Soviet Union/Union Sovietique;* Vol. 9, Part 2 (1982), pp. 212–24; Hill, M. R., 'Soviet Product Quality and Soviet State Standards', *International Journal of Quality and Reliability Management*, Vol. 2, No. 1, pp. 49–64 (1985). Hill, M. R., McKay, R., 'Soviet Product Quality, State Standards and Technical Progress', in Amann, R., Cooper, J. M., (eds), *Technical Progress and Soviet Economic Development* (Oxford: Blackwell, 1986), pp. 94–114.

1 Introduction

1. L'vov, D. S., in Akademiya nauk SSSR, Institut ekonomiki; *Ekonomicheskie problemy povysheniya kachestva promyshlennoi produktsii* (Moscow: Nauka, 1969) pp. 7, 8.
2. Ibid.
3. Lockyer, K. G., *Factory Management*, (London: Pitman, 1969) pp. 246–7.
4. Juran, J. M., Gryna, F. M.; *Quality Planning and Analysis*, (New York: McGraw Hill, 1970) pp. 1–4.
5. BS 4891: 1972 ('A guide to quality assurance') p. 3.
6. BS 4778: 1979 ('Glossary of terms used in quality assurance') pp. 3, 13.
7. Ibid., p. 10.
8. See BS 4778: 1979, p. 3. This standard also defines 'grade' as 'an indication of the degree of refinement of a material or product' (p. 9).
9. L'vov (1969), pp. 7, 8.
10. The number of publications on the Soviet economy is extremely large, and it is considered to be beyond the range of this present chapter to give a comprehensive account of all these sources. A useful indication of the development of the subject can be obtained from: Nutter, G., *Growth of Industrial Production in the Soviet Union*; National Bureau of Economic Research, General Series No. 75, Princeton University Press:, 1962; Dobb, M., *Soviet Economic Development since 1917*; (London: Routledge & Kegan Paul, 1966); Nove, A., *The Soviet Economic System*, (London: Allen & Unwin, 1977).
11. A clear account of this topic is to be found by R. W. Campbell, 'Problems of US/Soviet Comparisons', in Holzman, F.(ed.), *Readings on the Soviet Economy* (Chicago: Rand McNally, 1972).

Notes and References to pp. 3–5
183

12. Zaleski, E. *et al.*, *Science Policy in the USSR*, (Paris: OECD, 1969).
13. Amann, R., Cooper, J. M., Davies, R. W. (eds), *The Technological Level of Soviet Industry* (New Haven and London: Yale University Press, 1977).
14. Hutchings, R., *Soviet Science, Technology, Design: Interaction and Convergence* (London: RIIA/Oxford UP, 1976).
15. Amann, R., Cooper, J. M. (eds), *Industrial Innovation in the Soviet Union* (New Haven and London: Yale University Press, 1982).
16. Amann, R., Cooper, J. M. (eds), *Technical Progress and Soviet Economic Development* (Oxford: Blackwell, 1986).
17. See: Hanson, P., *Trade and Technology in Soviet–Western Relations* (London: Macmillan, 1981); Zaleski, E., Wienert, H., *Technology Transfer between East and West* (Paris; OECD, 1980); Hill, M. R., *East–West Trade, Industrial Co-operation and Technology Transfer:* (Aldershot: Gower Press, 1983); Schaffer, M.(ed), *Technology Transfer and East–West Relations*, (London: Croom-Helm, 1985); Bertsch, G. K., 'Technology Transfer and Technology Controls: a Synthesis of the Soviet–Western Relationship' in Amann and Cooper (1986), pp. 115–34.
18. See: Hough, J. F., *The Soviet Prefects* (Cambridge, Mass.: Harvard, 1969); Parrott, B., *Politics and Technology in the Soviet Union* (Cambridge, Mass. and London: MIT, 1983).
19. See: Granick, D., *The Red Executive* (London: Macmillan, 1960); Berliner, J., *Factory and Manager in the USSR* (Cambridge, Mass.: Harvard, 1957) Conyngham, W. J., *The Modernization of Soviet Industrial Management* (Cambridge: CUP, 1982).
20. Berliner, J., *The Innovation Decision in Soviet Industry* (Cambridge, Mass.: MIT, 1976) pp. 340–1.
21. Grant, J., 'Soviet Machine Tools; Lagging Technology and Rising Imports', in the US Congress Joint Economic Committee, *Soviet Economy in a Time of change*, Vol. 1 (Washington, DC: US Government P.O., 1979) pp. 554–80.
22. Treml, V. G., 'The Inferior Quality of Soviet Machinery as Reflected in Export Prices'; *Journal of Comparative Economics*, No. 5, Part 2 (June 1981) pp. 200–21.
23. Gorlin, A. C., 'Observations on Soviet Administrative Solutions: The Quality Problem in Soft Goods', *Soviet Studies*; Vol. 23 No. 2 (April 1981) pp. 163–81.
24. Grant (1979), pp. 562.
25. Berry, M. J., Hill, M. R., 'Technological Level and Quality of Machine Tools and Passenger Cars', in Amann, Cooper and Davies (1977), pp. 523–63, but particularly pp. 523–30.
26. Grant (1979), p. 561.
27. See: Berry and Hill (1977), pp. 523–63, but particularly pp. 530–56.
28. Ibid., pp. 547–50, 561–3.
29. Grant considers these types of machine tools as 'conventional', but it is the authors' opinion that they are better thought of as 'second generation' machines, with general purpose machine tools as 'first generation' machines and numerically controlled machine tools as 'third generation' machines.

30. The results of this survey are published in:
 Hanson, P., Hill, M. R., 'Soviet Assimilation of Western Technology: A Survey of UK Exporters' Experience', in the US Congress Joint Economic Committee, *Soviet Economy in a Time of Change*, Vol. 2 (Washington, D.C.: US Government Printing Office, 1979) pp. 582–604. This is a summary of the information available from the case studies; a full description of the case studies on machine tools is available in Hill (1983), pp. 49–74.
31. Treml (1981).
32. Shapiro, I. S.; *Smetnyi spravochnik po teplomekhanicheskom oborudivaniya electricheskikh stanstü* (Moscow: Energiya, 1968) p. 105 and (1977) p. 97. The 1976 rates, published in 1977, vary from a minimum of 21 per cent for gearcutting machines to 38 per cent for lathes for 'general destination' exports; and 38 per cent for gearcutting machines to 55 per cent for drilling and boring machines for 'tropical destination' exports. The authors are grateful to Professor Treml of Duke University, Durham, N. C. for the provision of this data.
33. Treml (1981).
34. See data presented in Hill (1983), p. 26.
35. See, 'T. I. Chesterfield Limited' in *Export Dynamics Case Studies*, British Overseas Trade Board Conference on 'Breaking the Export Profitability Barrier' at the Playhouse Theatre, Nottingham, March 1977, for examples of difficulties faced by technical barriers to export of certain British products to certain West European markets; and de Monthoux, P. G., *A Note on Standards and Industrial Marketing*, Discussion Paper 77–74, International Institute of Management, Berlin, September 1977.
36. Treml quotes *Veckans affarer*, No. 35, 10 October 1974, p. 62 for evidence on Swedish costs, and a small survey of American manufacturers carried out by himself.
37. See discussion of accessories offered by Soviet, compared with Western, manufacturers in export markets in a machine tool 'round table' discussion in *EKO*, 1982, No. 1, p. 59.
38. Chasin, J. B., Jaffe, E. D.; 'Industrial Buyers' Attitudes towards Goods made in Eastern Europe'; *Columbia Journal of World Business*, Summer 1979, pp. 81.
39. Since Soviet market shares for engineering products in Western markets have generally been lower than their market shares in other world regions. (See Hill (1983), p. 26).
40. See Woodward, C. D. (eds); *Standards for Industry* (London: Heinemann, 1965) for a collection of articles on standardisation practice in a mixed economy.
41. Each Soviet state standard (GOST) specification contains the statement 'non-observance of these requirements is against the law'. In the RSFSR, the continued manufacture by any enterprise of articles having a quality lower than that specified in the relevant state standard can lead to the dismissal of the director, chief engineer and chief quality controller, or their sentence to one year's directed labour, or up to three years loss of freedom. (Zakony RSFSR, Postanovleniya Verkhovnogo Soveta

RSFSR, 1960, p. 118, quoted in Andreev, B. G., *Ekonomicheskoe znachenie povysheniya kachestva produktsii*, (Leningrad: Lenizdat, (1968) p. 180). Furthermore, *Ekonomicheskaya Gazeta* prints frequent accounts of enterprise profits obtained from the sale of sub-standard products being confiscated by the state through the local inspection organisations of the State Committee of Standards. See also: Spechler, M. C., 'Decentralizing the Soviet Economy: Legal Regulation of Price and Quality', *Soviet Studies*; Vol. 22, No. 2; pp. 222–254 for a comprehensive account of contract law between enterprises, and the role of State Arbitrazh. Spechler's paper also includes accounts of several arbitration court decisions, some of which illustrate the impossibility of using comprehensive state standards for some types of consumer products.
42. *Pravda*, 3 October 1965.
43. January 1965, Decree of the Council of Ministers of the USSR, No. 16; October 1965, Decree of the Central Committee of the Communist Party of the Soviet Union and the Council of Ministers of the USSR, No. 729.
44. Boitsov, V. V., *Standartizatsiya v Narodnom Khozyaistve SSSR* (Moscow: Standartov, 1967) pp. 270–2.
45. *Standarty i kachestvo*, 1970, No. 12, pp. 3–6
46. Tkachenko, V. V., *Metodika i praktika standartizatsii* (Moscow: Standartov, 1967) p. 190; *GOST 1.1–68*, pp. 6, 7.
47. *GOST 1.1–68*, p. 10; *GOST 1.4–68*, p. 2.
48. *Standarty i kachestvo*, 1967, No. 6, p. 70.
49. Private communication, February 1985.
50. Decree No. 729, quoted in Tkachenko (1967), p. 258.
51. Kokhtev, A. A., *Osnovy standatizatsii v mashinostroenii*, (Moscow: Mashinostroenie, 1973) p. 124; Tkachenko (1967), pp. 119–25.
52. Tkachenko (1967), pp. 247, 258.
53. Ibid., p. 258. Tkachenko also notes that one half of this additional profit is intended for distribution to those members of the workforce engaged in the manufacture of approved products. See also Kokhtev (1973), pp. 124–6; Maev, F.R., *Standarty i kachestvo*, 1977, No. 4, pp. 14–17 and Lapusta, M. G. and Nikitin, P. N., *Stimulirovanie povysheniya kachestva produktsii* (Moscow: Profitzdat, 1980) p. 21.
54. Lapusta and Nikitin (1980), p. 21.
55. Ibid.
56. Ibid., p. 34.
57. Maev (1977), p. 15.
58. Ushakov, M. A., *Standarty i kachestvo*, 1983, No. 12, p. 9. The decree referred to is 'On measures to accelerate scientific and technical progress in the national economy'.
59. Isaev, I., *Planovoe Khozyaistvo*, 1983, No. 12, p. 16.
60. Ushakov (1983), p. 10.
61. Ibid., p. 9.
62. See Gosudarstvennyi Komitet SSSR po Standartam, *Attestatsiya promyshlennoi produktsii po dvum kategorii kachestva* (Moscow: Standartov, 1984) pp. 3, 4.
63. Ibid., p. 7.

64. Ibid. p. 8, 9.
65. See Decree of the Central Committee of the CPSU and the Council of Ministers of the USSR, 'On a Broader Diffusion of New Economic Methods, and the Strengthening of their Action on the Acceleration of Scientific and Technical Progress', published in *Pravda*, 4 August 1985, pp. 1, 2. A summary of the Decree has been published in *The Current Digest of the Soviet Press*; Vol. 38, No. 31, pp. 8, 9, 12. The Decree provides for mark-ups of up to 30 per cent of the wholesale price for highest category products, and discounts of 5 per cent, 10 per cent and 15 per cent respectively over a three year time interval for first category products. This price mechanism is due to be introduced alongside product attestation from 1986.
66. Private Communication, February 1985.

2 General Purpose Machine Tool Type Standards

1. The majority of these tests were originally developed by the German engineer, G. Schlesinger (*Testing Machine Tools*; Machinery; London; 1966) and the French engineer P. Salmon (*Machines – Outils, Reception Verifications*; H. Francois et fils; Paris; Fourth edition), and subsequently modified and adopted by individual companies, certain national standards organisations (including the Soviet All-Union Committee of Standardisation from 1940 onwards, and the British Standards Institution from 1970 onwards) and the International Standards Organisation. They are frequently referred to as alignment tests, or geometric tests, and include specifications of the tests, to be carried out, and maximum tolerances of alignment error for each test. In addition, accuracy requirements for a sample finished workpiece are also specified.
2. See Hill, M. R., *Standardisation Policy and Practice in the Soviet Machine Tool Industry*, Unpublished PhD thesis, University of Birmingham, 1970.
3. In 1965, for example, turning machines, including turret and capstan lathes, accounted for almost 30 per cent of total Soviet machine tool output for that year, while milling machines accounted for 12 per cent of total Soviet machine tool output (see Oznobin N. M. *et al.*, *Sovershenstvovanie struktury promyshlennogo proizvodstva* (1968) p. 136, quoted in M. J. Berry, *Research, Development and Innovation in the Soviet Machine Tool Industry*, unpublished research report, Centre for Russian and East European Studies, University of Birmingham (1974), pp. B7–B9.

The 400mm swing 1K62 centre lathe selected for comparison, and its variants, were produced in qualities of 13 000 per year (i.e. more than 50 per cent of the total turning machine output, and hence some 12–15 per cent of the total Soviet output in 1965, using Oznobin's previously cited proportions combined with a total 1965 output figure of 186 130) (*Narodnoe khozyaistvo SSSR v 1968 godu* (1969); p. 257). The output of the 6M82 range, also chosen for comparison, was more difficult to estimate however. Production planning data quoted in V. A. Anufriev et al.,

Notes and References to pp. 17–37   187

Krupnoseriinoe proizvodstvo frezernykh stankov (1965) suggest that a total of 10 machines of the 6M82 and 6M83 (1600 × 400mm table sized machines) were produced daily (i.e. 3000 machines annually).
4. The only British Standards which related to machine tool accuracy that were published at that time were BS 3800: 1964, which specified methods for testing the accuracy of machine tools, and a set of four standards specifying the accuracy requirements of gear cutting machines (BS 1498: 1954; BS 3013: 1958; BS3329: 1961; BS 3538: 1962).
5. Berry, M. J., Hill, M. R., 'Technological Level and Quality of Machine Tools and Passenger Cars', in Amann, R., Cooper, J. M., Davies, R. W. (eds), *The Technological Level of Soviet Industry* (New Haven and London: Yale University Press, 1977) pp. 530–63.
6. See definitions in: Lockyer, K. G., *Factory and Production Management* (London: Pitman 1974) pp. 50–64; Juran, J. M., Gryna, F. M., *Quality Planning and Analysis* (New York: McGraw Hill, 1970) pp. 1–4; L'vov, D. S. in Akademiya Nauk SSSR, Institut Ekonomiki, *Ekonomicheskie problemy povysheniya kachestva promyshlennoi produktsii* (Moscow: Nauka, 1969) pp. 7–8.
7. See Berry and Hill (1977).

3 Machine Tool 'Mark of Quality' Standards

1. Lapusta, M. G., Nikitin, P. N., *Stimulirovanie povysheniya kachestva produktsii* (Moscow: Profitzdat, 1980) p. 23.
2. Shteingauz, V. G.; 'Aktual'nye problemy dalneishego sovershenstvovaniya upravleniya kachestvom produktsii', *Izvestiya AN SSSR Seriya Ekonomicheskaya*, No. 3, 1983, p. 54.
3. Lapusta and Nikitin (1980), p. 23.
4. Shteingauz (1983), p. 54. 87 841 products were made to the highest grade of quality in 1981, and from 9220 factories in 1980.
5. Lapusta and Nikitin (1980), p. 23.
6. Ibid.
7. Ibid., p. 104
8. *Ukazatel' gosudarstvennykh standartov, 1982*
9. Ushakov, M. A., *Standarty i kachestvo*, 1983, No. 12, p. 10.
10. Treml, V. G., 'The Inferior Quality of Soviet Machinery as Reflected in Export Prices', *Journal of Comparative Economics*, No. 5, Part 2, (June 1981), pp. 200–21. The quotation from Treml cited in this paper draws on the views of V. K. Sitnin and Yu. V. Yakovets *(Ekonomicheskyi mekhanizm povysheniya effektivnosti proizvodstva* (Moscow: Ekonomika, 1978 p. 152). Treml also quotes L. A. Kostin (*Proizvodstvo tovarov narodnogo proizvodstva* (Moscow: Ekonomika, 1980) p. 86) to the effect that 'not all products that are awarded the seal of quality are competitive on the world market'.
11. Lapusta and Nikitin (1980), p. 199.
12. Shteingauz (1983), p. 55.
13. Ibid.
14. Ibid.

15. Ibid.
16. *Ekonomicheskaya gazeta*, 1984, No. 14 (April), p. 10.
17. Ibid.
18. See Berry, M. J. and Cooper, J. M.; 'Machine Tools' and Berry, M. J. and Hill, M. R.; 'Technological Levels of Machine Tools and Passenger Cars' in Amann, R., Cooper, J. M., Davies, R. W. (eds), *The Technological Level of Soviet Industry* (New Haven and London: Yale University Press, 1977) pp. 121–98, 523–63, especially pp. 93, 140–3, 523–30.
19. See Berliner, J. S., *The Innovation Decision in Soviet Industry* (Cambridge, Mass.: MIT Press, 1976) pp. 61–96.
20. Spechler, M. C.; 'Decentralizing the Soviet Economy : Legal Regulation of Price and Quality', *Soviet Studies*, Vol. 22, No. 2; (1970) pp. 222–54.

4 'Squirrel Cage' Electrical Motors

1. F. T. Bartho in *Industrial Electrical Motors and Control Gear* (London: Macdonald & Co., 1965) Ch. 2 claims that 'the general-purpose squirrel-cage will probably meet about 85 per cent of industrial motor application requirements'.
2. See Wall, T. F., *3 Phase Motors* (London: George Newnes, 1952) pp. 25–29 and Libby, C. C., *Motor Selection and Application*, (McGraw Hill; 1960).
3. See Bartho (1965), pp. 48–57.
4. BS 4999 in the UK, and GOST 183–74 in the USSR. See Table A.13 for a full list of requirements.
5. GOST 5.618–73.
6. Climatic Application Y and Article Category 3.
7. See the general Soviet state standard on 'Application for Different Climatic Regions'.
8. See GOST 10799–77.
9. Ermolin, N. P. and Zherikhim, I. P., *Nadezhnost' Elektricheskikh Mashin* (Moscow: Energiya, 1976) p. 118.
10. Cooper, J. M.; 'Is there a Technological gap between East and West?', Centre for Russian and East European Studies, University of Birmingham, 1984. (Prepared for a Conference on 'The East–West Economic Relationship in a Changing World Economy', Canadian Institute of International Affairs, Toronto, 1984.)
11. Ermolin and Zherikhim (1976), p. 151.

5 Automotive Products and Components

1. See BS AU 164.
2. Vlasov, B. V. et al., *Ekonomicheskie problemy proizvodstva avtomobilei* (Moscow: Mashinostronie, 1971) p. 46.
3. The recent Soviet passenger car output has been of the order of 1.3 million per year (see *Narodnoe khozvaistvo, 1922–1982*; p. 196).
4. Vlasov et al., (1971), p. 44.

Notes and References to pp. 71–86   189

5. *Avtoexport*, 1968, No. 12, p. 17.
6. Sutton, A. C., *Western Technology and Soviet Economic Development 1945–1965* (Stanford, California: Hoover Institution Press, 1973) pp. 197–8.
7. *Motor*, 28 July 1973, pp. 5–9.
8. Tarasov, A.M., *Avtomobil'naya promyshlennost'* – *narodnomu khozyaistvu* (Moscow: 1971) p. 53.
9. See *Motoring Which*, October 1965, pp. 106–127 for a detailed account of a road test on the 1599cc Vauxhall Victor 101.
10. *The Guardian*, 17 October 1973.
11. *Izvestiya*; 4 October 1973.
12. Tarasov notes that 'as a result of extensive tests carried out at the French state vehicle testing station in 1970, the Moskvich 412 was awarded an international safety certificate' (Tarasov (1971), p. 52).
13. *Avtomobil'naya promyshlennost'*, 1974, No. 11, p. 45.
14. *Avtomobil'naya promyshlennost'*, 1976, No. 1, p. 40.
15. *Avtomobil'naya promyshlennost'*, 1974, No. 11, pp. 41–3.
16. *Ekonomicheskaya gazeta*, 1974, No. 39, p. 2.
17. *Autocar*, 25 January 1975.
18. See *Pravda*, 2 July 1965; *Trud*, 16 August 1966; and Hill, M.R., *East–West Trade, Industrial Co-operation and Technology Transfer* (Aldershot: Gower Press, 1983).
19. See Hill (1983).
20. See Gutman, P., *Revue d'etudes comparatives est–ouest*, Vol. 11, No. 2 (June 1980), pp. 99–54 and Vol. 11, No. 3 (September 1980), pp. 57–100 and Hill (1983), pp. 49–101.
21. See Gutman (1980) and Hill (1983), pp. 49–101.
22. *The Guardian*, 27 January 1975.
23. *Autocar*, 25 January 1975.
24. Welihozkyi, T., 'Automobiles and the Soviet consumer' in US Congress Joint Economic Committee, *Soviet Economy in a Time of Change*, Vol. 1 (Washington, DC: US Government Printing Office, 1979) pp. 811–33.
25. Tarasov (1973), p. 13.
26. Vlasov (1971), p. 17.
27. Ibid., p. 20.
28. Ibid., p. 32.
29. Rhys, D.G., *The Motor Industry: An Economic Survey* (London: Butterworths, 1972) pp. 130–1.
30. Ibid., pp. 343–7.
31. Chase World Information Corporation (CWIC), *KamAZ, The Million Dollar Beginning* (New York: CWIC, 1974).
32. Hill, M. R., *The Industrial Application of Cylindrical Grinding Processes*, Department of Engineering Production, University of Birmingham (Report No. B/SR 8280), 1972 pp. 82–3.
33. Ibid.
34. Ibid.
35. Yagudin M. L., *Tekhnologiya proizvodstva dvigatelei vnutrennego sgoraniya* (Moscow: Mashinostroenie, 1967) pp. 187–92.
36. Hill (1972), pp. 82–3.

37. Converted from the Vickers Hardness scale using BS 860: 1967.
38. See *Izvestiya*, 21 July 1985.
39. See *Pravda*, 19 May 1985 and *Trud*, 26 July 1984.
40. See *Izvestiya*, 25 May, 1984. The VAZ 2108 has been named the 'Sputnik' (see *Pravda*, 22 December 1984).
41. Ibid.
42. See 'Draft Guidelines for the National Economy', published in *Pravda*, 9 November 1985.
43. See *Trud*, 26 July 1984, and *Izvestiya*, 1 January 1986 for a reference to the diesel powered versions of the VAZ 2108 and the Moskvich 2141 respectively.

6 Domestic Refrigerators

1. *'Journal of Consumer Research'*, 1982, Vol. 8, Part 4, pp. 456–9, and Vol. 9, Part 4, 1983, pp. 432–5. These articles concentrate their research on consumer acquisition patterns which prevail in both American (Oklahoma City) and Australian (Perth) Societies.
2. See *Which*, July 1968 particularly the quotation on p. 214, and also 'Thoughts on Fridges' which appears on p. 220.
3. See *Which*, May 1984, pp. 210–11.
4. These figures of production capacity, recorded in the mid-1970s, compare with those of leading capitalist countries in the first half of that decade. For example, USA (more than 6 million refrigerators in 1973); Italy (5 to 5.5 million 1972–3), Japan (2.6 to 4 million during the 1970s). See 'Mir Kholodilnikov Sevodnya i Zavtra', *EKO*, 1979, No. 6, p. 78.
5. See *Ekonomicheskaya Gazeta*, 1984, No. 29, p. 4; (June 1984).
6. *EKO*, 1979, No. 6, p. 26 provides the data on output and demand cited in the text. That source states that forty-three different models were available in the USSR during a seven-year time interval which covered the whole of the ninth, and the first two years of the tenth, five year plans. This breadth of model range would appear to differ from official policy at that time, however, which was attempting to rationalise from twenty-six, to six, types of domestic refrigerators. See Hutchings, R., *Soviet Science, Technology and Design* (Oxford: Oxford UP, 1976) p. 177.
7.

Refrigerator capacity	Year	Percentage of output
Up to 140 litres	1970	48.4
	1975	23.7
140–200 litres	1970	42.1
	1975	50.6
Greater than 200 litres	1970	9.5
	1975	25.7

(See *EKO*, 1979, No. 6).
8. During the 1st half of 1984, 1.5 million of the 4.4 million refrigerators

produced had a capacity greater than 200 litres (Compiled from output statistics given in *Ekonomicheskaya Gazeta*, 1984, No. 8, p. 11; No. 19, p. 4, No. 21, p. 6; No. 25, p. 4 and No. 31, p. 8.

9. See *Pravda*, 25 February 1983, in which I. Sadikov of the RSFSR Ministry of Trade gives details on defects found by the state quality inspectorate in a range of consumer goods. Two articles in *Ekonomicheskaya Gazeta* (April 1984 (No. 18), p. 9) and July 1984 (No. 30), p. 7) also refer to faults in refrigerators and their compressor units.
10. The above faults were pointed out in an article entitled 'Diktuyet Spros' which appears in *EKO*, 1979, No. 6, pp. 25–8. In 1976 nearly a quarter of all the certified refrigerators were rejected on account of one or other of these faults.
11. See 'Bolshie Tseli, Seriyuznie Zadachi' by Yu. V. Padobed in *EKO*; 1979, No. 6, pp. 28–32 and also J. M. Cooper 'Is there a Technological Gap between East and West?' (Prepared for a conference on 'The East–West Economics Relationship in a Changing World Economy', Canadian Institute of International Affairs, Toronto; 1984).
12. Cooper, J. M., 'The Civilian Production of the Soviet Defence Industry', in Amann, R., Cooper, J. M. (eds), *Technical Progress and Soviet Economic Development* (Oxford: Blackwell, 1986) pp. 31–50.
13. See *EKO*, 1979, No. 6, p. 41.
14. See *Ekonomicheskaya Gazeta*, 1984, No. 28, p. 21.
15. See *EKO*, 1979, No. 6, pp. 40, 41.
16. See the 'Husqvarra' model QR121P and the Zanussi model ZB2406 R (both larder type refrigerators). Also the Electrolux model RA513 (an absorption type of refrigerator) in Tables 6.1 to 6.4.
17. Unlike the 'larder type' refrigerators, most of the test samples contain chilled cabinets for the short-term storage of fresh food and unlike the absorption types, most of the refrigerators relied on the 'compression' principle for their operation.
18. Parts of BS3456, BS3739, BS6291, BS922 and 1691 for British refrigerators and GOST 16317–76 for Soviet refrigerators.
19. It is interesting to note in passing that Cooper estimates that more than half of the output of Soviet domestic refrigerators are manufactured in enterprises responsible to an industrial ministry located in the defence sector. (See note 12. above.)
20. See *Tass* report of 23 September 1986, published in *Moscow Narodny Bank Limited Press Bulletin*, No. 991 (15 October 1986), p. 10.

7 Cameras

1. See McKay, R., *State Standards and the Quality of Production in the Soviet Photographic Industry*, Working Paper No. 112, Department of Management Studies, Loughborough University of Technology, 1985, pp. 49, 50.
2. The production of cameras in pre-revolutionary Russia was probably very small when compared to imports, as camera production was not commenced in Moscow until 1882 (see note 1. above). On the other

hand, some 500 000 cameras were imported into Russia between 1889 and 1914 (See *Focal Encyclopaedia of Production*, Vol. 2).
3. See note 1. above, p. 7.
4. See Cooper, J. M., 'The Civilian Production of the Soviet Defence Industry'; in Amann, R., Cooper, J. M. (ed.), *Technical Progress and Soviet Economic Development* (Oxford: Blackwell, 1986) pp. 31–50.
5. See *Novye Tovary*; June 1982.
6. That is, manually adjustable for 'focus', 'range' and 'exposure'.
7. Further information on the appropriate attachments can be found in *Sovetskoe Foto*, February 1980, p. 42 and *Sovetsko Foto*, April 1981, p. 42.
8. See *Amateur Photographer*, 13 August 1969 ('Test Report on the Zenith 80' by N. Maud; pp. 53–6).
9. Haworth, J.P.; 'Zenith-80: A Review'; *British Journal of Photography*; 24 October 1969, p. 1010.
10. See note 8. above.
11. See note 9. above.
12. In 1967 'The Zenith E offers very remarkable value for money' and 'we have a true SLR selling at a very low price' (*Amateur Photographer*, May 1967). Over a decade later, the *Equipment Survey* (May 1980, p. 249) of the Royal Photographic Society also reported that 'The most liked thing about the Zenith is, not surprisingly, the price'. Tina Rogers of *Amateur Photographer* carried out a test report (6 December 1978, pp. 100–3) on the Zenith TTL model, the first through-the-lens (TTL) model of camera to come to Britain from the USSR. She remarked: 'We guess you'll be paying about £75 which will make the TTL the cheapest SLR with through-the-lens metering on the British market . . . As long as we are fairly close with our price estimate the camera will be good value for money. And it will sell.' As it happened, however, this price estimate was unrealistically low.

In the test reports carried out by *Amateur Photographer* magazine on five other models of Zenith similar praiseworthy comments about price were expressed by various authors involved, as outlined below:
   a) see Rex Hayman's Test Report on the Model EM carried out 28 July 1976.
   b) see John Wilmott's report on the Model ET carried out on 24 July 1982.
   c) see David Cocksedge's report on the ZENITH 19 carried out on 4 June 1983.
   d) see John Wilmott's report on the models 11 and 12XP carried out on 21 April 1984.
13. *Amateur Photographer*, 18 June 1983, p. 149.
14. *British Journal of Photography*, September 1980, pp. 343–4.
15. *Amateur Photographer*, 21 April 1984, pp. 66–8.
16. *Amateur Photographer*, 4 June 1983, pp. 60–3.
17. *Amateur Photographer*, 24 July 1982, pp. 62–4.
18. (a) 'The lens performed in much the same way as on other Zenith models – not exactly high class but perfectly adequately' (Test Report of the TTL model in *Amateur Photographer*; December, 1978).

(b) 'The specification and lens quality were and are excellent for the price bracket' (Test Report of the Model E, in *Amateur Photographer*, May 1967).
(c) 'As has been proved time and time again, is capable of very good results' (Test Report of the Model BM in *Amateur Photographer*, July 1976).
(d) 'Performance. Four stars here. Lens was close to excellent, and shutter speeds/exposure metering up to standard' (Test Report on the Model 19 in *Amateur Photographer*, June 1983).
(e) 'Acceptable and decent pictures' (Test Report of the Models 11 and 12XP, in *Amateur Photographer*, April, 1984).
(f) 'Can be looked at in a number of ways; it is a teacher, it is the cheapest SLR on the market, it is the basis of a budget system. It also takes good pictures' (Test Report of the Model ET in *Amateur Photographer*, July 1982).
(g) '... in no way can the reliability of models owned by members be criticised' (survey of 12 Zenith cameras, by J. Schofield, *British Journal of Photography*, May 1980).
19. See *British Journal of Photography*, September/October, 1980.
20. See note 8 above.
21. *Amateur Photographer*, July 1976 (Report on the Zenith Model BM).
22. *Equipment Survey* by the Royal Photographic Society, on minor brands of SLR cameras (September/October, 1980).
23. *Amateur Photographer*, 12 April 1984 (Test Report on Zenith 11 and 12XP).
24. *Amateur Photographer*, July 1982, Test Report on Zenith ET, and Royal Photographic Society's *Equipment Survey* May 1980 (Zenith TL).
25. 'Taking a picture with the ET is a seven stage operation' (*Amateur Photographer*, 24 July 1982).
26. See *Which* May 1981 ('Servicing and Reliability of Cameras').
27. *Practical Photography*, February 1978, pp.66–7.
28. *Amateur Photographer*, June 1983.
29. See 'Good Results from Cheap Cameras' in *Amateur Photographer*, 4 August 1984, pp.122–4.
30. 'Shooting on a Shoestring', *Practical Photography*, December 1979, pp.78–82.
31. 'It's based on a Voigtlander Brilliant, rather like the Rolliflex, but unlike the £100 to £200 Rolliflex, it costs about £11 including case' (see 'Shooting on a Shoestring', *Practical Photography*; December 1979, p.82).
32. Technical and Optical Equipment (London) Limited. (See p.18 of the company's illustrated promotional brochure).
33. *Amateur Photographer*, 13 August 1983, p. 96.
34. Statements by two owners of Lubitel cameras, one of ten years' duration, and another of twelve years, from a survey of a sample of owners of Soviet-made cameras living in the Loughborough area. This small survey was carried out by R. McKay, with the co-operation of local photographic societies.
35. **Example 1**. Page 42 of the October 1981 edition of *Sovetskoe Foto* carried an article which explained how 'distance' and 'focusing' scale modifications had been carried out on the Lubitel 166B by an amateur photographer from Leningrad.

Example 2. In a DIY article on photography entitled 'Polaroidski', photographic expert Peter Coupe explained how with a Lubitel camera body, a Polaroid swinger, a tube of Araldite and some patience he was able to make a form of instamatic roll-film camera for about £15 which otherwise would have cost in the range of £400 or more. See *Amateur Photographer*, 13 August 1983, pp.94–6.

Example 3. On page 43 of *Sovetskoe Foto* (published in July 1983) there was an article on new photographic techniques which gave details of how camera enthusiast V. Loberant from Kishinev in Moldavia modified his Lubitel model 166B for the fitting and connection of a flash-gun unit.

36. 'If you are prepared to fiddle with your camera in return for great versatility and an excellent lens then the choice is . . . the Cosmic Symbol . . . would be great fun for the enthusiast at any age.' (*Which*, December 1974, p. 358).

    'for £11 to £15 the Cosmic Symbol is the simplest of the multi-speed, multi-aperture, focusing cameras available . . . it's an excellent camera on which to learn all about photography' ('Shooting on a Shoestring', *Practical Photography*; December 1979; p.80) 'Very good optical class lens . . . ideal choice for children and beginners' (illustrated booklet of Technical and Optical Equipment (London) Limited).

    'The Cosmic Symbol is a small 35 mm camera which features a good range of shutter speeds and "symbol" focusing. Exposure is taken care of by a clever "weather symbol" indicator' ('Good Results from Cheap Cameras', *Amateur Photographer*, 4 August 1984, p.122).

37. 'The Cosmic 35 . . . took outstandingly good photographs of outdoor scenes . . . the camera which gave the least distorted pictures was the Cosmic 35' although it 'was particularly inconvenient to use' (all from 'Cheap Cameras', *Which*, November 1969).

38. 'The camera looks for all the world like a Zeiss Contax with all controls and functions being similar . . . Weight is quite substantial at 750 grammes . . . Accuracy was not perfect on the sample (of shutter) . . . tested but consistency of mode of operation were erring on the preferred side . . . On evenly toned subjects the camera settings provided by this exposure meter compared well with a reputable hand meter . . . At this point a sad feature was revealed, in as much as although the Kiev is a copy of the Contax, it is by no means a facsimile, particularly as far as lens mounting is concerned . . . a similar analogy is the Zenith 80, modelled on the original Hasselblads and which was erroneously reported in the popular press of the time of its introduction as being compatible with Hasselblad accessories of this era, whereas there was no matching at all, in practice . . . Briefly, not a lens of the professional standard to which we have become accustomed today, but definitely a good 'snapshooting, lens . . . fine for taking photographs with . . . Rangefinding was found to be accurate with the lens supplied, and may be expected to be so also with other lenses designed for the camera . . . It was a pleasant change to use once again a 'basic' camera, not one of the modern all-singing, all-dancing machines which may well become impossible to manufacture owing to materials shortages. Back to the hand knitting . . . there are sufficient detail differences in the Kiev to

Notes and References to pp. 123–9   195

make it another camera . . . it did all that was requested of it with a solid, almost stolid feel.'
39. *Which*, May 1979, pp. 263–7. This report refers to thirty-one 35 mm cameras. The Kiev 4 was found to have a weight of 765 grm, whereas the weight of most other cameras was within the range 200–600 grm.
40. See *What Camera*; 5 December 1981, p.5.
41. 'The basic construction (of the Zorki 4) is a strong diecast body . . . Despite the undoubted attractions of an SLR, there are still some photographers who prefer the coupled rangefinder, and few sophisticated cameras of this type, with interchangeable lenses, remain . . . the rangefinder gives an extremely good separation . . . . The lens is a 50 mm Jupiter 6. This is a well-known lens, of 6 element type, fully coated, and it was no surprise to find that the performance remained unchanged and as good as ever. . . . to summarise one could say that although old-fashioned the Zorki 4 has some old fashioned virtues. It can take good pictures while the price . . . is remarkably low for a coupled rangefinder camera taking interchangeable lens.' (See *Amateur Photographer*, 27 December 1967; pp.910–1). 'The Zorki is probably the cheapest of its type on the market. . . The camera is very heavy for its small size . . . [it is a] simple, straightforward camera . . . capable of producing excellent photographs. . . The machine looks and feels old-fashioned (but) the lens test results were very good indeed overall.'

8 Comments, Conclusions and Further Research

1. *Izvestiya*, 19 March 1986, p.2.
2. Hill, M. R.; *Export Marketing of Capital Goods to the Socialist Countries of Eastern Europe* (Farnborough: Wilton Publications, 1978) pp.85–135, 174–7, and Hill, M R.; *East–West Trade, Industrial Co-operation and Technology Transfer* (Aldershot: Gower Press, 1983) pp.49–74.
3. The 'creative' presentation of information by Soviet enterprises to higher organs in the administrative system has been discussed at length in the Western literature on Soviet industrial management. The major publications on this topic are: Granick, D., *Management of the Industrial Firm in the USSR*, (New York: Columbia University Press, 1954) pp.150–95. Granick, D., *The Red Executive* (Macmillan, 1960) pp.107–38, 239–84; Berliner, J. S., *Factory and Manager in the USSR* (Cambridge, Mass.: Harvard U. P., 1957) pp.310–96.
4. The sources quoted in note 3. above provide extensive accounts of problems in the administration of quality control in Soviet factories drawing particular attention to poor staffing and creative reporting. Many of the cases refer to the earlier stages of Soviet industrialisation, however, before the upgrading of the State Committee of Standards to its present status.
5. *Izvestiya*, 19 March 1986, p.2.
6. See Lawrence, P. A.; *Management in Action* (London: Routledge & Kegan Paul, 1984) pp.20–61, 83–112. In addition, for specific examples of manipulation of information in Western commerce, see Mars, G.,

Cheats at Work; (London: George Allen & Unwin, 1982). It is important to note that in both of these sources, the manipulative modes of individual and managerial behaviour are chiefly seen in terms of reporting on financial and production output information, rather than quality control. Nevertheless, it is not unusual for overt pressure to be placed on inspectors by production personnel when delivery schedules are tight and the quality control decision is borderline.

7. Hill and Berry (1977), pp.561–3. It is important to note that one British engineer considered commercial tolerances on multi-spindle turning machines to be slack, although 'improved' precision standards are now available for this equipment. (See Hill (1983), p. 56)
8. Gosudarstvennyi Komitet SSSR po Standartam, *Attestatsiya promyshlennoi produktsii po dvum kategorii kachestva* (Moscow: Standartov, 1984).
9. Private communication, February 1985.
10. *Pravda*, 4 August 1985, pp. 1–2. (See also *Current Digest of the Soviet Press*, Vol. 37, No. 31, pp. 8, 9, 12.).
11. See, for example BS5750: 1979 ('Quality Systems') for certification procedures followed by the British Standards Institution.
12. See, for example: Cooper, J. M.; 'The Application of Industrial Robots in the Soviet Engineering Industry', *Omega: The International Journal of Management Science*, Vol. 12, No. 3 (1984), pp. 291–98; Dolan, J., 'The Soviet Robotics Program' and McHenry, W.K., 'The Application of Computer Aided Design in Soviet Enterprises: An Overview'. Two papers presented at the *Workshop on Automated Manufacturing Systems in the USSR*, Illinois Institute of Technology, Chicago, Ill., 1985.
13. See Davis, N. C., Goodman, S. E., 'The Soviet Bloc's Unified System of Computers', *Computing Surveys (ACM)*, Vol. 10, No. 2 (June 1978), pp. 93–122; Snell, P., 'Soviet Microprocessors and Microcomputers' in Amann R., Cooper J. M. (eds), *Technical Progress and Soviet Economic Development* (Oxford: Blackwell, 1986) pp.51–74.
14. See, for example Schaffer, M. (ed), *Technology Transfer and East–West Relations* (London: Croom Helm, 1985) *passim*; and Goodman, S.E., ('Technology Transfer and the Development of the Soviet Computer Industry') in *Trade, Technology and Soviet–American Relations*, edited by B. Parrott, (Bloomington, Indiana: Indiana University Press, 1985) pp. 117–40.
15. *EKO*, 1982, No. 1, p. 53 (quotation from the Director of the Ivanovo Carding Machine Factory).
16. Ibid., p.55.
17. Ibid.
18. Ibid., p. 70.
19. Ibid., p. 78.
20. Ibid., pp. 71, 72.
21. Ibid., p. 50.
22. Ibid., p. 70, 71.
23. Ibid., pp. 60, 61, 65–7.
24. Ibid., pp. 57, 59.
25. Ibid., pp. 65, 72–4.

26. Ibid., pp. 26, 27.
27. Ibid., pp. 31.
28. Matalin, A. A., Frenkel, B. I. and Panov, F. S., *Procktirovanie tekhnologicheskikh protsessov obrabotki detalei na stankakh s chislovym programmnym upravleniem* (Leningrad: izd. Leningradskogo universiteta, 1977).
29. 'Improved' precision for turning machines, and 'normal' precision for milling machines.
30. See Matalin *et al.* (1977), pp. 38–74.
31. *The FMS Magazine*, April 1985; pp. 101–103 (V. N. Vasiliev, 'Implementation of FMS in Soviet Industry').
32. Hill, M. R.; 'FMS Management – The Scope for Further Research', *International Journal of Operations and Production Management*, Vol. 5, No. 3 (1985), pp. 5–20.
33. Ibid.
34. See Cave, M. J., 'Computer Technology', in Amann, Cooper & Davies (1977); pp. 377–406, Cave, M. J., 'Innovation Aspects of the Management Automation Programme in the Soviet Union' in Amann, R. and Cooper, J. M. (eds), *Industrial Innovation in the Soviet Union* (New Haven and London: Yale University Press, 1982) pp. 212–40 (especially pp. 231–3) and Conyngham, W. J., *The Modernization of Soviet Industrial Management* (Cambridge: Cambridge University Press, 1982) pp. 117–24.
35. See Conyngham (1982), p. 124 for a comment on the high quality of Soviet applied mathematics.
36. The earliest comprehensive account of the Soviet industrial research infrastructure is provided in Amann, R., Berry, M. J. and Davies, R. W., 'Science and Industry in the USSR', in Zaleski, E. *et al.*, *Science Policy in the USSR* (Paris: OECD, 1969) pp. 376–585.
37. See sources quoted in note 34. above.
38. Ibid.
39. Based on one of the present authors' experience of supervising various university-supported projects on the industrial application of computer-aided production management systems.
40. Prokhorenko, V.A., Reinshtein, G. M.; *Uskorenie vnedreniya konstruktorskikh razrabotok s pomoshch'yu EBM*, Belarus'; Minsk; 1980.
41. For example, Prokhorenko and Reinshtein, pp. 17–27 make little reference to VDUs and plotters, referring mainly to tape input and microfiche output.
42. See Prokhorenko and Reinshtein (1980), pp. 5, 6.
43. See Cave (1977).

Bibliography

AMANN, R., BERRY, M. J., DAVIES, R. W., 'Science and Industry in the USSR', in Zaleski, E. *et al.*; *Science Policy in the USSR* (OECD, Paris, 1969) pp. 376–585.
AMANN, R., COOPER, J. M., DAVIES, R. W. (eds), *The Technological Level of Soviet Industry* (Yale University Press, New Haven and London, 1977).
AMANN, R., COOPER, J. M. (eds), *Industrial Innovation in the Soviet Union* (Yale University Press, New Haven and London, 1982).
AMANN, R., COOPER, J. M. (eds), *Technical Progress and Soviet Economic Development* (Blackwell, Oxford, 1986).
ANUFRIEV, V. A. *et al.*; *Krupnoseriinoe proizvodstvo frezernykh stankov* (Mashinostroenie, Moscow, 1965).
ANDREEV, B. G., *Ekonomicheskoe znachenie povysheniya kachestva produktsii* (Lenizdat, Leningrad, 1968).
BARTHO, F.T., *Industrial Electrical Motors and Control Gear* (Macdonald & Co., London, 1965).
BERLINER, J., *Factory and Manager in the USSR* (Harvard, Cambridge, Mass., 1957).
BERLINER, J., *The Innovation Decision in Soviet Industry* (MIT Press, Cambridge, Mass. 1976).
BERRY, M. J.; HILL, M. R., 'Technological level and Quality of Machine Tools and Passenger Cars', in Amann, R., Cooper, J. M., Davies, R. W. (eds) *The Technological Level of Soviet Industry* (Yale University Press, New Haven and London, 1977) pp. 523–63.
BERTSCH, G. K., 'Technology Transfer and Technology Controls: a Synthesis of the Soviet–Western Relationship' in Amann, R., Cooper, J. M. (eds), *Technical Progress and Soviet Economic Development* (Oxford: Blackwell, 1986), pp. 115–34.
BOITSOV, V. V., *Standartizatsiya v Narodnom Khozyaistvo SSSR* (Standartov, Moscow, 1967).
CAMPBELL, R. W.; 'Problems of US/Soviet Comparisons' in Holzman, F. (ed), *Readings on the Soviet Economy* (Rand McNally, Chicago, 1972).
CAVE, M. J., 'Computer Technology' in Amann, R., Cooper, J. M., Davies R.W., (eds); *The Technological Level of Soviet Industry* (Yale University Press, New Haven and London, 1977) pp. 377–406.
CAVE, M. J., 'Innovation Aspects of the Management Automation Programme in the Soviet Union', in Amann, R., Cooper, J. M. (eds); *Industrial Innovation in the Soviet Union*, Yale University Press, New Haven and London, 1982) pp. 212–40.
CHASIN, J. B., JAFFE, E. D., 'Industrial Buyers' Attitudes towards Goods made in Eastern Europe'; *Columbia Journal of World Business*, Summer 1979.
CHASE WORLD INFORMATION CORPORATION (CWIC); *KamAZ; The Million Dollar Beginning* (CWIC, New York, 1974).

Bibliography

CONYNGHAM, W. J., *The Modernization of Soviet Industrial Management* (Cambridge University Press, Cambridge, 1982).

COOPER, J. M.; The Application of Industrial Robots in the Soviet Engineering Industry', *Omega: The International Journal of Management Science*, Vol. 12, No. 3 (1984), pp. 291–8.

COOPER, J. M., 'Is there a Technological gap between East and West?' (Centre for Russian and East European Studies, University of Birmingham, 1984). (Prepared for a Conference on 'The East-West Economic Relationship in a Changing World Economy', Canadian Institute of International Affairs, Toronto, 1984.).

COOPER, J. M., 'The Civilian Production of the Soviet Defence Industry', Amann, R., Cooper, J. M. (eds); in *Technical Progress and Soviet Economic Development* (Blackwell, Oxford, 1986, pp. 31–50).

DAVIS, N. C., GOODMAN, S. E., 'The Soviet Bloc's Unified System of Computers', *Computing Surveys (ACM)*, Vol. 10, No. 2 (June 1978), pp. 93–122.

DE MONTHOUX, P. G.; *A Note on Standards and Industrial Marketing*; Discussion Paper 77–74 (International Institute of Management, Berlin, September 1977).

DOBB, M., *Soviet Economic Development Since 1917* (Routledge & Kegan Paul, London, 1966).

DOLAN, J.; 'The Soviet Robotics Program'; Paper presented at the *Workshop on Automated Manufacturing Systems in the USSR* (Illinois Institute of Technology, Chicago, Ill., 1985).

ERMOLIN, N. P., ZHERIKHIM, I. P., *Nadezhnost' Elektricheskikh Mashin* (Energiya, Moscow, 1976) p. 118.

GOODMAN, S. E., 'Technology Transfer and the Development of the Soviet Computer Industry' in Parrott, B (ed) *Trade, Technology and Soviet–American Relations* (Indiana University Press, Bloomington, Indiana, 1985) pp. 117–40.

GORLIN, A.C., 'Observations on Soviet Administrative Solutions: The Quality Problem in Soft Goods', *Soviet Studies*; Vol. 33, No. 2; (April 1981), pp. 163–81.

GOSUDARSTVENNYI KOMITET SSSR PO STANDARTAM, *Attestatsiya promyshlennoi produktsii po dvum kategorii kachestava* (Standartov, Moscow, 1984).

GRANICK, D., *Management of the Industrial Firm in the USSR* (Columbia University Press, New York, 1954).

GRANICK, D., *The Red Executive* (Macmillan, London, 1960).

GRANT, J., 'Soviet Machine Tools; Lagging Technology and Rising Imports', in US Congress Joint Economic Committee, *Soviet Economy in a Time of Change*, Vol. 1 (US Government PO, Washington, DC, 1979) pp.554–80.

GUTMAN, P.; *Revue d'etudes comparatives est–ouest*; Vol. 11, No. 2 (June 1980), pp. 99–154 and Vol. 11, No. 3 (Sept. 1980), pp. 57–100.

HANSON, P., *Trade and Technology in Soviet–Western Relations* (Macmillan, London, 1981).

HANSON, P., HILL, M. R., 'Soviet Assimilation of Western Technology: A Survey of UK Exporters' Experience' in US Congress Joint Economic

Committee, *Soviet Economy in a Time of Change*, Vol. 2 (US Government Printing Office, Washington, DC, 1979) pp. 582–604.
HAWORTH, J. P., 'Zenith-80: A Review', *British Journal of Photography*, 24 October 1969, p. 1010.
HILL, M. R., *Standardisation Policy and Practice in the Soviet Machine Tool Industry*, Ph.D thesis, University of Birmingham, 1970.
HILL, M. R.; *The Industrial Application of Cylindrical Grinding Processes*, Department of Engineering Production, University of Birmingham (Report No. B/SR8280), 1972.
HILL, M. R.; 'The Contribution of Soviet State Standards to the Assessment of Soviet Product Quality', *Soviet Union/Union Sovietique*, Vol. 9, Part 2 (1982), pp.212–24.
HILL, M. R.; *East–West Trade, Industrial Co-operation and Technology Transfer* (Gower Press, Aldershot, 1983).
HILL, M. R., 'Soviet Product Quality and Soviet State Standards', *International Journal of Quality and Reliability Management*, Vol. 2, No. 1, pp. 49–64, (1985).
HILL, M. R., 'FMS Management – The Scope for Further Research', *International Journal of Operations and Production Management*, Vol. 5, No. 3, (1985), pp. 5–20.
HILL, M. R., MCKAY, R., 'Soviet Product Quality, State Standards and Technical Progress' in *Technical Progress and Soviet Economic Development* (edited by R. Amann and J.M. Cooper) (Blackwell, Oxford, 1986) pp.94–114.
HOUGH, J. F., *The Soviet Prefects* (Harvard University Press, Cambridge, Mass., 1969).
HUTCHINGS, R., *Soviet Science, Technology, Design: Interaction and Convergence* (RIIA/Oxford University Press, London, 1976).
ISAEV, I., *Planovoe khozyaistvo* 1983, No. 12 p. 16.
JURAN, J. M.; GRYNA, F. M.; *Quality Planning and Analysis* (McGraw Hill, NY, 1970).
KOKHTEV, A. A., *Osnovy standartizatsii v mashinostroenii* (Mashinostroenie, Moscow, 1973)
KOSTIN, L. A.; *Proizvodstvo tovarov narodnogo proizvodstva* (Ekonomika, Moscow, 1980).
LAPUSTA, M. G., NIKITIN, P. N.; *Stimulirovanie povysheniya kachestva produktsii* (Profizdat, Moscow, 1980).
LAWRENCE, P. A., *Management in Action* (Routledge & Kegan Paul, London, 1984).
LIBBY, C. C., *Motor Selection and Application* (McGraw Hill, 1960).
LOCKYER, K. G., *Factory Management* (Pitman, London, 1969).
LOCKYER, K. G., *Factory and Production Management* (Pitman, London, 1974).
L'VOV, D. S. in Akademiya Nauk SSSR, Institut Ekonomiki; *Ekonomicheskie problemy povysheniya kachestva promyshlennoi produktsii* (Nauka, Moscow, 1969).
MAEV, F. R.; *Standarty i kachestvo*; 1977, No. 4, pp. 14–17.
MARS, G., *Cheats at Work*; (George Allen & Unwin, London, 1982).
MATALIN, A. A., FRENKEL, B. I., PANOV, F. S., *Procktirovanie tekhnologicheskikh protsessov obrabotki detalei na stankakh s chislovym*

programmnym upravleniem (izd. Leningradskogo universiteta, Leningrad, 1977).
MCHENRY, W. K., 'The Application of Computer Aided Design in Soviet Enterprises: an Overview'; Paper presented at the *Workshop on Automated Manufaturing Systems in the USSR* (Illinois Institute of Technology, Chicago, Ill., 1985).
MCKAY, R., *The Quality Levels of Asynchronous Electric Motors in the USSR*, Working Paper No.93, Department of Management Studies, Loughborough University of Technology, 1984.
MCKAY, R., *State Standards and Quality Production in the Soviet Photographic Industry*, Working Paper No. 112, Department of Management Studies, Loughborough University of Technology, 1985.
NOVE, A., *The Soviet Economic System* (Allen & Unwin, London, 1977).
NUTTER, G., *Growth of Industrial Production in the Soviet Union*, National Bureau of Economic Research, General Series No. 75 (Princeton University Press, 1962).
OZNOBIN, N. M. et al. (eds), *Sovershenstvovanie struktury promyshlennego proizvodstva* (Moscow, 1968).
PADOBED, YU. V., 'Bolshye Tseli, Seriyuznie Zadachi', *EKO*, 1979, No. 6, pp. 25–8.
PARROTT, B., *Politics and Technology in the Soviet Union* (MIT Press, Cambridge, Mass. & London, 1983).
PROKHORENKO, V. A., REINSHTEIN, G. M., *Uskorenie vnedreniya konstruktorskikh razrabotok s pomoshch'yu EBM* (Belarus', Minsk, 1980).
RHYS, D. G., *The Motor Industry: An Economic Survey* (Butterworths, London, 1972).
SALMON, P., *Machines-Outils: Reception, Verification* (H. Francois et fils, Paris, Fourth Edition).
SCHAFFER, M. (ed), *Technology Transfer and East–West Relations* (Croom-Helm, London, 1985).
SCHLESINGER, G., *Testing Machine Tools* (Machinery, London, 1966).
SHAPIRO, I. S., *Smetnyi spravochnik po teplomekhanicheskom oborudivaniya elektricheskikh stantsii* (Energiya, Moscow, 1968 and 1977).
SHTEINGAUZ, V. G., 'Aktual'nye problemy dalneishego sovershenstvovaniya upravleniya kachestvom produktsii', *Izvestiya AN SSSR Seriya Ekonomicheskaya*, No. 3, 1983.
SITNIN, V. K., YAKOVETS, YU. V.; *Ekonomicheskyi mekhanizm povysheniya effektivnosti proizvodstva*; Ekonomika; Moscow; 1978.
SNELL, P., 'Soviet Microprocessors and Microcomputers' Amann, R., Cooper, J. M. (eds) in *Technical Progress and Soviet Economic Development* (Blackwell, Oxford, 1986) pp.51–74.
SPECHLER, M. C., 'Decentralizing the Soviet Economy: Legal Regulation of Price and Quality', *Soviet Studies*; Vol. 22, No. 2, pp. 222–54.
SUTTON, A. C., *Western Technology and Soviet Economic Development 1945–1965* (Hoover Institution Press, Stanford, California, 1973).
TARASOV, A. M., *Avtomobil'naya promyshlennost' – narodnomu khozyaistvu* (Moscow, 1971).
TKACHENKO, V. V., *Metodika i Praktika Standartizatsii* (Standartov, Moscow, 1967).
TREML, V. G., 'The Inferior Quality of Soviet Machinery as Reflected in

Export Prices', *Journal of Comparative Economics* (June 1981), No. 5, Part 2, pp. 200–27.

USHAKOV, M. A., *Standarty i kachestvo*, 1983, No. 12, p. 9.

VLASOV, B. V. *et al. Ekonomicheskie problemy proizvodstva avtomobilei* (Ekonomika, Moscow, 1971).

WALL, T. F., *3 Phase Motors* (George Newnes, London, 1952).

WELIHOZKYI, T., 'Automobiles and the Soviet Consumer' in US Congress Joint Economic Committee, *Soviet Economy in a Time of Change Vol. I* (US Government Printing Office, Washington, DC, 1979) pp. 811–33.

WOODWARD, C. D. (ed), *Standards for Industry*, (Heinemann, London, 1965).

YAGUDIN, M. L., *Tekhnologiya proizvodstva dvigatelei vnutrennego sgoraniya* (Mashinostroenie, Moscow, 1967).

ZALESKI, E. *et al.*, *Science Policy in the USSR* (OECD, Paris, 1969).

ZALESKI, E., WIENERT, H., *Technology Transfer between East and West* (OECD, Paris, 1980).

Index

Amann, R.   21n, 182n, 183n, 187n, 188n, 191n, 196n, 197n
Andreev, B. G.   185n
Anglo–Soviet Working Group on Metrology and Standardisation   15, 16
Anufriev, V. A.   186n

Bartho, F. T.   188n
'BCPM' Electric Motors   53–9, 60, 61
'BelAZ' Trucks   36, 81, 83
Berliner, J.   4, 183n, 188n, 195n
Berry, M. J.   4, 21n, 22n, 182n, 183n, 186n, 187n, 188n, 195n
Bertsch, G. K.   183n
'Biryusa' Refrigerators   95, 105, 108, 109
Boitsov, V. V.   185n
British Standards Institution   9, 15, 16
Broaching Machines   19–22, 27–9, 167
'Bukovinka' Knitting Machines   36

cameras   111–25, 191–5n
Campbell, R. W.   182n
cars   68–77, 90, 91, 188–90n
Cave, M. J.   197n
Chase World Information Corporation   198n
Chasin, J. B.   184n
Communist Party of the Soviet Union   3, 14, 185n, 186n
computer-aided design and manufacture (CAD/CAM)   134, 138–41
Consumers' Association   73, 74
Conyngham, W. J.   183n, 197n
Cooper, J. M.   182n, 183n, 187n, 188n, 191n, 192n, 196n, 197n
'Cosmic' Cameras   111, 124, 194n
Council of Ministers of the USSR   10–14, 185n, 186n
crankshafts   86–91

Davies, R. W.   21n, 182n, 183n, 187n, 188n, 197n
Davis, N. C.   196n
De Monthoux, P. G.   184n
diesel engines   82, 83
Dobb, M.   182n
Dolan, J.   195n
drilling and boring machines   19–22, 25, 29, 38–47, 152–4

electrical motors   50–67, 175–81, 188n
'Electrolux' Refrigerators   98, 99, 191n
'Elektrim' Electric Motors   53–7
Ermolin, N. P.   188n

'Fagor' Refrigerator   104, 105
'Fenner' Electric Motors   55–7
'Fiat' Cars   71, 74–7
flexible manufacturing systems (FMS)   134–8
Frenkel, B. I.   197n
'Frigidaire' Refrigerators   98, 99

'GAZ' Trucks   36, 81, 83
gearcutting machines   19–22, 26, 29, 31–4, 38–47, 167–71
'GEC' Electric Motors   55–9
Goodman, S. C.   196n
Gorlin, A. C.   4, 183n
Gosudarstvennyi Komitet SSSR po Standartam (Gosstandard SSSR)   see State Committee of Standards
'Gram' Refrigerators   100, 101
Granick, D.   183n, 195n
Grant, J.   4, 5, 183n
grinding machines   25–7, 29, 31–4, 38–47, 155–66

Gryna, F. M.   182n, 187n
gudgeon pins   86–91
Gutman, P.   189n

Hanson, P.   183n, 184n
Haworth, J. P.   192n
Hill, M. R.   182–4n, 186–9n, 195n, 197n
Hough, J. F.   183n
'Husqvarra' Refrigerators   104, 105, 191n

'Indesit' Refrigerators   102–5
Isaev, I.   185n

Jaffe, E. D.   184n
Juran, J. M.   1, 182n, 187n

KamAZ Trucks   37, 83, 91
'Kiev' Cameras   122, 124, 194n, 195n
Kokhtev, A. A.   185n
Kolomensk Heavy Machine Tool Factory   46
'Kosior' Machine Tool Factory, Khar'kov   43–5
Kostin, L. A.   187n
Krasnoyarsk Engineering Factory   95, 97, 109
'Krasnyi Proletarii' Machine Tool Factory   36, 41

'Lada' Cars   see 'Zhiguli' Cars
Lapusta, M. G.   37, 185n, 187n
Lawrence, P. A.   195n
Lathes   17–24, 29, 31–4, 38–47, 142–8, 172–4
'LEC' Refrigerators   98, 99
'Leroy-Somer' Electric Motors   53, 54, 58–61
Libby, C.   188n
Lockyer, K. G.   1, 182n, 187n
'Lubitel' Cameras   111, 121, 122, 193n, 194n
L'vov, D. S.   1, 2, 182n, 187n

McHenry, W. K.   195n
machine tools   4–6, 17–45, 142–74, 186–8n

McKay, R.   191n, 193n
Maev, F. R.   185n
'Mark of Quality'   11–15, 35–8, 83–6, 95–110, 130, 131
Mars, G.   195n
Matalin, A. A.   197n
'MAZ' Trucks   81
'Miele' Refrigerators   100, 101
milling machines   17–22, 24, 31–4, 38–47, 149–51
'Moskvich' Cars   69–74, 91

'NEMA' Electric Motors   55–61
Nitikin, P. N.   185n, 187n
Nove, A.   182n
numerical control   38, 49, 134–8
Nutter, G.   182n

'Opel Rekord' Cars   71
'Ordzhonikidze' Machine Tool Factory, Moscow   41, 42
Orsha Grinding Machine Factory   42
Oznobin, N. M.   21n, 186n

Padobed, Yu. V.   191n
Panov, F. S.   197n
Parrott, B.   183n, 196n
'Parvalux' Electric Motor   53, 54
'Philco' Refrigerators   102, 103
planing and shaping machines   21, 38–47
Prokhorenko, V. A.   197n

'quality attestation'   11–5, 130, 131

refrigerators   92–109, 190n, 191n
Reinshtein, G. M.   197n
'Renold' Electric Motors   55–7
Rhys, D. G.   189n

Salmon, P.   186n
Schaffer, M.   183n, 196n
Schlesinger, G.   186n
Shapiro, I. S.   184n
Shteingauz, V. G.   187n
Sitnin, V. K.   187n
Snell, P.   196n

'Snowcap' Refrigerator *see*
  'Biryusa' Refrigerators
Spechler, M. C.   185n, 188n
Spillman, R.   122
'Sputnik' Car   190n
Srednevolzhsk Machine Tool
  Factory   41
State Committee of Planning of the
  USSR   13, 14
State Committee of Science and
  Technology of the USSR   13
State Committee of Standards of
  the USSR   10–15, 38, 185n,
  195n
'Super Ser' Refrigerators   102, 103
Sutton, A. C.   189n

Tarasov, A. M.   189n
Tkachenko, V. V.   185n
Treml, V. G.   4, 6, 36, 37, 183n,
  184n, 187n
'Tricity' Refrigerators   100, 101
trucks   77–85, 90, 91, 188–90n
'TSV' Trucks   36, 83

Ushakov, M. A.   185n, 187n

'Vauxhall Victor' Cars   71
Vil'nyus Grinding Machine
  Factory   45
Vlasov, B. V.   188n, 189n

Wall, T. F.   188n
Welihozkyi, T.   189n
Wienert, H.   183n
Wilmott, J.   119, 120, 192n
Woodward, C. D.   184n

Yagudin, M. L.   189n
Yakovets, Yu. V.   187n
Yaroslavl Engine Factory   83

Zaleski, E.   183n, 197n
'Zanussi' Refrigerators   98–103,
  108, 191n
'Zenith' Cameras   111, 119–21,
  192n, 193n
Zherikhim, I. P.   188n
'Zhiguli' Cars   69, 74–7, 91
'ZIL' Trucks   36, 81, 83–6
'Zorkii' Cameras   123, 124, 195n